Praise for *The Brat and the Bullfighter* . . .

"A magically lyrical memoir . . . This clever narrative dares the reader to suspend disbelief in order to acknowledge truth and insight can be more clearly revealed through a perspective other than human."
—Patricia Wood, author of *Lottery*

"*The Brat and the Bullfighter* is an exquisitely written ballad between a horse and a woman that unfolds slowly and beautifully in two parallel memoirs."
—Carol Odell, LICSW, author of *Girl, Groomed*

"Erin shares how horses are the ultimate guides, shaping our creative, emotional, and even love lives. They provide a unique framework and lens through which to view life. A lens that is spiritual and, at times, terrifying. But always, horses are a gift."
—Christy Cashman, author of *The Truth about Horses*

"An unforgettable tale about finding those who heal us."
—Lisa Cheek, author of *Sit, Cinderella, Sit*

THE BRAT AND THE BULLFIGHTER

A Love Story

Erin O'Malley

SHE WRITES PRESS

Published in 2026 by
She Writes Press, an imprint of The Stable Book Group

32 Court Street, Suite 2109
Brooklyn, NY 11201
https://shewritespress.com
Library of Congress Control Number: 2026904067
ISBN: 979-8-89636-354-5
eISBN: 979-8-89636-355-2

Interior Designer: Kiran Spees
Printed in the United States

A work of memory and imagination.

To Mom and Dad, Kathy and Ed O'Malley—

Thank you for always saying maybe,
which I always knew meant yes.
For sleepovers, the puppy, riding lessons, European road trips,
and every adventure and whim in between.
For the challenges that shaped me
and the sacrifices that gave me everything.

And to Q, Ole, Arty, Xairel, and Bella—

Oh, my pretty horses. You stole my heart and became my home.

I love you all.

Every love story is a potential grief story.
If not at first, then later.
If not for one, then for the other.
Sometimes, for both.

—Julian Barnes, *Levels of Life*

1

I'm neither a meteorologist nor a love guru, but I know thunderstorms require three key ingredients: moisture, lift, and instability. The same might be said of love at first sight. I can't speak for anyone else, but I've been struck by a coup de foudre arrow three times. What follows is the story of the third and unexpectedly life-changing one.

1971: Heilbronn, Germany

Once upon a time, there lived a little girl. When she was not yet two years old, she told her mother she wanted a horse. But not just any horse. The horse, she told her mother, must be a white horse.

Her mother knew the little girl had not recently seen any white horses. In fact, she wasn't sure the little girl had seen any horses at all. Still, she documented the request in a letter to her own mother.

"She wants a horse," she wrote. "But not any horse will do. She insists it be a white horse."

1971: Loire Valley, France

Once upon a time, there also lived a little French boy. He grew up in the Loire Valley, not so very far from where the little girl lived but also near the Cadre Noir of Saumur. Whether by matter of proximity to the prestigious riding academy or divine providence, he grew up with a strong inclination toward classical dressage: a discipline and belief system where harmony trumps obedience. Finesse trumps flash. Compassion trumps competition.

Like the little girl, he'd grown up loving horses and, in his youth, had taken every opportunity to seek them out. He knew, as did the girl, that horses can be much kinder, much more understanding than other creatures—especially other children.

When he reached young manhood, he had put in the time and toil to gain the skills and, most of all, sensibility to become a riding instructor. What he lacked, however, was the desire to settle down and land of his own on which to do so. He was young, after all, and a growing sense of wanderlust led him down a different path. He became a mounted guide, leading small groups of adventurers on high-altitude horseback tours through the lush *alpage* and coniferous forests of the Alps, as well as leisurely rambles across the windswept beaches and salty marshes of the Camargue.

But life, no matter how good or bad, never stays the same.

2007: Palo Alto, California

When the little girl had grown up in height and years, her path crossed that of this now-mature Frenchman's—not at a stable or a ranch or anywhere to do with horses. They met at a wine bar. He asked what she'd like to drink. Not in a rakish way, but because he was the bartender.

She asked for a glass of white wine. But not just any white wine.

"I'll take anything," she said, "*except* an oaky California chardonnay."

He tilted his head and raised an eyebrow.

"Please," she added.

What he delivered made her smile. "*Merci.*"

Soon, she ordered another glass of the same, and at some point, someone said something about horses.

The earth shifted on its axis.

May 25, 2009: Gilroy, California

Two years later, the Frenchman had given up pouring wine for a living and was once again working with horses. The transition had begun soon after he poured that perfect glass of white. When he became that grown-up little girl's dressage trainer. My dressage trainer.

Recently, he'd taken on a new client and wanted me to meet her and her white horses. But not just any white horses. These were Iberian horses. But not just any Iberian horses.

These were Lusitanos.

His client's ranch was nestled amid the garlic farms of Gilroy, the garlic capital of the world. It was her home, her oasis, her Shangri-la.

As the Frenchman and I passed through the property's ornate wrought iron gate, the smell of garlic gave way to eucalyptus and freshly turned soil. An ostentation of peacocks greeted us. Next came the dogs. So many dogs: all breeds, all sizes. I could hardly keep track except for the three standard poodles. They stood out. Clipped to tidy perfection, they buzzed about this woman as her personal valets.

She stood six feet tall, confidence radiating from every tiny pore of her chiseled, flawless face. In my mind, I christened her Amazonian Aphrodite as my own confidence shrank.

I looked down at my clothes. My leather paddock boots were dry and cracked, my breeches dusty, my shirt covered in horse saliva and snot. I tried to find a clean place to wipe my hand before shaking hers.

Unconcerned, she shook my hand generously. "Let's go meet the boys."

We headed to the stallion barn. A camel walked by, followed by a pig, then a donkey. A herd of Texas longhorns bellowed hello from a nearby pasture.

On the way, Aphrodite explained how she had recently acquired four new Lusitano stallions. She already had a dozen other horses. But to choose these four, she'd spent more than a year networking with various breeders, visiting Brazil, watching hundreds of videos, and riding innumerable horses before narrowing the field. These were the best.

She stopped us outside the barn, where each horse had its own hand-painted nameplate and engraved wooden tack box, and instructed one of the grooms to lead them out.

"One at a time, please," she said.

I was feeling as if I'd been given backstage passes to the Academy Awards until the first horse emerged from the barn. This was no Hollywood awards show. This was the court of King Louis XIV.

The sun had arrived.

In Greek mythology, Helios drives the sun across the sky in a golden chariot drawn by four white horses. The lyric poet Pindar called them fire-darting steeds. They were Pyrois, Eous, Aethon, and Phlegon.

Aphrodite's new stallions were Xeque, Xairel, Zap, and . . . I'd heard him before I saw him. Iron hooves on asphalt. A shrill scream.

"This is our youngest stallion," she said. "His name is Artilheiro. But we call him Dragon."

She emphasized the second syllable with a long, drawn-out *o* sound. *Dra-GŌN.*

As in Oh. My. God.

He let out another ear-piercing whinny. Snorted. Curled his lip. Stomped his front feet. This horse could breathe fire.

He was the most magnificent creature I'd ever seen.

In other mythologies, white horses symbolize good over evil. They offer the promise that darkness will pass. That life will return after death. I didn't know it then, but one day, this white horse was going to save me. That day, May 25, 2009, he simply wounded me.

In English, *Artilheiro* means "gunner." In mythology, it doesn't really mean anything unless you add a birthdate to the equation. This Artilheiro was born on December 15, 2004. This Artilheiro was a Sagittarius—the centaur, the archer, the fire starter. And boy oh boy, did he live up to his name and sun sign. Before I could do anything about it, he'd drawn back his bow, released, and bam! Bull's-eye. My heart was ablaze.

The three key ingredients were there. Moisture (I could have cried). Lift (a heat so intense it could have launched a hot-air balloon into space). Instability (remarkably, more his than mine).

This is where my story becomes inextricably linked to his. But since his story is very much his own, not mine, you should hear it from him. Through his eyes. In his voice.

But before I pass the mic, believe one thing. Above all, this is a love story.

2

December 15, 2004: São Paulo, Brazil

On the day I was born, two things happened: I took my first wobbly steps on legs as thin and knobby as the bamboo stalks that swayed outside the foaling barn. And Mother told me she had only six months to teach me all she knew about life. The second thing turned out to be a lie. Or no. That's not right. She never would have lied to me. She simply didn't know better.

To her credit, I still learned much in the time we did have. Much beyond the conventional instruction—nursing, grazing on well-managed pastures, frolicking with other carefree foals. Mother was an exceptional teacher because she was a keen observer and an even better listener. She taught me to listen to the herd. To humans. To everything around me, including the wind.

She said I'd been born of the gentlest wind, Zephyr. My duty was to listen to it. Feel it. Let it guide me. As if it carried—through summer's warm caresses, autumn's faint sighs—the collective unconscious of our kind, imparting great knowledge of the past and present. She told me it spoke of our ancestry. Of battles fought. Bullfights won. Owners kind and cruel. Of love, of loss. Of art. And music. Of anything I could imagine.

"Open your mind. Eavesdrop on the world," she said. "You will hear and see the most amazing things. And one day, it will lead you to your destiny."

She also told me few horses listened to the wind anymore. Perhaps because they felt powerless to change their lot in life. Most in our herd had surrendered to a simpler existence—content to graze and laze in a sunny pasture, somehow knowing they had it better than most.

"You are different, Artilheiro. Your knowledge and experience will soon surpass mine. Of this I'm certain."

I wish I could have shown her she was right. But also, I wish she had been wrong.

3

My name is Erin O'Malley, and I'll shank a bitch for calling my horse a brat. It's lazy, ignorant, and reckless. No horse deserves that.

And it's not that I mind four-letter words. I use them all the time. *Shiv*, for example, has a nice ring. But *brat*. *Brat* is different. More than a word, it's an assumption. A fallacy. A misconception that's clung to me like a spider monkey my entire life, a byproduct, at times, of my own temperament, but also of where I'm from. Or *not* from.

When asked where that is, my answer is all over the place.

1970: Camden, New Jersey

I was born at Our Lady of Lourdes Hospital in Camden, New Jersey. Not with a silver spoon in my mouth or a bevy of horses in a family stable at my disposal. My first address was on a narrow street called Beechwood Place in Bellmawr, New Jersey. Not far but far enough from Camden and not to be confused with Belmar.

We lived in a white two-bedroom attached house that, according to my mom, had "a nice little backyard" and was walking distance to my maternal grandparents. And my maternal great-grandparents (the two still kicking). And a dozen other next of kin.

Mom-Mom and Pop-Pop Levins were quintessential grandparents. Kind. Patient. In love with babies. My (great) Granny McCartney veered more toward Wicked Witch of the West. She preferred little boys to girls (not in a kinky way), ate butter by the stick (no bread required), and smoked enough cigarettes a day to remain the size of a squirrel till the day she died, at age ninety-three.

Of my great-grandfather Levins, I have but one recollection. He wore a patch over one eye, and we called him Pop-Pop with the Sore Eye. Never anything else. I'd always assumed the eye was missing or otherwise defective. Turns out, neither was the case. Apparently, he'd had some sort of cataract procedure and was only supposed to wear the patch temporarily. But he liked the look of it, so kept it as a permanent accessory. Definitely odd, but also kinda badass. I should have called him Pop-Pop with an Eye for Fashion.

In the near-year I lived in that little white house, Pop-Pop Levins dubbed me Funny Face—a nickname I did not mind. My brother and I—nearly, but not quite, Irish twins (he was thirteen months older)—shared one of the two bedrooms, and by all accounts, I wasn't an unopinionated baby. To his credit, I did not get shanked.

Also in that time, my dad said goodbye to his teaching job at an elementary school a few blocks from his childhood home in South Philly—just across the Delaware River. And a couple of weeks shy of my first birthday, my little family said goodbye to our big extended family and boarded my first transatlantic flight bound for Germany. My mom said I cried and puked and most certainly became everyone's favorite passenger. My dad had reenlisted in the military, and change was afoot. I had officially become an army brat.

I don't remember everything about the move. But what I will never forget is the horse.

Not long after we got settled in our new living quarters, my mom bought my brother and me a spring-loaded Wonder Horse, the kind of thing that would give any self-respecting helicopter parent a heart attack nowadays. When I later asked why she got it, she said, "You were very active, and I probably just thought you'd like it. And you did. You were little, but you rocked it back and forth with no fear."

She said I was the same with real horses. "You were never afraid of them."

Maybe that's because I came out of the womb knowing them. At least that's how I've always felt. As if they somehow belonged to me. Not in terms of possession, but profound connection. Like a memory that's just out of reach—fuzzy at the edges, yet familiar enough that I feel warm and safe just sensing it's there.

I think that bouncy plastic horse awoke something dormant in me. The way stress can reactivate the chicken pox virus and cause shingles, only in this case with less itch and irritation. I'd say less pain, but I'd be lying. Whatever it was inside me, I couldn't escape it. I couldn't outrun it. When you love something too much, there's always pain.

4

My name is Artilheiro do Vouga, and I am a Puro Sangue Lusitano. For millennia, my ancestors carried warriors into battle, confronted bulls in arenas, danced before kings. We are known for our fearlessness and loyalty to our riders as much as for our athleticism and versatility. These were lessons Mother burned into me. She taught me to be proud of my heritage and showed me what it was to be generous of heart, indomitable of spirit, and above all, brave.

2005: São Paulo, Brazil

They called my mother Obsessão, and she was as beautiful and brave and passionate as her name. Not only did she teach me all she could, but she loved me with everything she had. And I mean everything. The last thing she ever did in this life was save mine.

I was five months old, not yet weaned, and this is how I remember my mother's love.

I remember the sky. The sun, though it awoke late that morning, delivered a palette of endless *manacá-da-serra* blossoms. At the horizon, a thin shock of white bled into pale plum, pink, periwinkle.

I remember the grass. Mother's milk was my favorite, but there was a peace in the hours spent nibbling the rich, sweet blades that covered the hundreds of acres we shared with the other mares and foals of our herd. There were no stallions; they lived upwind in the red-roofed stone stables.

I remember the creek. It snaked through our pasture, and though once bloated and rushing, it seemed to have tapered to a trickle overnight. Mother assured me it would soon return to its fuller figure. I needed only to believe, embrace the changing seasons, and relish the coming of a cooler, drier Brazilian winter.

I remember the flies. They were thick by afternoon, buzzing in my ears, crawling up my nose, licking at my eyes. My young tail was too stubby for adequate combat, so I tried to escape them by tossing my head and trotting over the narrow ridge that led down to the cool, emaciated creek. I was still tossing my head when I nearly collided with him.

I'd disturbed his daybed, and a guttural chuff blew from a cavernous yawn. His teeth clacked and, as if time slowed, I watched a fly drift onto a wiry whisker sprouting from his white muzzle. He swatted at it lazily, revealing the sickle-curved tips of long, sharp claws.

But I didn't know what the ripple of muscle under his fur meant, the twitch of his tail tip, and Mother, who'd followed close behind, acted fast. She flew past me, a blur of white. Her nostrils flared red as she reared and struck out at him, her hooves making dull thwacks against his meaty flesh. It was a horrible clash of claw and hoof, until it wasn't.

My brave, beautiful, brilliant Lusitano mother killed that cougar and saved my life. But by morning, she, too, was gone. My own flesh had gone unscathed. Not a blemish on me. But deep within, my heart had ruptured, and a scar began to grow, thick and hard and tight around it.

5

1971: Heilbronn, Germany

Losing a mother is painful, even if only to distance. Because no matter how old you get, no matter where you find yourself, mothers always mean home.

That first year my little family was in Germany, my mom attempted to curb her homesickness by promising to write a letter to her mother, and vice versa, every day. While they may have preferred to pick up the phone, writing letters was much more economical. In 1971, the international calling rate was $1.50 per minute. Today, that'd be $11 per minute.

By some miracle, my mom saved all those letters, and I'm glad she did. She generally delights in getting rid of junk, and ironically, I only learned of their existence during a different kind of purge.

"We're getting to that age," she said.

Ugh. Stop. I don't want to hear it.

"So, I'm getting things organized, dividing things up between all you kids, clearing clutter."

After donating about a million *National Geographic* magazines to one of my friend's schools and not donating about a million Legos to the same school after my younger brother told her that Legos of that *vintage* could contain lead, she started in on the photos. She put together four boxes, one for each sibling. When she handed me mine, I was sure it contained lead. There were so many photos, including a few of me and my older brother with our Wonder Horse. I suppose she could have stuck these photos—or even just one—in his box, but really, that made no sense: He outgrew horses as soon as he outgrew the Wonder Horse. Maybe even before.

I could tell I was little, but with no date on the back of the photo, I asked if she might remember when it was.

"Funny you should ask," she said. "I was just reading some old letters . . ." When she said "some," she meant hundreds from that year and beyond.

Besides learning my brother and I got into our mom's lipstick and painted the town (read: ourselves, the walls) red, and that I loved to shove pieces of my parents' chenille bedspread up my nose, I got an answer to my Wonder Horse question, and then some.

April 17, 1971

. . . we probably would have taken Eddie for a pony ride. We could have even taken Erin for a ride. She really loves animals—you can't believe how excited she gets every time she sees a dog, cat, or even birds. I know she would love ponies.

April 22, 1971

In one of your letters, you said you'd really know Erin is a genius if she got on Eddie's horse and rode it. Well, she still hasn't managed to get on it herself but she screams until I put her on it. Then she really can ride it herself. Of course she scares me to death but she doesn't even want me to hold her. Her feet don't even touch the bars but she holds the handle and rocks it back and forth. So, she's almost a genius—I'm sure it won't be long until she finds a way to get on it herself.

June 18, 1971

. . . and then you'll hear [a cassette tape accompanied this letter] about Erin climbing up on Eddie's horse and riding it. I wish you could have seen Eddie because I told Erin the horse was sleepy and he went over and hugged his horse and kept telling Erin to get off. That was the first time she managed to climb up on it by herself. She's really a smart little girl.

In all modesty, I know getting up on a plastic horse at eighteen months of age *is* as genius as it sounds. I mean, right up there with curing cancer and ending world hunger. My point is not to brag but more so to highlight what I believe to be true: My love of animals, of horses, was somehow preordained. Or maybe just out of my control.

6

2005: São Paulo, Brazil

Without Mother, life became at once dull and sharp.

I don't remember the sun the morning after she died. Only the pungent zing of petrichor as the barn workers hurried to bring us in from pasture. News had come of a sudden, unexpected storm, and when the heavy metal barn doors clanked shut behind us, the lights flickered as an angry hail rattled the roof. Through a window, I saw branches from the nearby jaboticabas bend and contort like circus acrobats while the workers darted across the courtyard in search of shelter. Their hands covered their ears to shield them from the loud, stinging downpour.

Out that same window, I saw Mother, too. Had I not known better, she could have been a mound of dirt. They'd draped her with a stiff gray tarp, anchored by equally stiff gray stones. Unfortunately, neither the tarp nor the stones proved a match for the tempest, which yanked and yanked until it snapped loose a corner to reveal a lifeless forelimb streaked in crimson. Like spatter from a painter's brush, it told the story of her violent but valiant end.

Another gust and the tarp sank back in place. All went silent as if God himself had taken a deep breath and held it. Not another pellet fell.

Next to me, a mare comforted her snorting foal. She'd placed herself between him and an open window and as she reached to nuzzle his neck, tiny white beads spilled from her forelock. Next to her stood another mare, then another, and another, all the way down the length of the wide, vaulted room. Each was tethered by a rope and halter to metal rings on the stone wall. The foals were not constrained, but few ventured far from their mothers' sides, where each dipped its head to nurse.

Out of sync, I lifted mine high, wrinkled my nose, and sucked in the air. I wanted to catch Mother's sweet scent but smelled only earth and damp. Instinctively, I cried out like the stallions. A long, high-pitched scream that said I wanted her back and wished so hard I'd not been bothered by the flies. That I'd not run off to cool myself by the creek. That I'd helped her fight.

None of the others seemed to notice my distress. What would it have mattered anyway? I wandered to a far corner, collapsed, and tried to find warmth in the rough straw strewn across the hard floor. Only the corner was dank, and a cold draft blew in through a barred window. It felt more like a cell than a shelter. I closed my eyes and tried not to tremble.

7

As an army brat, I knew a thing or two about loss. The more times I moved, and the more goodbyes I said, the more pieces of me I left behind, the more walls I built. Not so much to keep people out as to keep myself closed off. If I never cared in the first place, no one could hurt me when they left, or I left.

Is it better to have loved and lost? I don't know. After all these years, I just don't know.

8

2005: São Paulo, Brazil

Two days after Mother's death, the old routine carried on as if nothing had interrupted it. Two barn workers led us out to our pasture, as often was the case, to the sound of urgent cries from the stallion barn. Though I'd rarely seen the stallions up close, I felt an odd kinship with them. I wondered if they missed their mothers, too, and if they were anything like my sire and grandsire.

Mother had told me my sire was a dressage champion, imported from Portugal to Brazil. She'd found him not only magnificent to look at, with a coat so white he appeared luminescent, but also of a gentle nature. Had it been his choice, he may have taken her out on a gallop through the forest or for a splash in the creek. He was the antithesis of certain other, more aggressive stallions at the ranch, who would carelessly mount a mare, have their way, and bid farewell with a vicious chomp on the rump.

She didn't speak of him often, but it was comforting to know he'd not been rough with her and that the memory of their brief encounter was a good one. When she told me the story, I promised her I would strive to be the same. What I didn't say was dressage and prancing around an arena with a top-hatted rider sounded stuffy and boring. Especially so compared to bullfighting, which, instead, sent a quiver of excitement through me.

Mother had never known her sire, but she had known of him. As many had. He belonged to a famous Portuguese *cavaleiro*. In fact, my grandsire was as famous, if not more so, than his owner. You see, there are three essential elements to a good bullfight: the *cavaleiro*, the bull, and the horse. While the *cavaleiro* is important, he is not as important as the bull. And while the bull is very important, neither he nor the *cavaleiro* is as important as the horse. A good horse can make a career, and for this *cavaleiro*, my grandsire was that horse, a master at outmaneuvering the bull at close range during the short *bandarilha* stage of the fight. Together, they were superstars of the *corridas de touros*, renowned for their remarkable unity, artistry, and courage.

"*As multidões podem torcer pelo cavaleiro,*" she said. "*As multidões podem torcer pelo touro. Mas nunca uma multidão aplaudiu mais alto do que seu avô.*" Crowds can cheer for the rider. Crowds can cheer for the bull. But never did a crowd cheer louder than for your grandsire.

I told her I wanted to be just like him. I wanted to be a bullfighter. Her reaction surprised me. I thought she would be happy, proud of my choice, but her expression changed at my declaration.

She took a moment before saying, "*Você é seu próprio cavalo, Artilheiro. Você pode ser o que quiser ser. Mas saiba disso: Existem dois lados na corrida de touros.*" You are your own horse, Artilheiro. You can be whatever you want to be. But know this: There are two sides to the *corrida de touros*.

I didn't understand and wanted to know more, but she said we would talk about it another time. When she felt I was ready.

I never did hear the other side of the story. At least not from Mother. And without her by my side, without all her stories, days became weeks, weeks turned into a month, and around my six-month birthday, mares were separated from foals, foals were separated by fillies and colts. I knew the pain of each split but shared little empathy. If anything, I felt envy. They'd all had extra time with their mothers, and their mothers would live to foal again.

I now lived in a new field with four other young stallions. We were all gray, but of course, I was the most handsome and most ornery. At a year old, life had already hardened me, and I had learned to pin my ears to get more hay and narrow my eyes or hint at a kick to tell the others to keep their distance. It wasn't that I didn't want friends, but the other four had coupled off to form deeper friendships. They spent their days following each other around, play rearing, grazing side by side, gnawing at one another's itches.

As usual, I was busy pretending to ignore them when I noticed the deer that day. He had jumped the fence from an adjacent field and was headed to nibble at the grapelike fruit that had fallen from the jaboticabas. The others either didn't notice him or didn't care that he'd invaded our space. I can't exactly explain why, but he annoyed me. His dainty hops. His fuzzy rump. I lowered my neck, and as he appeared on my left side, my ears went flat, and I gave chase.

I was so fixated on the young buck, I didn't notice the open pasture gate and almost flew straight out of it as a barn worker rushed to slam it shut. I suppose he hadn't expected my ill will toward the animal. But what can I say? My instinct to fight or flee simply took over, with no option of an in-between. As a Lusitano, I was born brave. But as a Veiga-bloodline Lusitano, I was forged across centuries to be a warrior. My intention was to kill. I had not wanted the deer near me, just as I had not wanted many things near me since Mother's death.

I slid to an abrupt halt, dust encircling me as if I'd arrived via the touch of a magician's wand. The spike had jetted off and escaped through the trees. I doubted he would return.

It took me a moment to notice, but the worker was softly calling my name. "Artilheiro. Artilheiro."

Did I know him?

Only feet away, he reached out his arm. I wasn't sure if he intended to catch me or simply touch me, but I swung around in a furious high and tight pirouette and took off in the opposite direction. *Catch me if you can,* I thought. But he didn't give chase. Instead, he exited through the gate and headed a short way back up the path to where a large boulder offered him a decent seat. From this new perch, he stared out over the field. I returned to grazing, looking over now and again. I can't say how long he stayed, but long enough for the sun to shift in the sky.

9

1981: Heidelberg, Germany

We never stayed very long in one place.

I was eleven when we moved to my seventh "hometown." It was the summer of 1981 and by then, I had two new siblings, Meggan (eight) and Patrick (one). As a family of six, we scored an *oversize* stairwell apartment on South Gettysburg Avenue in Patrick Henry Village, a military base not far from downtown Heidelberg, Germany. "Oversize" meant we had four bedrooms *and* a two-bedroom maids' quarters. Living large!

Not far from our abode, which came with a balcony and wacky set of neighbors, was a chapel, a movie theater, a Foodland, a library, a bowling alley, a rec hall, a middle school, an elementary school, a baseball field or two . . . and that was just on base.

From our balcony, we had a view of the A5 Autobahn, beyond which stretched fields and fields of white asparagus and red strawberries. Beyond the fields were quaint towns and cozy restaurants, where I lapped up *Schnitzel mit Pommes frites oder Späetzle oder Kartoffelsalat*. There were so many new tastes and sight sensations. So many new adventures to be had.

I immediately signed up for drawing and tae kwon do classes at the rec hall. I even found a barn in Sandhausen, a small town not far away, where I started taking weekly riding lessons. When winter arrived, we traveled south and hit the slopes of the Austrian Alps, where we didn't take T-bars or rope tows. Instead, we took trains to the top of runs. They were that long and glorious!

What more could I have wanted?

Well, according to my diary, six months after arriving on that foreign soil, there was something still missing. Something I wanted more than anything.

January 1, 1982
It's a new year! What a day this has been. Last night, the New Year's Eve party band was so loud. I didn't get to stay up until dawn. We're still in Chiemsee and we're going back home tomorrow. I hope this new year will bring me good luck and a friend.
Signed,
Erin O'Malley
P.S. I have a friend already! Winnie!

Winnie was my West Highland white terrier. I say "my" because three moves back, when I was five and living at Fort Hood, Texas, I'd decided I wanted a dog. After having consulted *The New Book of Knowledge* encyclopedia (I was fascinated by those big white books), I chose a Westie. Really for no other reason than I thought it was the cutest breed. And white. I liked white.

My parents later told me their first thought was, *Where the heck are we going to get a Scottish dog in the middle of Texas?* But a week later, an ad for a litter of Westies appeared in the local paper. You can call it coincidence. I call it fate. Winnie was meant to be mine. And Winnie had indeed become my rock, my one and only constant companion. Dogs rule. And perhaps that's also why I had a Snoopy diary. I liked dogs better than people.

January 19, 1982
It's my twelfth birthday! Yay! I love my presents. They are all great! [. . .] At school nobody even knew it was my birthday and didn't say, "Happy Birthday, Erin!" That made me sad. Well at least Snoopy is happy skiing!

At the bottom of this particular entry is an illustration of Snoopy skiing, with Woodstock sitting on his head. Both dog and bird are wearing goggles, but only Woodstock is smiling and presumably happy. To my present self, Snoopy's mood is unclear. He was drawn without a mouth and the goggles add an air of mystery. Maybe my newly twelve-year-old self was trying to be positive. Or simply hopeful.

January 20, 1982
My second day of being twelve. It's pretty neat. I feel good except for the fact that I don't have a friend.

Dear God! Now this is getting pathetic. Someone, get this kid a friend already! This is both hilarious and depressing. Thank Christ for Winnie and those horseback riding lessons.

January 23, 1982
Tonight there was a sixth-grade mass. I brought up the offerings. It was embarrassing! I had horseback riding today. I rode Paulty. Saturday is my favorite day because I get to sleep late. Tonight I can go to bed late because I don't have CCD tomorrow because of the sixth-grade mass.

January 30, 1982

It's Meggan's birthday! She's nine years old. We got our pictures taken today. I also had horseback riding. Need to get a crop for riding lessons! I rode Baskil today and like him very much. When we were cantering Baskil started galloping and just before that he bucked because Frau Biard hit him with the whip. It was fun! I still wish I had a friend though.

If I could go back in time, I'd hit Frau Biard with a whip.

February 20, 1982

Horseback riding! I love it!

Some things never change. I still love riding horses. But lest you worry too much, some things do change. I did make a friend. Actually, many friends.

10

2005: São Paulo, Brazil

Mother had been right. The river did eventually return to its fuller form, and though I had no control over it one way or the other, the man on the boulder continued to return, again and again, to our pasture.

His name, I learned, was Nuno.

He was not a barn worker. Or at least, not any longer. He had paid his dues, starting as a barn hand but working his way up to groom and now on the path to becoming one of the training program's riders. I could tell he had an affection for horses. It was evident in his gentle manner.

Nuno would arrive early, right after we'd been turned out for the day, to stroll through the pastures, always stopping and standing still should one of us show enough curiosity to approach him. I didn't understand at the time but now believe he was watching to see how our bodies were maturing, eager to see how our personalities were forming, what natural talent we might display. He didn't always stay for long, but his early morning presence was consistent, and I took a certain degree of comfort in that.

Atlas and Allegro, one of the colt couples, often approached him. Their eyes stayed soft and kind as they bent their necks to accept his hand, which scratched their withers or brushed flies from their eyes. I figured he liked them best and so kept a cautious distance.

Deep down, I wanted him to like me, too. I wanted to greet him with a casual cool, a nonchalance. But something held me back. It was an internal tug-of-war that pulled me to and fro. I simply wasn't sure whether I could trust him. Or, really, any human.

Weeks passed until, one morning, Nuno changed his routine. Instead of strolling through our field, he sat down on a small stump not far from the gate and waited. He did the same thing the following morning and the one after that. I kept an eye on him and the other foals, who always let their curiosity guide them to him.

On the fourth morning, I relented and walked closer to get a better look at this strange young man. He didn't move when I approached. He looked down, took a deep breath, and let his shoulders drop an inch. I stretched out my neck and nudged his flat cap with my nose. When it shifted, I flinched. He didn't. He kept planted to that stump, seemingly mesmerized by his dusty leather paddock boots.

I put one foot forward and nudged his cap again. From beneath it rose a clean, fresh scent mixed with a breathy bitterness when he chuckled. He opened his hand and produced a carrot. I snatched it without hesitation and ran away. Not too far, but well out of reach. I swung my head as if drawing a question mark in the air, stopped abruptly, and reached down to tear a few bites of grass. Locking eyes with him, I trotted back. Where there'd been one carrot, I hoped for more.

Still on his stump, he reached into the pocket of his well-worn nubuck vest and pulled out another chunk of carrot, and then another. His movements were unhurried, even as I continued with my grab-and-go dance. He laughed again and eventually stood.

I pranced over to him, my head high, and for the first time, we stood face to face. His skin was a rich brown, his eyes black. He was much smaller than I had realized, almost childlike in stature. I didn't budge when he carefully raised his hand to stroke my neck. It was the first human touch since Mother had died that didn't feel cold or obligatory.

"*Obrigado, valente. Obrigado.*" Thank you, brave one. Thank you.

We stood together a moment longer before he turned, walked out the gate, and left for the day.

This exchange was repeated the following day, and every day thereafter. It became our ritual. And what I came to appreciate most about Nuno was how he seemed to understand when to approach me and when to let me come to him. I can admit now I wasn't an easy, straightforward foal, yet he never held that against me. On the contrary, he was up for the challenge and even sympathized with my situation. One day, he whispered to me he was an only child and had lost his parents when he was ten years old. Horses had been his salvation.

I felt a camaraderie with Nuno. And slowly, I began to trust him.

I shouldn't have.

One day, he, too, would let me down. And my faith in humans would take an icy turn.

11

1984: Berchtesgaden, Germany

The cow bell rang at a dark 6:00 a.m. We hustled out of our bunks and made quick work of bundling up in long underwear, wool sweaters, anything to fight off the January cold and despite knowing warmth would be short-lived. Soon enough, we'd be stripping down to our shorts and T-shirts for the morning run-and-dip ritual.

I was, unfortunately, not on kitchen duty that morning, a coveted assignment, as no one stopped us from spooning globs of peanut butter into our mouths and stuffing extra handfuls of trail mix into our pockets. Anything calorie-rich and quick to chow down or easy to stow.

Still, I had an extra spring in my step upon reaching the dining room.

They'd remembered.

"Happy birthday to you! Happy birthday, dear Erin!" sang Mr. White's eighth-grade honors English class at full volume while presenting me with a glorious stack of pancakes.

A single lit candle stood in the middle of the golden-brown pile. Planted like a flag on a mountain peak, it marked this momentous and practically newsworthy occasion: Erin O'Malley had turned fourteen.

"Make a wish! Make a wish!"

Unlike when I turned twelve, I wasn't writing in my diary and wishing for a friend. That birthday, I was midway through a weeklong outdoor-education program ("Project Bold") at Hinterbrand Lodge in Berchtesgaden, Germany, and my friends were gifting me not only with song and carbohydrates but also a journal they'd all signed.

I keep that journal tucked away in an attic box, along with everything else I refuse to throw away. When I do bring it out into the light of day, I still smile at all the "friends forever" sign-offs and goofy inside jokes. "Minus the dip!" "Wasn't it marvie?" "Captain Caveman!"

But there's one entry whose "outsider" honesty always grabs.

Dear Erin,
You are so lucky to have a boyfriend. I wish I had one. You are also lucky to be in the "in" crowd. All I can really do is just sit and look out at your world with the eyes of a dreamer.
Your friend,
C.G.

I didn't know "C.G." well, but I don't think we were so very different. We both had feathered hair. Both played violin; I'd bet money she managed it better than I. Both wore glasses. I remember swapping them on the bus down to Hinterbrand.

"Oh, everything is blurry," she said.

"Oh, everything is dirty," I replied.

The words flew from my mouth before I could snatch them back. Not cool.

Before that trip, I'd never considered myself part of any crowd, least of all an "in" crowd. But Hinterbrand had created a different world for me. A world in which, for the first time, I was able to let my guard down and tell my shyness to go fuck itself.

I never found out exactly why the school had chosen our class to go on this adventure, but I'm grateful it did. The lodge had been welcoming American students since the seventies when the Department of Defense Dependents Schools-Europe (DoDDS-Europe) created the program, where kids ran through the snow, did push-ups in cold creeks, traversed rope courses, took trust falls, cross-country skied, hiked, sledded, and—if anything like my group—bartered with fellow students to get more M&M's in their trail mix.

Hinterbrand was dubbed an outdoor-education center, but it offered us a much broader education.

The lodge was steeped in history. Maybe even haunted by ghosts. Countess Carolina zu Ortenburg had it built in 1903 to commemorate her being the first woman to summit Hoher Göll. Later, it was used as a hideaway for German nationalist writer Dietrich Eckart and as a political base for the Nazi party. An old photo, circa 1935, showed Adolf Hitler, Hermann Göring, and Reich war minister Werner von Blomberg strolling its sunny grounds.

Before we got to the lodge, we toured Oberammergau, where once every ten years, the pastel-painted town performs the Passion Play to honor its vow to God for sparing its citizens and ending the Black Death. In 1934, Hitler applauded the production for its anti-Semitic overtones. By 1984, some changes had been made to correct its misrepresentation of Jews. But not enough. After forty years and a world war, still not enough. Even as a teenager I understood that.

The one place I didn't want to visit on that trip, but later realized I couldn't have done without visiting, was the Dachau Concentration Camp Memorial. We arrived a bus full of teens cracking jokes. We left silenced.

Humans can plot evil in even the sunniest, most beautiful of places.

12

2007: São Paulo, Brazil

Despite Mother's advice, I'd not given much consideration to the humans on the farm. They let us out. They brought us in. They fed us. Occasionally, they said a kind word or lingered to watch us play in the field. In a sense, they seemed inconsequential. I hadn't quite realized how much we needed them, and how we were there only because of them.

My perspective began to shift after meeting Nuno and forming a new kind of bond and friendship. I paid closer attention to their comings and goings. To the way they moved and carried themselves. To the way they spoke to one another, to us.

Some smiled and laughed often. Others, never. Some hurried along in a haphazard manner, running back and forth. Others, like Nuno, appeared more deliberate and focused in their actions. I saw it all. From my stall.

Yes, my stall.

Not only had I grown several inches and a whole new set of teeth, but gone were the days of meandering in the rolling pasture hills. I now lived in the red-roofed stallion barn. One day, my small herd had grazed as usual in our pasture. The next, we were moved into four-by-four-meter stalls. Our tiny, new square worlds, where we spent the majority of our days. Isolated from one another.

The adjustment had not been easy, especially for my fellow inmates Atlas and Allegro. For days after the transition, they cried to one another from behind iron bars. I felt for them. I knew what it was like to suddenly lose someone you love.

It marked the end of an era. Never again would we—not even Atlas and Allegro—be let out together into the same pasture. Instead, we were given a few short hours of turnout each day into small, individual gravel paddocks behind the barn. The time allowed us to stretch our legs and, as small compensation, afforded me a better vantage point for my new-found diversion: people-watching.

Among the regular cast of characters was Gustavo, the groom. He was responsible for scrubbing the amber urine stains from my coat and braiding my thickening mane and tail. Armed with all variety of sprays and lotions, he took pride in keeping me shiny and bright. But that's not all I knew about him. If there's one thing people love to talk about, it's themselves.

His wife, I learned, had the most delicate of noses. She could detect the slightest hint of urine and complained incessantly about how the wretched smell clung to his hair, his clothes, his boots.

"*Você cheira a Fandangos sabor peixe podre!*" she complained. You smell like rotten fish-flavored Fandangos!

Her olfactory sensitivities had become so extreme, Gustavo sought special permission from ranch management to launder his work clothes in the barn's industrial washers. At the end of his shift, he would change into a spare clean outfit and spritz himself head to toe with one of our lavender detangling sprays. Whatever it took to placate "*la diabla.*" The she-devil.

There was also Lucca, the much-loved young man who delivered our thrice-daily feedings. Unlike Gustavo, he never spoke of a wife but rushed around as if one were impatiently waiting for him. He arrived early, fed fast, and, when he stopped for lunch, rarely ate. Instead, he spent the time scribbling ideas into a tattered spiral-bound journal.

Lucca had a second job as a bartender at the local tavern, where he was renowned for his curious concoctions. Cachaça-based this. Hibiscus-infused that. More precious than a diary, his journal was a treasure map of secret formulas for bringing pleasure, if only temporarily, to an otherwise plebeian existence. His drinks were one of the few things Cesar, our stall mucker, ever talked about.

Older than the other men, Cesar didn't move fast or reveal much about his life outside the barn, but he did a decent job keeping my stall clean. That was good enough for me.

Beyond occasional entertainment, my eavesdropping also provided a decent education on the workings of the ranch, its history, and *the* family. If there's another thing people love to talk about, it's other people.

The family owned and ran the ranch—the same family who'd done so for generations, passing the proverbial reins from father to son, father to son. Certain long-established traditions persisted through the years, like setting each privileged child in a saddle before they could walk. Others had evolved, some to the point of extinction.

The patriarch was no longer the first to check on the horses each morning or the last to walk the stables at night and bid each steed, "*Boa noite.*" Good night. Though the original equine residents had been as much a part of the family as any wife, son, or daughter (at times, possibly more so), priorities had changed. What had been born of a passion for the horse had slowly transformed into a passion for other things.

The current proprietor was a grandson of the ranch's founding father. He resided with his wife, son, and two daughters in the sprawling white house at the top of the ridge. Not far from the stables, pastures, and arenas, but far enough. They were a family of riders, save for the mother. She didn't much care for the outdoors and preferred a pair of delicate strappy high heels to a stiff tall boot. Then again, she was quite short—a detail I noticed when she stopped to visit with Nuno one day while he was brushing me in the crossties.

With staccato rhythm, she sashayed into the barn and, once in front of us, rose on tiptoes and tilted her head, as if the combined contortion gave her a better vantage point.

"*Bonito, esse aqui,*" she said. "*Um perfil perfeito.*" Beautiful, this one. A perfect profile.

"*Sim,*" Nuno agreed. He quit with the comb and turned to properly greet her. "*É muito sensível e generoso. Um bom menino.*" Yes, and very sensitive and generous. A good boy.

I've no doubt he would have said more about my natural talent, perhaps asked about next steps in my training program, but before he could say another word, one of the men in black interrupted.

An adjunct to the family, he was one of a posse of broad-shouldered men who only ever wore black suits, dark sunglasses, and grimaces. When not shadowing or shuffling the family in and out of black SUVs that hurried in and out of the property's black iron entry gates, the morose group stood with hands clasped behind their backs, waiting. For what? I can't tell you. But what I can tell you is that they had no clue how to interact with horses. I found it peculiar the way they walked through the barn, constantly checking the bottom of their shoes.

The man bent uncomfortably low to whisper into the tiny woman's ear. "Ah" was all she said before shooing him aside and turning to place a bejeweled hand on Nuno's arm. Her scent, redolent of soap and citrus, filled my nose.

"*Continue com o bom trabalho. E, por favor, mande um abraço para a vovó Karla.*" Keep up the good work. And please, say hello to Grandma Karla.

Nuno nodded, thanked her, and said of course he would pass along greetings to his grandmother. He knew the family missed her, but he also knew what they really missed was her cooking, the warmth of which had brought everyone—the family, the riders, the workers—together in a way not much else did. It was hard to believe it had been almost a year since her departure, especially after so many years, almost a lifetime, of service and devotion in their kitchen. She, too, missed the family. They had been good to her, but she'd left the ranch for good reason. I knew because I had heard the story told here and there, in bits and pieces, many times.

From an early age onward, Karla had done more than suffer great losses. She had endured them, never complaining, always working hard, and with an unwavering belief in God's greater plan. Her husband had died young, under strange circumstances. Or at least that's the vague phrase that got bandied about, and Nuno had learned not to ask more. On her own, she had raised her only daughter and was pleased when she married Nuno's father, a soft-spoken and gentle barn hand. The happy couple had lived with their beloved Nuno in a nearby village until the devastating car crash that killed them both. Nuno's survival was hailed a miracle, and, drawing from a faith few could imagine conjuring, Karla never cursed God for taking her only child. Rather, she thanked him for protecting her grandson Nuno.

She was gracious and grateful and took nothing for granted. Food, she had always said, was her gift, and she raised her station in life to new heights with a passion that transcended filling bellies and ascended to feeding souls. Her genial manner and flair for flavors in the kitchen was a thing of local legend, and when one of the family's business acquaintances, João, came to the ranch for an extended weekend getaway, he quickly learned why.

The day of his arrival, she had baked passion fruit pastries to complement a champagne welcome and, against protocol—her young assistant had taken ill—delivered them herself to the lounge, where guest and family had convened. In a moment that could have been plucked from a romance novel, João lifted the sweet treat from her tray and to his lips, politely, but almost in a rote, absentminded manner. A second later, he was fully present. He stared at Karla; she unapologetically stared back. But just as he thought to raise his glass to acknowledge her triumph, she turned and disappeared down the hallway. For João, it had been love at first bite.

Their courtship was brief. They were of an age, and they knew what they wanted. Marriage made sense and so, too, did a move to João's large and comfortable São Paolo penthouse apartment. Karla hated to leave Nuno but was reassured of her decision when he told her what a wonderful example she had set. Her marriage and move gave him hope. She had shown him if you work hard at what you love, you will be rewarded. Maybe not right away, but one day.

13

"Choose a job you love, and you'll never have to work a day in your life," someone once bullshitted.

The things I love to do are often the most work. I'm not saying they aren't rewarding, but to imply they are somehow not work is hogwash. It's like saying if you love someone, your relationship will be a cakewalk.

1977: State College, Pennsylvania

Before moving to Germany that second time, I'd also lived in Georgia (for ten months), Texas (three years), Pennsylvania (one year), and New York (three years).

I was in second grade in Pennsylvania and, at the time, wanted to be a veterinarian when I grew up. Not only because I loved animals but because I liked the way the word and all its syllables rolled off my tongue. It was never *vet*, always *veterinarian*. As if the profession were calling to me: *vet-ERIN-arian*.

Too bad I have a vasovagal response to blood and needles. A real phlebotomist's dream. And too bad by the time I grew up, I (a) never could have gotten into vet school and (b) no longer had a clue what I wanted to be. At least not in terms of real life. I still had plenty of dreams.

But back then, imagination (or naivete) ruled, and animals were kinder and more interesting than most kids. And even some adults.

We'd moved there from Texas so my dad could finish up his master's degree at Penn State. In Texas, I'd attended St. Joseph Catholic Academy, where a little boy used to torment me at recess. I told my older brother, and one day, he and his friend came to *help* me on the playground.

"So, what's this kid doing to you?" they asked.

"He throws kickballs at my head," I said, pointing to the offender.

The two looked at one another before turning to me to ask, "That's it!?"

"Well, he . . ." I trailed off.

They started laughing, along with another dozen kids who'd swarmed around us. Humiliated, I didn't say another word, only wished to be home with Winnie. Or under a rock.

In Pennsylvania, I attended Our Lady of Victory Catholic School, where I didn't have kickballs thrown at my head but where I made my first macramé plant holder and received my First Holy Communion. Only the body of Christ for me, no blood. Too young, I was told. Thank Christ . . . oh wow, he does listen.

But as for the body? Honestly, I was a bit disappointed. I'm not sure what I was expecting Christ to taste like, but I don't think cardboard was high on my list. After the priest said, "The body of Christ," but before I could finish making the sign of the cross, Christ was already clinging to the roof of my mouth like a giant, unwanted popcorn kernel. I tried to chew, swallow, dislodge him with my tongue, but in the end, all I could do was let him slowly dissolve. And then, just when I thought he was gone for good, he rose again.

As bad breath.

That year, I was also introduced to Fla-Vor-Ice popsicles and a heated driveway. The Fla-Vor-Ice made my throat itch and turned my tongue and teeth all shades of wrong. The heated driveway could have proved useful—State College saw the most snowfall in its recorded history that winter: 98.2 inches!—but sadly, someone had accidentally switched it on during ninety-degree summer temps. We knew something was amiss when the asphalt started bubbling up like burnt cheese in a forgotten fondue pot.

I felt bad watching my dad shovel the driveway, but I loved the snow. Freshly fallen, it smelled of magic. A tabula rasa of possibility! There was nothing better than donning a one-piece snowsuit and moon boots and taking Winnie out into the backyard to make snowmen and snow angels. And of course, the snow gave me a perfect excuse to wear my favorite coat to school.

I'm not sure where my mom found it, but my best guess is the Narnia wardrobe. All purple velvet and embroidery, it stretched all the way to the floor. And with its cloak-and-dagger hood and cuffs trimmed in ivory faux fur, it made me feel like a princess and wizard wrapped up into one. Magic!

Unlike St. Joseph's, Our Lady of Victory did not require us to wear uniforms. Even at that tender age, I had opinions about fashion, and I quite liked getting to choose what I wore. What I did not like was my teacher, Mrs. Herr, calling my coat "gaudy."

At the end of the day, she was helping me button up before I rushed to catch the bus.

"Well, isn't this gaudy?" she said.

"Gaudy," I repeated to myself all the way home. I wanted to ask my mom what it meant.

After she told me, I said I didn't like Mrs. Herr anymore.

"Are you sure she didn't say bulky?" she asked, suggesting I'd misheard.

My mom was always doing that. Giving people the benefit of the doubt.

Like the year before. When a neighbor showed up at our front door to tell my mom I'd cut off her daughter's eyelashes. Because I was jealous of them. My mom actually asked me if I had. What?! The kid did have pretty blue eyes and long lashes, but I'm sorry, who lets someone cut off their eyelashes? And also, this is the same neighbor kid who cut the eyelashes off all her own baby dolls (a known fact!) and whose brother drank his pee in front of us neighborhood kids.

"Mmm," he said, licking his chops. "It's still warm."

But I digress.

"No, Mom. I know what *bulky* means. She said *gaudy*."

"I think she just misspoke. I'm sure she didn't mean your coat was ugly. And maybe she just doesn't realize purple is the color of royalty and luxury, creativity and imagination."

My mom was also always doing that. Telling me I had a great imagination. It was a diversionary tactic she coupled with hot chocolate and cookies, and it worked. It didn't hurt that my mom had an incredible imagination and memory, too.

"You kids have always loved dressing up and playing pretend. One day, you and Eddie would be wearing your hats with the three sides and feathers, boots, and have long blocks in your belts as swords. You told me you were old soldiers, and your horses were the two living room chairs. You even put blankets over the backs of your chairs as saddles.

"And remember the old toy bull on wheels?" she continued. "You and Eddie pretended you were at a bullfight. He was the matador in his black hat and red cape, and you were a fair maiden sitting in the stands. You wore a big sun hat and a white shawl. You threw fake roses at Eddie."

Snuggled up with Winnie in my bed, warm and cozy and protected from the snow, I could listen for ages while she told stories of us kids dressing up and playing pretend. I could sometimes even pretend I didn't care what other people thought. Sometimes.

14

1992 to mid-2000s: São Paulo, Brazil

Nuno wasn't like most other people in the horse business. He possessed rare patience. The kind this ranch once personified under the benevolent rule of its early horse-loving progenitor. The kind that had been lost, little by little, over the years as the onetime retreat from São Paulo's raucous urbanity slowly morphed into a lucrative international breeding business. Now, time was money and not to be wasted on deep affection for, sentimental attachment to, or kid-glove patience with a four-legged commodity.

This blinkered, short-sighted view went against not only Nuno's nature but nature itself. Of course, careful quality time spent with a horse was never a waste. It was an investment in a sound future, of both body and mind. Push us too hard, too fast, to turn a quick profit, and it would not only risk our health and diminish our beauty but also make us, the descendants of those who once carried kings, pawns in a display of mechanical puppetry. And to what end? The oohs and aahs of a largely uninformed clientele?

For Nuno, the work was not about the showiness, the entertainment, the accolades. It wasn't even necessarily about the ride and most certainly not about hopping up and spurring on. Rather, it was about the well-being of the horse. *That* always came first. It was his love for us, our history, and our unique stories that made him special and such an extraordinary trainer. He had an authentic curiosity and desire to learn combined with raw talent and instinct. His goal was to understand what made us tick.

What made us nervous, frightened, hesitant. What made us willing, loyal, devoted. He wanted to see the world through our eyes.

If his parents' untimely passing offered even the slightest grace, it might have been that it forced him to develop an incredible capacity to be alone. I think it helped him relate to us. Perhaps us stallions most of all. He knew solitude and was quite content with minimal human interaction. So long as he had his horses and his books.

Vovó Karla worked long hours, every day but Sunday. And after school, Nuno's routine was to help feed the horses, a chore he'd volunteered for, before racing back to their small one-room apartment over the family's garage. Once there, he would pour a glass of milk, pull his favorite chair to the window, sit, and read. He loved his books and the adventures they took him on. They led him to distant times and faraway places and, one day, straight into the most unlikely of fellowships.

After finishing at the barn, Nuno stopped at Karla's kitchen in the big house to grab a sweet to go with his milk. He deftly snuck in, but as he attempted to slink out unnoticed, he tripped on a slippery antique rug. "Stolen" *sequilhos* flew through the air and Nuno fell to his knees, landing directly at the feet of the current proprietor's father. Nuno looked up slowly. The Old Man looked down, his lips parting, as if about to deliver an admonishment, when instead his attention was drawn to something beside the boy.

There, having fallen out of Nuno's school bag, was a well-worn copy of *White Stallion of Lipizza*.

"You speak English?" the Old Man asked.

"*Perdão?*" Nuno responded, not understanding. Pardon?

"*Achei que talvez você falasse inglês.*" I thought perhaps you spoke English.

"*Não,*" Nuno said, embarrassed. "*Gosto das ilustrações.*" I like the illustrations.

The Old Man reached to pick up the book. "*Eu estive lá.*" I've been there.

Nuno's eyes widened.

"*Sim, para a Escola Espanhola de Equitação em Viena.*" Yes, to the Spanish Riding School in Vienna.

"Oh!" Nuno exclaimed. "*Você montou num Lipizzaner?!*" Did you ride a Lipizzaner?!

The Old Man laughed. "*Não. Mas eu os visitei.*" No. But I visited them. "*Você gostaria de ver por si mesmo?*" Would you like to see for yourself?

Nuno nodded with excitement.

"*Vem. Eu vou te mostrar.*" Come, I'll show you.

He led the boy down a long hall and into a grand study. Photos covered nearly every inch of its walls. From sepia-toned images of bygone coffee harvests to colorful shots of his grandchildren on horseback. It was a panorama of the Old Man's family history, meticulously preserved.

He pointed to a single framed photo, but noticing it was too high for Nuno to see clearly, he reached up, removed it from its mount, and handed it to the boy. Nuno stared at the image. Though a much younger man stared back at him, Nuno recognized the Old Man immediately. He was standing in front of the Hofburg Palace, dressed in a full-length fur coat. Behind him was a line of beautiful high-stepping Lipizzaners in full regalia. Steam rose from their nostrils.

Young Nuno's questions began that evening and never stopped. Their friendship was fated, sealed by a common interest. Over the years, the Old Man shared his vast collection of books on horses and history. Some denser than others. Many in foreign languages. Nuno did his best to translate, understand, and apply the theories he learned. Or he modified or disagreed with them entirely when he tried to put something into practice with a real-life horse. Because, yes, the Old Man also invited Nuno to ride with him.

Together, they took long trail rides, traveling in their minds to the battlefields of ancient Greece or the grand riding academies of the Renaissance and waxing poetic about classical masters and their various works.

Nuno learned from the Old Man to inhabit other worlds and characters. At first, he would latch on tightly to one technique, then to another, and another . . . until one day, he had an epiphany. He could pick and choose and create his own method and philosophy. Experience taught him that the beauty of horses is our capacity to offer a never-ending education. And, perhaps, a new daily challenge. With us, he knew he would never be bored. And contrary to wanting to rush our training, he cherished every moment of the process.

Those years of kinship with the Old Man were good. But nothing is permanent, and one evening after a long ride, the Old Man fell asleep on a well-loved chaise longue that overlooked his vast ranch. He awoke on the other side to greetings from Nuno's parents. Of that, Nuno was certain.

Now, years later, while Nuno did his best to appease the new powers that be, he also did all he could to stay true to us horses. He encouraged short but consistent training intervals that, in time, he knew would bring amazing results and offer proof of his patient program. And what horse wouldn't prefer this approach to the hurry, hurry, hurry and more, more, more of those methods used on other horses in the barn? I was so glad to have my Nuno.

By contrast, the family's patience was thin. They rarely visited the stables if they weren't riding, and when they did ride, they were always in a rush, often snapping orders at the barn workers. In turn, the grooms—Gustavo was one among many—would rush to tack their selected horse, which one of the staff riders would promptly warm up. The family simply didn't have time for mundane bending and stretching. Their preference was to strut into the barn in their shiny boots and starched tops, climb aboard, and launch straight into the more advanced collected work. Perhaps their time was limited. Or perhaps they just felt it was better spent sipping caipirinhas, eating hearts of palm, or riding around in a black SUV.

All this is not to say they treated us badly. There was certainly no conscious abuse. It was more a lack of warmth, an indifference that gave the horse-rider relationship—if you could call it that—all the depth of a tawdry one-night stand. *Wait, what's your name again?* If one horse failed to impress, they knew there were others. I couldn't give you an exact count, but they had many of us to choose from. Hundreds, perhaps.

Barn life offered a new network of horses. The white stone walls of my stall may have prevented me from seeing the stallions on either side of me, but I carefully watched those across the aisle. Many were unfamiliar faces and new personalities, ranging from the vacantly content to the irritably restless. An odd black or bay appeared in the mix, but most were gray. The ranch specialized in grays. In particular, Veiga-line grays like me.

Born the color of ash and smoke, I'd been given a fitting name. My younger coat had resembled a battlefield of low, gray artillery bursts rising and dissolving into a nubilous sky. In time, it would brighten to a nacreous white, but at the moment, it made me a dead ringer for the mount in Jacques-Louis David's *Napoleon Crossing the Alps*. The Versailles version, naturally. Or so said the slight but mighty proprietor's wife, whom I dubbed Dona.

As promised, Dona did return to visit. Here and there and never for long, but long enough to reveal that, in addition to a fondness for silly shoes and giant jewels, she had a thing for Napoléon Bonaparte. Years before, she'd commissioned a replica of David's painting. It hung on the short wall of the covered arena.

While I could agree to the color comparison, I saw none of myself in his face. First, that horse lacked my Roman nose. Second, his expression, all wide-eyed and gaping-mouthed, was wrought with fear. I had no desire to look or feel that way, and under Nuno's tutelage, believed I never would.

But what did I know? Just as the fragments of life around me had started to coalesce into a pretty picture and predictable routine, in the background, the tide was turning. Capricious winds portended a coming storm.

15

Did you know rain alone has no scent? It's only when raindrops hit dry soil and water dances with earth that rain's petrichor aroma is created. Like a kiss from a prince, the rain awakens sleeping microbes in the soil, which then release a chemical odorant called geosmin, the primary compound responsible for rain's earthy smell.

While I love the smell of rain, I'm not a huge fan of storms, which require instability. There's always this element of the unknown, which can be great for adventure seekers (sometimes me), not so great for stress cases (almost always me).

As a kid, every time I moved, I felt a bit like a leaf in a storm. I was never quite sure which way was up or exactly how I'd land, but at the very least, my parents were able to tell me when change was coming. I wasn't left to wonder.

It's hard to *tell* a horse when change is coming.

As prey animals, horses don't like surprises. They thrive on routines. They like being fed at the same time, turned out at the same time, exercised at the same time. They even like taking naps at the same time every day. I've known many a horse who enjoys a mid-morning, postprandial snooze. This predictability feeds calm and relaxation. It gives them a sense of stability and security.

This dependency on routine is also why it's so upsetting and frightening for horses when we move them from place to place, especially if they have to go alone. The stress of it can cause dehydration, colic, gastric ulcers, behavioral changes, depression.

I'm sure plenty of people will want to argue that the more you expose your horses to different things, the more they'll become comfortable with change. I'm not here to argue that point. I'm not trying to say horses don't like adventures. I think horses have all sorts of diverse interests and many may greatly prefer a trail ride to trotting in endless circles in an arena. I'm simply saying, we owe it to them to be ever mindful of their nature and best interests.

Horses have long memories. Likely longer than humans do. I think once we establish trust with them, they enjoy human interaction. They know their people. And it's one reason I cherish all interactions with them. Riding a horse is amazing, but so is grazing a horse.

I'll never understand people who prefer to arrive *every* day at a barn and have their horses already tacked up. For me, the time I spend picking their hooves, brushing them, bathing them is an investment in the relationship that pays off not only when I sit in the saddle but also when I'm in their paddock, stall, leading them down a lane or into that dreaded steel box of a trailer. I can't promise them everything will be okay, especially in the steel box, but I can promise them I'm not just along for the ride. Why? Because I love them.

16

2008: São Paulo, Brazil

Nuno's father and the Old Man had more than a few things in common. They both loved Nuno. They both loved horses. And they both loved Maysa Matarazzo. She had a voice for storytelling, and her songs, so rich in the contradiction, the pleasure-pain of *saudade*, held a special place in their hearts and, by osmosis, Nuno's. And now, mine.

When I think of Nuno, I think of him singing those songs. He carried them like a locket around his neck and shared them like a treat from Vovó Karla's kitchen.

Most mornings, I heard him before I saw him. At first, the sound was faint. A phrase or two mixed with the shuffling of pebbles on the path outside my stall window. I'd perk and lift my head to whinny greetings. Often, as he rounded the corner to the front of the building, he stopped to say hello to the stable hands, but, with a full day's work ahead for all of them, he didn't linger and would promptly pick up where he'd left off, entering the aisleway with a song and a smile.

The other riders liked to tease him, telling him to join the twenty-first century and quit with the insufferable torch songs.

"*Não mais Maysa!*" No more Maysa. They wished for anything but Maysa.

Nuno didn't care. He laughed along with them and then sang louder. His voice was far from perfect, but his tone and intention and conviction in what he loved settled me. When he sang of love and longing, I believed every word. Because he was confident, I grew more confident. Because he was happy, I was happy. I took the goodwill he gave and reflected it back. It's what horses do, and it's why my training with him saw an easy progression from hand walks around the ranch and longeing in a round pen to work in hand and, finally, under saddle. This final *work*, it seemed, was to be my *destino*.

You see, the history of the Lusitano as a saddle horse is a long one. In fact, many would argue we are the oldest saddle horse in the world, first mounted some five thousand years ago. Chosen—if I were to venture a vain guess, and I shall—for our willingness, athleticism, intelligence, versatility, and courage. In the millennia since, we only continued to prove our worth, whether on the battlefield, in a farmer's field, or against a bull in a ring. We may be a rare breed, limited in numbers, but we are abundant in talent, sensitivity, and emotion.

With a Lusitano, there is little room for trainer or rider error. Not because we are obstinate and slow to learn. Quite the opposite. Our responsive, giving nature requires the patience, precision, and steadiness of a funambulist. And Nuno had long been preparing me the best way he knew how: slowly but surely. With him, I never felt hurried or forced. My sensitivity was paramount. My trust, a thing to be earned.

From my early days in pasture through the transition to the big barn, Nuno had made the most important investment of all: time. With him, I began to trust everything would be okay, and when it came time for the saddle, he didn't change pace. First, he made sure I was comfortable with his weight draped over my back, with the saddle, girth, bridle. Then, when he eventually put a foot in the stirrup and threw a gentle leg over my back, I appreciated his slight frame. He did little to disturb my balance.

His way was to ask, allow me to consider the question, and give me the space to process and respond. He made a point of giving many breaks, often bringing me to a full halt, dropping the reins, and letting me stand, blinking and thinking. He waited for me to sigh, lick my lips, and stretch my neck to the ground. That way, when he would take up the reins again, I was calm and ready. Maybe even curious to see what was next.

He never scolded for trepidation or a *wrong* answer to a request. And he always praised me for the smallest accomplishment, with kind words and gentle strokes down my neck.

Most rides took place within the confines of the large arena or smaller covered manège, where we maneuvered around a dynamic obstacle course of other riders and their mounts. But my favorite rides were those through the forest that bordered the ranch. No other horses. No other people. But never alone.

Hundreds, maybe thousands of birds lived along the soft dirt trail that weaved beneath a cooling canopy of trees. Sometimes I would catch movement in the brush or a flash of red or yellow or blue in the branches above. Their music was the constant, and oh how captivating. They kissed and whistled, tweeted and cawed. At once joyous and crazed, they echoed and amplified Nuno's love songs, which of course he sang at full volume.

Those were good days. Looking back, I choose to remember Nuno for who he was and not what he later became to me. To him, the songs were gifts to be shared. The birds were gifts to be enjoyed. And I was a gift to be cherished. I think his modest upbringing had been strange manna; it led him to see *and* appreciate beauty in the simple things: a ride in a forest on a handsome horse surrounded by a chorus of mocking-birds and a bouquet of fresh mango.

If only everyone could have been more like Nuno.

17

Songs and scents are the best souvenirs, wouldn't you agree?

Every time I hear "Little Red Corvette," I'm fifteen again, in Germany. Crammed into the back seat of, well, a little red Corvette. Next to my first real boyfriend. On my first real date. Headed to my first lame school dance at Heidelberg High. The windows are open. The song is blasting. And I've never felt cooler in my life.

I hear "Kiss" and it's New Year's Eve 1994. I'm twenty-three, in Paris for grad school, and at a humid party in Montmartre. Like something out of an eighties music video, scaffolding climbs the inside windowed wall of the bel étage apartment. My two grad school roommates and one of their kid brothers are somewhere, but I'm not fussed to find them. I'm dancing like nobody's watching. In other words, I'm happy drunk. And I just don't care.

That Paris New Year's Eve ranks second only to that of 1999. When I hear *that* song, I'm twenty-eight, again in Germany, but this time, surrounded by my immediate family and looming, mile-high portraits in the traditional Volkskunst style. In one, there's a mountain guide from the Wilder Kaiser Mountains ("*Bergführer aus dem Wilden Kaiser*"). He's wearing culottes, hiking boots, and a coil of climbing rope over one shoulder. In another, there's a violin maker from Mittenwald ("*Geigenbauer aus Mittenwald*"). He's got a long Ulmer pipe casually dangling from bearded lips as he holds the head of a violin in one hand, a gouge in the other. Behind both men, in the distance, are the Alps.

But whatever bygone eyes may be upon us, my brothers, sister-in-law-to-be, and I don't care. Fueled by a few (too many) Weissbier, we're slapping the dance floor—owning it!—in the main dining hall of the Lake Hotel at the Armed Forces Recreation Center at Chiemsee.

Originally commissioned by Adolf Hitler as an Autobahn rest house, the Chiemsee complex opened in 1938. The Germans used it as a hospital during the war, and the U.S. Army took it over at the end. So long as I live, I doubt I'll have a more memorable New Year's Eve.

That's the power of a song. A power surpassed only by that of a scent, the most powerful of which, for me, is that of a horse.

Sweet and earthy, the smell of a horse takes me elsewhere. Whether to a calmer state of mind or, like with Proust's madeleine, to a different time. One whiff and I'm suddenly ten years old again, mucking frowsty stalls in the heat of a Hudson Valley summer. It's 1980. I'm at the United States Military Academy riding stables in West Point, New York, at my first riding camp.

Every morning, I hop out of the station wagon, wave goodbye to my mom, and report in for barn duty. The camp organizers are no dum-dums. From day one, they've stressed good horsemanship isn't only about riding. It's about learning what it takes to care for horses. Thus, our morning curriculum includes hands-on lessons in shit shoveling, aisle sweeping, tack cleaning, and hoof picking. By noon, I'm dirty, thirsty, and hungry, but I've loved every minute. Plus, lunch has never tasted so good. In the immortal words of John Houseman for Smith Barney, it's because, through good old-fashioned hard work, I "earn it."

There's not a cloud in the sky, and a group of us free laborers—er,

I mean, young grasshoppers—plop down in the shade beneath a canopy of oaks. A creek trickles behind us. It's the perfect picnic spot.

I open my baby-blue plastic lunch box and pull out a neatly wax paper–wrapped cheese sandwich, a Tastykake Chocolate Cupcake, and an apple (I'll save that for one of the horses). I twist off the top of my thermos of chocolate milk, take a giant swig, and smile. Can life get any better than this?

Why, yes! Yes, it can. Because after lunch, I'll be tacking up Guy, a sweet schoolmaster Thoroughbred, and going for a ride. "Back in the saddle again . . ."

18

2008: São Paulo, Brazil

Unlike Nuno, the ranch's head trainer, Senhor Matos, did not sing songs of love and longing. In fact, he did not sing at all. The sound and scent I associated most with him was stale, labored breathing. He was a man of excesses who carried much weight, both in his breeches and business affairs. He gave new meaning to the term *full seat* and stomped about the ranch with an air of discontent, deriving his joy in life from finding fault and doling out criticisms. Praise from him was infrequent and often disingenuous or backhanded.

Looking across an arena, he might yell to a rider, "*Adorável piaffe*"—Lovely piaffe—only to add, "*Eu treinei ele bem, né?*" I trained him well, no?

He was smug. Of that, I had no doubt. But did his attitude belie something else? Even with his overinflated ego and belly to match, he seemed to recognize how his acknowledgment could brighten a rider's day. Or maybe I am giving him too much credit. It was tough to read his emotions. He hid them well behind dark glasses and a mustache as thick and black as a stirrup leather.

Wherever Senhor Matos went, so, too, did Socrates, his one-eyed, equally paunchy white bulldog. The poor thing had gotten too close to the backside of an agitated Lusitano one day and *smack*! Faster than anyone could have thought to react, a hoof hit his wrinkled face. Small graces, the horse had been unshod. Otherwise, Socrates would have lost more than an eye. And Senhor Matos, perhaps more of his mind.

Reacting to the accident, Senhor Matos let loose a barrage of verbal vitriol so concentrated and cruel I never saw that horse's frightened eyes regain their previous luster. Like those of the stone horse who stood sentry at the entrance to the stallion barn, his, too, went blank. Poor, poor Allegro. First to lose Atlas, then his self-confidence. All because his instinct had been triggered.

Ever after, Socrates wore a black velvet eyepatch. He didn't seem to mind, but at times, I did. Mainly when potential clients, always from America, greeted him with an "Ahoy!"

Senhor Matos grinned and said, "Ah. Hoy." I had to hope he, like I, was cringing inside, but he never let on. He had an undeniable talent for playing to a crowd, especially one he wanted something from. Perhaps that's why he let the tired salutation slide. Or he just didn't care.

The same visitors fawned over the higher-level stallions, whom the ranch's established riders paraded around. A procession of fine breeding. Occasionally, they ventured to peek into the stalls of us younger stallions. A few pointed to me and nodded their heads. I didn't have a problem with that. But when one thought to reach through the bars to pat me, I didn't hesitate to reach back with an equally impolite nip. The audacity!

Alas, with or without clients, the man-dog duo trundled into the barn together each day—Senhor Matos always expecting to be handed a fully groomed and tacked horse, and Socrates, a treat. I never saw either not get what he wanted. One thing the ranch did not lack was toadying riders and dutiful barn hands. In one way or another, they all sought to please the man who had the family's ear on perks and promotions.

Exactly how he'd come to secure his role as confidant and coach was not immediately clear. The story came across in bits, like the left-over luncheon *farofa* that fell from his mustache when he yelled at a rider to "*Respire!*" (Breathe!) as he simultaneously sucked all the air from the arena. A factoid here. An anecdote there. Someone mentioned he trained in Germany. Someone else said Portugal. There was talk he competed in the European dressage circuit and innuendo he never made it to the top levels because he never found *the* horse to take him there. Did I wonder why? No, of course, I didn't. Yet, whatever his past, he did not lack self-confidence, only delicacy and decorum.

As barn rumor had it, Senhor Matos even campaigned against Vovó Karla's marriage, saying she was making a poor life decision as he feigned concern about her giving up her culinary art. And for what? To marry a boring banker? Of course, everyone knew the real reason for his protestations. He didn't want to lose Karla because he didn't want to lose his favorite *pastels*, filled round and tight with ground beef, cheese, chicken, whatever his rapacious appetite desired.

If ever the subject arose, Nuno always knew better than to engage, saying only, "*Ela está feliz. Isso é tudo que importa.*" She's happy. That's all that matters.

Now, I realize my biggest mistake had been in thinking Senhor Matos was peripheral to my life. A background character who mildly entertained but lacked even the utility of Gustavo, Lucca, and Cesar. In my mind, I belonged to Nuno and he to me. He had become more than just my friend. He was my family. My person.

My perspective changed on a bright, warm, near-perfect day. Nuno had foregone arena work to take me on a short ride through the forest. He sang. The birds sang. And by the time we returned, I had worked up enough of a girth sweat to warrant him relieving me of my tack and releasing me into one of the large outdoor arenas for a roll. First the forest, then a roll! Two of my favorite things. Life was sweet.

I dropped to the dirt, fast and hard. Down. Over. Up. Legs thrusting my body from one side to the other until, satisfied, I extended my forelegs and heaved myself up, shook, and raced around the arena, bucking, screaming, tossing my head.

Nuno was smiling, laughing, right until he raised his hands to the side of his head and made horns with his index fingers. I thought, *Is he serious? Does he not remember from whence I came? Or wait. Is this a test?*

With that thought came a sudden shift in the wind and there, right beside Nuno, stood my grandsire. I blinked, thinking the arena dust had blurred my vision, caused me to hallucinate. But no, there he was. Seemingly as real as the bright sun in the blue sky and the coarse sand beneath my hooves. Just as Mother had described him. His thick white neck framed by a running braid of silver mane woven with red and green ribbons. His muzzle and eyes, dark like smudged charcoal. His ears alert, flicking back and forth. His haunches lowered. Ready for action. *But how? And what?* Before I could react, he was gone.

Nuno, oblivious to my preternatural apparition, bent forward and began to snort and paw at the ground in a threat display. I'm not sure who it surprised more, but when he suddenly charged toward me, I did not dart away but instead met him head-on, emboldened by the unexpected visitation. Before we collided, he zigged, I zagged. Round and round we went, circling one another again and again until, abruptly, Nuno stopped.

Outside the arena, Senhor Matos stood staring. I'd been so focused on the game I'd missed his approach. And he'd stayed silent as a cougar observing his prey, but now he raised his thick paws and slapped them together in three metered beats of applause. *Clap. Clap. Clap.*

"Bravo," he said.

I arched my neck, snorted, and passaged straight to Nuno, who offered me a treat. It was part of our routine and a reassurance to me. I stopped, bent low, and took it with carefree relaxation. A curtain call bow, of sorts.

With his arms resting on the arena fence, Senhor Matos casually raised a wrist, pointed to me, and said, "*Me diga de novo. Quem é esse?*" Tell me again. Who is this one?

"Artilheiro," said Nuno.

And there it was. The spark of recognition.

"*Ah, esse é o que ela gosta,*" Senhor Matos nodded. Ah, this is the one she likes. "*Eu vou montar ele amanhã.*" I shall ride him tomorrow.

Crack! As if a whip had reached out to snatch it, Nuno's smile fell from his face and along with it, ill-considered words from his mouth. He went into immediate defense mode.

"*Ele não está pronto. Preciso de mais tempo com ele.*" He's not ready. I need more time with him.

Senhor Matos bristled. He was not about to have an amateur rider and trainer tell him what he could or couldn't do with one of the family's horses.

He pushed the gate open in a showy, deliberate manner and stepped into the arena, also in a showy, deliberate manner. As the gate slammed shut behind him, he seemed oblivious to Socrates's near decapitation. His focus was elsewhere. He walked past Nuno, heading straight for me.

I froze . . . ears forward, feet firmly planted . . . until he reached out to touch me. Too close! I reared, high over his head, letting my front legs flail and threaten. Startled, he stepped back, caught his heel in a rut, and landed on his wide bottom with a palpable thud.

Nuno rushed to help, but Senhor Matos waved him off while threatening to fire whoever hadn't properly groomed the arena.

"*Eu poderia ter torcido um tornozelo!*" I could have twisted an ankle!

Socrates, who'd been whining on the other side of the gate, somehow managed to squeeze under it. He shuffled toward his master, who, with effort, had risen and was dusting himself off.

Together, they headed toward me. My only option was to keep as far away as I could, for as long as I could. I was quick to feint, pirouette, and run away. The more they hinted at chasing, the more I darted and spun and snorted until, eventually, my coat began to lather and they finally relented.

"*Pegue-o,*" Senhor Matos said to Nuno. Catch him.

My relief was brief.

Before turning to leave, he added, "*Prepare o cavalo para mim às nove da manhã.*" Have him ready for me at 9:00 a.m.

It was an order, not a discussion, and Nuno knew better than to protest.

"*Claro,*" Nuno said. Of course.

After dog and head trainer were gone, Nuno did not call my name, did not walk toward me. He stood in the center of the arena, eyes down, almost as if he'd forgotten I was there. I snorted, still feeling the effects of the adrenaline. He didn't move, just stood there breathing in through his nose, out through his mouth. We stayed apart like that for several minutes, and when I finally did approach him, he didn't reach out to grab me but let me stand beside him, unbothered. I nudged his shoulder. Then his cap. He opened his palm to offer me a piece of browning apple. I don't much care for imperfect apples, imperfect anything, but I took it and did not run when he raised his hand to stroke my damp neck.

"*Desculpe, Artilheiro. Me perdoe,*" he said. Sorry, Artilheiro. Forgive me.

To me, he'd done nothing wrong, and for a moment, I let myself believe everything would return to normal. Or better still, that my bullfighting days were set to begin.

Neither was true.

Rather than dissuade Senhor Matos, my unwillingness to be caught had incensed him, challenged his ego. The next day, he relegated Nuno to grooming, tacking, and longeing me and took it upon himself to take over my training, riding and breaking me to his liking. Certainly not mine.

I began to learn a lot. Not about riding but about people.

Senhor Matos's riding lacked elegance. While his hands were not wildly unsteady, nothing about him was light. He was all drill, drill, drill. Demand, demand, demand. He preferred domination to the dance and was bereft of the selflessness and forbearance required to be a good partner. He did not allow me a beat to process his requests. If my responses were not instantaneous and correct, he only asked louder. With his booming voice, stinging whip, or jabbing spur. I wanted to scream, *I heard you the first time. Give me a second!* I am no slouch, but I am also not a robot or a mind reader.

Under his tutelage, which, sadly, continued long past that first day, my progress took a steady dive. When the bridle came off at the end of each day, I'd stand in the crossties shaking my head, first trying to rid my mouth of the feel of heavy hands and, next, my mind of the perpetual question, *What was that all about?* I tried and tried to do what was asked, but the nagging never stopped, and my anxiety grew. Like when Mother died, life had again become at once dull and sharp.

The training intensified with each passing week. My back tensed and tightened. My gaits grew shorter, choppier. I started to lose my spring, become flat and unimpressive. Worse still, I never once met a bull or even another man pretending to be one. I started to second-guess myself, my abilities, my intuition. Without a voice, my only recourse was to act out or shut down. Most often, I chose the latter. Much had been expected of me, the son of a dressage champion, grandson of a tauromachy legend, and I was not quite rising to the occasion or, rather, meeting the unreasonable expectations.

Senhor Matos may have held the title of head trainer, but more than anything, he was a businessman. And the most lucrative business of the day was to produce horses who demonstrated an ease for collection and capacity to shine in the dressage arena. In other words, easy-riding, fancy-prancing mounts clients could show off to their friends, family, and—let's be honest—rivals. His program was based on deception.

I knew I had all those qualities and more. Not only did I have a natural talent to collect and deliver a comfortable ride, but I could also explode from a standstill into a high-powered sprint, stop in an instant, back, pivot, do it all over again. I was multidimensional. But I was being pushed too far, too fast, too young. I didn't yet have the physical strength or mental maturity for sustained collection under saddle. The new exercises, which pushed me into a false frame, were overdeveloping the underside of my neck while straining my back.

To the undiscerning eye, I may have looked the part. To the ranch's tiny, citrus-smelling matriarch, however, the disconnect was clear. Dona may not have been a horsewoman in the usual sense, but she had an eye for art, and this was not that. Too bad she faulted the horse and not the rider. What spell Senhor Matos had put her under, I still don't know. But whereas he'd lost his campaign to convince Karla to stay, his criticisms of me had taken root and he seemed to be winning the battle to sour her infatuation.

"*Ele é teimoso.*" He is stubborn. "*Ele nunca será fácil de montar.*" He will never be easy to ride. "*Ele se agita. Ele não piaffe.*" He jigs. He does not piaffe.

"É uma pena," she said. "*Para olhar, ele é perfeito. Como uma pintura.*" It's too bad. To look at, he is perfect. Like a painting.

"*E é por isso que ele terá um preço muito bom no leilão.*" And that is why he will bring a very good price at auction.

A good price at auction? They wanted to sell me? But why? Once again, if only I'd been able to air my grievances and debate that a piaffe requires forward motion, maybe she wouldn't have rolled over as easily as Socrates did for a liver treat. I mean, why would anyone—ahem, Senhor Matos—face me into a wall with nowhere to go?

It's no secret I disliked the man, but I'd also begun to regard her beloved Napoléon and his mount with aversion. Their *Alps* painting hung on that same piaffe wall, and if that weren't bad enough, their faces were everywhere, reflected in the mirrors lining the long sides of the arena. I couldn't even look at myself without having that horse's red, battle-weary eyes staring back at me. I worried I'd begun to look more like him, less like myself.

The only reprieve was Nuno's evening visits. He always returned to the barn after hours to check on me and sneak me a carrot or two. He was careful not to get caught by Senhor Matos, who did not believe in giving rewards for *nothing*. Luckily, the fat man was generally long gone. Off, I imagined, entertaining visitors or, more likely, eating a pie. Or three.

I can assure you those rewards were not for nothing. Nuno's consistent, caring visits calmed me, kept me going. And as he left each night, he would repeat something the Old Man had once told him.

"*O que sofremos não é importante, apenas como suportamos isso.*" What we suffer is not important, only how we bear it.

I knew he wasn't saying it only for my sake.

19

Growing up, I wanted a hometown. I wanted to belong. But then, after I did grow up, all I wanted to do was keep moving. To escape. To reinvent. And yet, as the saying goes, wherever I went, there I was.

Still lost.

But also, still proud.

Proud of *who* I came from.

I admit, when I travel, I often tune out the safety demos on flights. I've heard them a million times, and I know how to fasten my seat belt, look for the nearest exit, put on an oxygen mask. But while I'm waiting to board a flight, one thing can catch my attention and give me pause.

"Families traveling with small children are welcome to board first. So, too, are active-duty military members. We thank you for your service."

Born in 1921, my Pop-Pop O'Malley belonged to the Greatest Generation, and during the Second World War, he enlisted in the navy and served in the Pacific. More specifically, he was stationed on Guam. Until he died at the age of ninety-seven, he wore his U.S. Navy veteran's baseball cap with pride.

My dad served in Vietnam before reenlisting in 1970. His generation is the Silent Generation. Maybe that's why he never spoke much about Vietnam. Frankly, he never spoke much about his job at all, even though he served for twenty years.

Back in the eighties, there was an ad campaign whose slogan was "Army. Be all you can be." I remember kids at my high school saying, "because that's all you can be." At the time, I was at a *regular* public school. Not with other military brats but just brats.

I wanted to tell them to shut up and that they didn't know what they were talking about. But I said nothing. Not because I belong to the Silent Generation, but maybe because I also don't belong to the Greatest Generation. I'm a Gen Xer. The Forgotten Generation. Invisible.

Sounds about right.

20

2009: São Paulo, Brazil

Mother taught me a trick. Not a circus one like bowing, but a coping one for when I was feeling lost or out of sorts. She said times would not always be good, but they'd also not always be bad. Like the weather, life can change from one minute to the next. A cloudless sky might turn into a pelting storm, but the darkest day could also be turned right side up with a single ray of sunshine. The trick? Embrace impermanence and persevere.

After two months spent up against that wall, I heard Maysa again. I'll never forget. It was a Sunday. The only day of the week I didn't usually see Nuno. And yet, his voice was distinct and the tune a comfort.

He approached my stall, his smile wide, his black eyes bright.

"*Bom dia, valente. Vamos dar uma volta?*" Good morning, brave one. Shall we go for a ride?

My ears shot forward, but when he entered my stall with the halter, I unconsciously recoiled. Just the week before, Senhor Matos had begun to assign other riders to work with me and the training had intensified. Instead of two hours of riding each day, it had become two hours twice a day. No sooner had I recovered from a taxing morning session than Nuno was tacking me up again . . . for someone else to ride me. And while he continued to promise everything would soon be okay, I saw no sign of improvement until this. Out of nowhere, shall *we* go for ride? Why had Senhor Matos suddenly granted Nuno permission to ride me again?

As if reading my mind, Nuno answered.

"É seu aniversário, Artilheiro." It's your birthday, Artilheiro. "*E meu.*" And mine.

My birthday? My birthday! Why, yes, I was four years old. But his birthday?

"*Sim, meu aniversário também.*" Yes, my birthday, too. "*Alguém nos deu um presente muito especial.*" Someone has given us a very special gift.

It was everything about his demeanor that helped me understand immediately. This had nothing to do with Senhor Matos. It was *her* doing. Dona had orchestrated this reunion. I had underestimated her, not given her enough, or really any, empathetic credit. Under that cool exterior, did there beat a warm heart? Perhaps the test all along had been of Senhor Matos. Perhaps she had seen through his charade and now understood Nuno and I were meant to be together.

"*Pronto?*" Ready?

He stood at my side. He'd thrown a halter over his right shoulder like a purse and reached up to place his left palm flat against my forehead. He knew that touch relaxed me, and as I lowered my head, he slid the halter on and up over my ears.

"*Hoje será um dia para lembrar,*" he said. Today will be a day to remember.

It was still early, but the air had not cooled or thinned much overnight and the temperature was already on the rise. Nuno didn't bother with a saddle or bridle and instead hopped up bareback with just the halter and a lead rope for reins. He was in no rush and took me on the long loop through the forest, never asking for more than a walk. We stopped at the end of the trail so I could soak my legs in the cool, shaded creek.

He was right. It was a birthday to remember.

Two days later, the trucks arrived.

21

1985: Heidelberg, Germany

Trucks were always arriving. Okay, maybe not always. But generally every two to three years. Trucks meant packing up furniture, knickknacks, mementos, but most of all, trucks meant change and leaving behind life as I knew it. A life I was expected to say goodbye to. Sometimes, as my dad wrote to one school guidance counselor, on short notice.

April 2, 1985
Heidelberg American High School
Attn: Guidance Officer (Mrs. Ray)
Dear Mrs. Ray,
During our telephone conversation I had with you about six weeks ago, we discussed the early departure of my son Edward and daughter Erin from Heidelberg High School. At that time, you said that if Ed and Erin remained until 15 May, they would receive full credit for the academic year. You also said I would have to inform you in writing of our expected departure date about thirty days beforehand.

Attached is a copy of my orders to Ft. Meade, MD. Currently, my availability date is 19 May 1985, which means my family will receive a Port Call sometime between 19 and 29 May 1985. With this departure window in mind, it looks like

17 May 1985 will be the last school day for Edward and Erin, although it may be possible for them to attend a few more class days if we do not leave until the following week.

Thank you very much for your assistance.

Sincerely,

Edward P. O'Malley

Four years earlier, I hadn't been thrilled to leave West Point and my weekly riding lessons, biweekly gymnastics lessons, and seasonal ice-skating, skiing, swimming, tennis, soccer.

I loved the colorful upstate New York autumns, its snow-white winters and lightning bug summers. I cheered from Michie Stadium's peanut gallery at the Army football games (Go, Army! Beat Navy!). Every game, I bought a tired pom-pom and a pack of grape Bazooka gum. It was my ritual. In the heat of summer, I swam in Round Pond, and after the 1980 Winter Olympics at nearby Lake Placid, I skated across its icy surface, proudly wearing my ice-skating Roni (Iroquoian for "raccoon") beanie. I even once ate gravel at Round Pond. It was not my ritual. Just my neurosis.

It happened during an overnight Girl Scout camping excursion. My marshmallow slipped off my stick while I was roasting it over the campfire, and when given a graham cracker and chocolate to make my s'more, I was too shy and embarrassed to tell anyone I needed a new marshmallow. So I assembled and ate the whole damned thing. Gravel and all. What a weirdo.

But perhaps most memorably at West Point—at least, historically speaking—I hung yellow ribbons around my fifth-grade classroom and said "welcome home" to a handful of the returning Americans who'd been held hostage in Tehran for 444 days. The Thayer Hotel at the United States Military Academy had served as a waypoint after their release, and for some reason, they came to visit our small elementary school. I could have sworn one of them said, "If I never have to see another yellow ribbon . . ." I had a little one pinned to my shirt and I put my hand over it.

Oh, childhood!

West Point had been a dreamy place to spend those years, and it was sad to leave. But Heidelberg . . . Heidelberg brought a whole new level of sad. With the exception of the occasional bomb threats at school and anti-American "Yanks, go home!" insults hurled at us by some from the younger generation of Germans, when it came time, I really (really) didn't want to leave Heidelberg.

Not my friends. Not my boyfriend. Not my quirky neighbors.

Not the weekend *Volksmarches*. The downtown *Hauptstraße*. The holiday *Christkindlmärkte*.

Not the *Wiener Schnitzel, Dampfnudeln, Heiße Schokolade*.

Not even the summer-hire program where I'd been one of two kids not assigned to the main headquarters at Campbell Barracks, where everyone else boasted of watching videos all day. Instead, I'd been assigned to an accounting office in the middle of a corn field. It took me three bus rides and a creepy ten-minute walk to get there. My job? Getting paid $2.10 an hour to endure a thousand paper cuts shoving forms into file cabinets more stuffed than a Thanksgiving turkey, all while watching the permanent staff busily file their nails. From a young age, I was groomed to fear office jobs.

But also from a young age, I was afforded many incredible experiences.

When we flew out of Frankfurt am Main airport in late May 1985, Simple Minds' "Don't You (Forget About Me)" was topping the charts. Nope. I would never forget you, Heidelberg. I was already counting down the days until I could return.

22

2009: Miami, Florida

Twelve. Four thousand. Nine. Thirty-three. These were the numbers going round and round in my head after I was taken away from the only home I'd ever known.

We were twelve of the ranch's finest young Lusitano stallions. Loaded into trailers. Hauled to a noisy airport. Unloaded onto a hot tarmac. Crammed into narrow shipping stalls. Hoisted into the belly of a cargo plane for a bumpy, stressful four thousand-mile flight. After nine long hours, we landed with a jolt and a faceless voice broadcasting, "Welcome to Miami."

Off the plane, we were brought to a large windowless concrete structure. A barn like none I'd ever seen. Stall after stall, it was a maze of other lonely, fearful horses, until we reached our own lonely, individual, windowless stalls. I didn't know it at the time—how could I?—but the next thirty-three days and nights would unfold to become the longest of my life. Import quarantine, they called it.

But hold on. I'm getting ahead of myself. I need to take a step back. Back to two mornings after my birthday.

I'll never know if Nuno knew the plan all along and was trying to protect me. Or if he, too, had ulterior motives. But when the trucks and trailers pulled up, he didn't appear upset. Quite the opposite. He seemed excited, propelled almost by the anxious whinnies coming from the stallions.

The ranch was abuzz. A nervous energy blew through the aisleway like wind across a treeless plain. Each horse huffed and puffed and stomped its feet. One after the other down the row. Feeding off and into the collective frenzy. Though an unusual herd, we were a herd nonetheless, and we all knew something strange was happening as we watched the ranch staff racing around.

Senhor Matos was barking orders at whomever crossed his and Socrates's path. Nuno was directing the truck drivers on where to park and what supplies to load. Gustavo was pulling around a cartload of shipping boots and sheepskin halters. Even Dona and her husband had come down to oversee the orderly chaos. They went from stall to stall, nodding their heads, giving each horse a parting pat.

When they arrived at my stall, the man gave me a quick pat and was on his way to the next horse. Dona lingered a moment longer, leaning in to whisper, "*Me deixa orgulhoso, Artilheiro.*" Make me proud, Artilheiro.

Like the others, I'd been braided and booted and was starting to get hot. It was time to get us moving. One by one, we were led out and loaded onto one of two long trailers with the hope, I suppose, of getting the right horses next to one another to avoid any personality or hierarchical clashes. Allegro was the first stallion to go. They should have known better. I watched from my stall window as he balked at the ramp, his eyes wide and white with fear. Atlas was next, and then each horse down the line until they reached my stall. Apparently, they saved the best for last.

Gustavo haltered me and led me out past the stone horse sentry. I pranced and kicked, trying to rid myself of the shipping boots. They felt funny. Not uncomfortable, but unnatural. I'd only ever worn them once before and couldn't comprehend the need on such a warm summer day.

Before reaching the trailer, I stuck my nose high in the air and let loose a shrill, quivering scream. It was not to Gustavo's liking and when he snapped my lead rope, I yanked back hard enough to send us both reeling sideways. Nuno came running from around a corner, grabbed the rope, and yelled for Gustavo to go.

"*Pegue o resto do feno. E rápido!*" Get the rest of the hay. And fast!

To me, he turned and said, "*Tudo vai dar certo. Confie em mim.*" It will be okay. Trust me. "*Eu estarei com você a cada passo do caminho.*" I'll be with you every step of the way.

I'd never given Nuno any trouble loading before. Never. But that day, I gave it a second thought. Could I trust him to be there for me? Every step of the way? I didn't have a choice in the matter. I took one last look around before relenting and following him up the ramp. I saw the red-roofed barn, the jaboticabas, the big white house in the distance, framed by blue skies and green pastures.

To begin, but only to begin, Nuno was true to his promise. He did fly with me. Not only on the plane but in the cargo hold, where he had to wear a heavy jacket to keep warm. He'd never been to the United States before and had a hard time concealing his excitement, quite pleased Senhor Matos and the family had seen value in his service and decided the auction would be a good experience for him. And, no doubt, for them.

Ladies loved Nuno. And the family, who catered to a predominantly female clientele, had finally realized the jewel they had in him. He was a true asset at client functions and dinners. Cute, approachable, and, above all, single. He also didn't drink, as did others. He enjoyed listening, not solely out of duty but with genuine interest. And when given the chance, he took pride in sharing the history of the ranch.

The Old Man had taught him well, and, as it turned out, Nuno was a born storyteller. His English was still rudimentary, but improving, and his passion for the ranch and the horses was a magnet. Even when he stuttered, stumbling between languages to find the right words, his audience didn't tune out but leaned in, suddenly desperate to know how a quest to produce the perfect cup of coffee had led to the importation of Lusitano stallions and mares from Portugal. And eventually, the birth of a successful breeding business that exported horses to faraway lands. Like Florida.

Nuno's storytelling talents, however, were of no use at the quarantine facility. How could they be? He was not there. He may have promised to be with me every step of the way. But no, he was not. Not for every step. Not for every mindless hour in my too-bright, too-tight, but supposedly state-of-the-art cell. And not for every poke and prod from the vets and attending staff who didn't speak Portuguese and only sang Pitbull. "Rain Over Me" was right. *Ay ay ay. Por favor.*

Most days, I stared into space, trying to ignore the music and constant *whomp-whomp* of the ceiling fans, wishing they did more than spin the thick, hot air in circles. I couldn't wrap my head around my new existence. *Who cages a bullfighter?! Am I even a bullfighter? What fight have I ever won?*

Without a choice, I'd been forced from my home. First loaded onto a truck. Destination unknown. Then crammed into a metal box and hoisted into a huge metal barrel. Destination unknown. Now left in another box all alone to undergo government-mandated quarantine. Parole date unknown.

We'd taken off from Viracopos International Airport with one vet inspecting us and arrived in Florida with another taking vitals and making sure we'd managed to make it through the flight unscathed. At the time, one horse had been hurried away to be given intravenous fluids. So nervous, he'd refused to drink during the entire flight and had begun to show signs of colic. Luckily, the fluids helped, and he was back to himself by the following day. Well, as much as possible under our new lockdown.

Welcome to muggy Miami, I thought, *where you'll be tested for all variety of diseases.* From the exotic dourine, glanders, and piroplasmosis to the more common but highly contagious equine influenza. If you pass, it's on to the contagious equine metritis (CEM) part of your stay, where you'll be test-bred to two unsuspecting mares.

A stallion's quarantine period can vary from four weeks to two months or longer. I got lucky. The mares came into season sooner rather than later, and I tested negative for all diseases. Still, it was one of the worst experiences of my young life.

23

1985: Severna Park, Maryland

We touched down at John F. Kennedy International Airport, and it may as well have been Mars. More than a fish out of water, I felt like an alien in this new world. I'd grown accustomed to pristine streets and autobahns, and when we headed onto the Jersey Turnpike, all I could think was, *Welcome to the United States of Billboards, Graffiti, and Garbage.*

What happened to *Give a hoot, don't pollute*?

I'll put it this way. There's a cocktail called the Jersey Turnpike. It's for losers. Lose a bet, take this shot, and head directly to the nearest toilet. Or emergency room. If you haven't heard of it, it's when the bartender dumps any spilled liquids from the bar mat into a shot glass and, if your rival really hates you, rings out any nearby bar rag as the cherry on top. Retch.

"And what's that smell?" I asked as we crossed over the Walt Whitman Bridge and into Philadelphia. "It smells like a butthole!"

Turns out it wasn't a butthole, but close to it. It was the *known* Old Hickory bourbon smell that wafted up from the nearby Publicker distillery, where sour mash was being killed, I mean, distilled. World-famous stink. Awesome.

Nothing against South Philly. I'd always loved visiting my grandparents' row house. Built in the 1840s by a family named Blood, it had its own smells. Especially down in the basement. That's where my Pop-Pop stored his ham radios, computers, photography equipment, woodworking saws, watercolor paints and canvases, whatever accoutrements matched his hobby du jour. He once sawed off the top of his thumb on one of those saws while building me a dollhouse. Don't worry, that wasn't one of the smells, and also, the nearest ER doc sewed it back on. The only problem was the thumb never quite bent in the same way. Ever after, my Pop-Pop looked like a perpetual hitchhiker.

Hanging in that house was an old framed photo of him on a tall, ribby, swaybacked nag. By my grandfather's youthful face, I'd guess it was taken well before the war.

I've asked around, but no one seems to know where the photo was taken. It's not in the city, but maybe a borough? They're on a dirt road, and behind them is a long flat field that stretches out to reach a row of small houses in the distance. There may be a church with a spire in the mix. But really, I don't care if there's a church or houses. It's the horse that captures my imagination. It may be the angle of the shot, but there's no tail visible. My guess is it had been docked, and maybe he'd been a cart horse. Perhaps even a milkman's horse, like the one my dad used to tell me about.

When my dad was a kid, the milkman still made deliveries on the avenue. The milkman, his cart, and his trusty steed. The horse was so well trained and obedient, all the milkman had to do was whistle and whoa. The horse would walk on and stop before the next house.

Years later, when the cart became a truck, the milkman told my dad he missed his horse. It was actually faster and easier for him to do his job with the horse.

"Now, I gotta get in and out of this damn thing," he said of his truck.

I bet the kids missed the horse, too. Every once in a while, a parent or grandparent might hold up a little one to pet the horse, give it a carrot. The milkman didn't mind and neither did the horse.

I wish I'd been around when milk was delivered by horses. I wished for a lot of things. But that summer, maybe what I wished for most was distraction. And in retrospect, what I should have wished for harder was for someone to take me to Live Aid.

Sure, it wouldn't have been at Wembley, where Queen blew the roof off the stadium, inspiring a sea of arms to sway and clap in unison—*ga ga, goo goo, blah blah*—by giving what would later be called the greatest live performance in the history of rock and roll. But still, it would have been amazing. I'd have been giddy seeing me some Tom Petty, Bryan Adams, Madonna, The Cars . . . Plus, my grandparents lived less than two miles from JFK Stadium. Less than two miles!

Could've, should've, would've.

Besides that, the rest of the summer went by in a blur of thick East Coast humidity, my new *As the World Turns* and *General Hospital* daytime drama addictions, a few long weekends down the shore with cousins, and unimaginably good corn, tomatoes, and peaches. They don't call it the Garden State for nothing. And as a result of that summer and my lack of insistence, Jack Wagner later became my first concert experience, not Live Aid. Christ.

I still missed my friends in Germany terribly, but mostly I spent hours dreading starting at a new school. Not that I hadn't done it before, but this time was going to be different. I wasn't going to be on a military base, with other military brats. I was going to be at a regular public high school. Classes didn't worry me so much. I loved studying. But one thing had my stomach all tied up in knots: lunch.

It was always the worst time of day at any school, but when I started at Severna Park High School, the cafeteria became a veritable torture chamber. Khakis to the left of me. Polos to the right. There I was, stuck in the middle. Where would I sit? Who would sit next to me?

On my first day, I walked in with my brown paper lunch bag and, phew, found an empty table. I was alone for maybe three minutes when someone sat down next to me. Like, not just at the same table, but *right next to me.*

"Hi, my name is Wanda. What's yours?" she said through her braces.

"Hi, I'm Erin."

"Wanda be friends?"

If it's not what she said, it's what I heard. And Erin didn't Wanda be friends. Don't get me wrong. I was *not* cool (Wanda wasn't the only brace-face). But Wanda seemed desperate. And desperation felt uncool in a way I wasn't down with.

The next day, I skipped the cafeteria and walked out the front door. I found a tree and sat under it. I did that every day until it got too cold. Then, I went to the library. You weren't supposed to eat in the library, but I carefully hid my cheese sandwich, eating it in panicked bites when no one was looking. It pained me to break the rules, but it would have pained me more to try to endure that lunchroom.

Besides Wanda, not many other people said anything to me at school. No one asked me if I was new. They either didn't care or hadn't noticed me. The school was quadruple the size of Heidelberg High. From what I gathered, most of the kids had been born in the area and grown up together. They moved in cliques like fish in schools.

I felt invisible. But also, awkwardly visible.

And it didn't get much better as the year progressed. Except for Sara. She was another transplant. Her family had moved from

Minnesota a few months into the school year and Mrs. Zukauskas, our English teacher, was kind enough to pair us on a group assignment. A friendship was born.

Sara and I mostly hung out at her house or mine, watching movies, painting our toenails or faces, listening to music my older brother would have mocked. But every once in a while, we'd brave the world. And more than once in a while, we'd find out the world was not so brave, but just full of a bunch of douchebags.

I'll never forget the time I let her convince me to go to a party. When we walked in the door, I heard, "What are *you* two doing here?"

The question had come from a girl with a giant mole between her nose and lip. She was drunk. Disorderly. And despicable. I wanted to remind her it was not a Halloween party but that she'd have made a great witch. Instead, I turned to Sara and said, "This place sucks. Let's get out of here."

Not long before we'd also gone to a football game. As we were walking through the crowd to find seats, another Severna Park sophisticate screamed, "Wide load coming through!"

My friend struggled with her weight, already subsisting on nothing but lettuce leaves and Tab cola. If you've ever tasted Tab, you know how hard she was trying. She didn't need to be berated by these ignorant kids who knew nothing yet felt free to say anything.

Then again, how would they have known otherwise? More disgusting were the complicit adults. Plenty heard the insult and not only did they say nothing in my friend's defense, but worse, they laughed along.

This. Place. Was. Officially. The. Worst. Ever.

That year, I also struggled with deciding what to do about horseback riding, if anything.

During our New Jersey stay, my relatives had asked if I was

planning on finding a new barn once we settled in Maryland. Settled? What were we? Pioneers?

"Maybe," I said.

Every time we moved, I tended to give up things I'd done before. Generally, this was because there were several times I tried otherwise only to be relegated to beginner levels, despite my experience. *Prove yourself, kid*, was the implication. And I was tired of proving myself. Exhausted, really.

Even before leaving Germany, I'd considered giving up riding. But that was only because my old barn had closed down and I hadn't been overly enthused about the new one. It had been much less friendly, much more uppity. It was the first time I'd been made to feel inferior, like a second-class citizen, for not having my own horse.

Now, very much *unsettled* in Maryland, I wasn't sure if my psyche could take more snubbing. And so, the question of finding a new barn lingered . . . until before too long, it was definitively answered.

24

2009: Wellington, Florida

Yes, that's me! Well, at least I think that's me.

I was halfway through my morning timothy flake when they came for me. And by *they*, I mean one of the clog-clad staff whose name I never bothered to learn. So perhaps it was a tad unfair of me to judge him butchering my name.

Halter in hand, he opened my stall door and said, "Artill-hero! Time to go."

I hadn't a clue where but, as always, hoped for home.

Together, we clopped back through the corridor of lonely horses. Some different, some the same as when I'd arrived. To my surprise and delight, we headed straight through the exit doors, out of the windowless lockup, and into the bright glare of a boundless blue sky. I blinked and blinked. Half trying to adjust my eyes. Half in disbelief of what I was seeing.

Nuno! He greeted us, reached for my lead rope, and, stroking my neck, gave me a once-over from head to haunches.

"*Você está bem? Você parece bem.*" Are you good? You look good.

Words of apology trickled out after.

"*Sinto muito.*" Sorry. "*Essas eram as regras.*" Those were the rules.

In one way, his excuses buzzed in my ears like flies in a field. In another, I didn't care. I was happy to see him, to be out in the sun, to be going home. His quick exam finished, he led me around the building. Another trailer awaited us, and I didn't dare hesitate. I walked straight up and in.

Not an hour later, we turned through the gates of a sprawling equestrian facility. So, not homeward bound. The truck and trailer wound around the property's perimeter, and I took in arena after arena. There were so many I lost count. But when we pulled to a stop, I couldn't take my eyes off the last one.

A lone rider was jumping an enormous, sweaty chestnut under a relentless, high-noon sun. Obstacle over obstacle, they flew . . . until the horse stopped dead, refusing to move forward. Something had unsettled him, but instead of caring about or considering what, the rider went into an apoplectic fit. She yelled and kicked and wrenched his neck to her knee, making him spin round and round in tiny, tight circles.

I was glad when the trailer doors swung open and I could focus on the two long white barns before me. Each large enough to house a hundred horses. Nuno led me into the nearest one and introduced me to another *new* stall. The shavings were deep. The hay net was full. But what interested me most was the window. Once again, I had a view, and I could see I was not alone at check-in. More trailers continued to arrive, with more people leading more horses into their own new accommodations.

Another Brazilian breeder had also flown in a selection of its top sale prospects. As the testosterone level began to rise in the barn, so, too, did the volume. Not only from horses stomping and whinnying but also from old human friends reuniting with hugs and kisses and new acquaintances sharing names and how-do-you-dos above the cacophony.

I was happy most of the conversations were in Portuguese. I paid close attention to all within earshot. This was it. The big event. The culmination of all the training, travel, pokes, and prods. In two days, the previews would begin. Then the showcase. Then the auction.

From all the barn chatter, I learned the small pool of potential buyers had received photos and short videos of all the horses, and the breeders had invited them to schedule appointments to meet and test ride any they liked. The one stipulation: Only one ride per horse was permitted. Understandable in a sense, and completely nonsensical in another. A single ride to decide a yea or nay on a purchase? To decide a horse's worth? Its fate?

I thought, *What if no one chooses me?* And yes, it was a fleeting thought. And the wait to find out wasn't long.

The first previewers arrived early the next morning, and I was quick to weary of their ceaseless small talk. The self-promotion circulating the barn was dizzying. Riders boasting about their skills. About the world-renowned clinicians they'd ridden with. About the lavish barns they owned, or time spent in Portugal or Brazil. Funny, I didn't hear a single one speaking Portuguese.

The grooms from the other breeding barn told every visitor how much their horses were looking forward to new adventures with their soon-to-be new owners. I wasn't certain any of the other horses felt the same, but I knew I wasn't looking forward to any of it. I still just wanted to go home. Back to Brazil. Back to the ranch. Back to my small room with a view. A better view than this one, which faced the two tryout arenas.

There was one arena for each breeding barn, and each had half a dozen young stallions going around at the same time. A bit crazy considering most of the horses had been under saddle only a couple of months, and all of us were newly out of quarantine and under pressure to perform in strange surroundings.

Nuno was dressed to impress. He wore our ranch's requisite red vest along with a white polo, white breeches, and tall black spit-shined boots. Before my first appointment, he led me to a nearby grassy field for a quick warm-up ride. The goal was to take off a bit of the overnight, cooped-up edge, but not having been ridden for nearly a month, it had the opposite effect. I was amped.

A crowd of onlookers began to assemble. The women caught my eye. Mainly because they sparkled. Their hands adorned with diamonds. Their riding attire dipped in ostentation. Glittery helmets, glittery boots, glittery belts. Meanwhile, the men, most of whom were not dressed to ride, wore plaid pastel jackets and straw fedoras to shield their bald heads.

I watched three other horse-and-rider combos going around the arena. One rider had her horse's head cranked so tight toward his chest it was a miracle he didn't topple over. Another horse kept spooking at the same corner of the arena. Nothing crazy, but enough to spook the rider into dismounting and handing him back to a groom.

Closest to us, another groom from our ranch was helping an older woman dismount. She appeared frazzled, complaining loudly about the horse's trot.

"He's too bouncy," she barked.

My take? If she couldn't handle the young horse's trot and needed help down, she shouldn't have gotten up in the first place.

Behind me, someone called my name.

"Artilheiro?" said a bedazzled woman. She squinted at a piece of paper in her hand before looking back over at me. "This is Artilheiro, correct?"

Nuno nodded and motioned for her to enter the arena.

"Smaller than I'd imagined," she added.

Though middle-aged, she spoke with the rattle of a geriatric and, once mounted, rode with a similar fragility and shakiness. She was constantly adjusting herself in the saddle. Not in a good way. She jiggled the reins and wiggled her legs and hips as if to signal . . . but for what? I couldn't tell.

Fortunately, we only walked. And not for long.

"I just don't know what to think of him," she said after hopping off. "He didn't seem to want to do what I asked."

"What you ask him to do?" Nuno said.

"Well, I don't know. Maybe trot. Maybe piaffe."

Nuno took the reins and said only, "Have a good day."

Next up was a very tall, lean man. I wondered if his feet might scrape the ground once mounted. He said nothing to me or Nuno but put the reins over my neck, pulled them taut, and climbed aboard. His feet did not scrape but hung lower than my belly and instead of clicking or squeezing, he raised those feet and gave me a rough kick that jolted me forward. His riding was heavy-handed, robotic, and completely devoid of feel or finesse. I was relieved when he, too, hopped off within ten minutes. Nuno hurried to take the reins, which the man dropped into his hands, still without a word. No thank-you, no nothing. He simply walked away, moving on to the next poor horse.

Nuno tried to reassure me, "*Relaxa. Tudo ficará bem.*" Relax. Everything will be okay.

I couldn't tell if he was talking to me or himself, but there was no time for relaxing. The next rider was already approaching. Unlike the bedazzled crowd, she wore no glitter, yet her broad smile carried a certain sparkle. She extended one hand to shake Nuno's, while using the other to cram a pack of cigarettes into the pocket of her denim shirt.

She spoke fast. Much too fast.

"Only one horse has played me up today. Skirted clear across the arena. Everyone gasped, 'Oh my God!' like it was some crazy surprise. Between you and me, I kind of liked him for it."

She paused, cocked her head.

"You're not understanding a word I'm saying, are you?"

"*Perdão?*" he said. Pardon?

She slowed down. Way down. "I can see . . . you're different. And I can see . . . you like this horse . . . and he likes you."

Nuno nodded.

"So, tell me. Any advice?"

Nuno finally understood. "He's young. If he is afraid, I let him look."

She laughed and patted him on the shoulder. "*Obrigado.*" Thank you.

To me, she said, "*Olá,* you." The first person to say hello to me.

She didn't swing her hand in front of my face to pat my nose—a move I never liked—but instead stroked my neck. The smell of smoke and tar clung to her hands, her breath, her clothes. Clothes that consisted of faded jeans, dusty cowboy boots, and a helmet she called "horseshit." Her blue eyes, framed by deep crow's feet, told me she'd seen a thing or two. I wondered if she knew any bulls.

She didn't immediately mount but led me around the arena. First in one direction and then the other. She was careful to pay attention to the other riders, who weren't doing the same, and didn't say another word until she took me to the mounting block. There, she looked me in the eye and said, "How about you show me what you've got, and I'll do my best to avoid these nincompoops."

Again, unlike the others, she took her time. She walked me for a good long while, testing how I moved under slight shifts in her weight. When she asked me to trot, she bent slightly forward and gave a gentle squeeze with her legs. She did not kick. As Nuno did, she gave me a chance to answer before throwing more "aids" at me. She did not try to hold me back in canter but let me open up the gait around the arena, giving bystanders a taste of my speed and power.

Once off my back, she told Nuno, "He's definitely not straightforward . . . which I don't mind. But there's something about him I can't quite put my finger on."

"Tomorrow," he said. "You try again tomorrow."

She started to nod but halted abruptly when she saw two men watching from the sidelines. One, with rubicund cheeks, was big and out of shape. So, of course, I figured him for an instructor. His cowboy hat sat atop his big head like a child's party favor, and his fuzzy mustache could have doubled for a goatskin *xairel*—a piece of fur that sits behind a traditional Portuguese saddle and over a horse's loins to help keep a rider's jacket clean. His sidekick, a slighter man, was dressed top to bottom in khaki. He looked more ready to go on safari than a ride. So, of course, I figured him for the money man. Yeah, I'd been picking up some lingo in the barn aisles.

"Let me get back to you," she told Nuno.

Cowboy and Safari approached her as she left the arena. They were keen to know whether she liked me. Or for that matter, if she liked any horse.

"Well, you were watching. What did you think?"

"Probably not good for a beginner?" Safari said.

"None of these horses are good for beginners. But you know who I really like?" she said.

The men leaned in.

"The gray stallion. He's fantastic."

With the exception of one palomino, one buckskin, and one black stallion, all the horses at the event were gray. The men should have known better. This was big business, and she had to be careful about what she said. Even to her clients.

Turns out Boots, as I came to call her, was related to one of the biggest Lusitano buyers in California and also the foundational trainer for a couple who'd made several purchases at the previous year's auction. Both breeding barns, particularly mine, were interested in a repeat performance. And while Nuno had been instructed to treat everyone well, he'd been given permission to grant her special dispensation. Boots had a knack for choosing quality and wasn't afraid to ride anything.

That same day, I had three more riders try me out. None were too terrible, but as the afternoon dragged on, most seemed more interested in the happy hour menu. Champagne cocktails and bacon-wrapped dates were calling to them. And let's face it, I was ready for some grass and alone time.

The next day, morning broke and my soul died a little more. The humidity level had risen, and an even larger crowd had gathered to watch, point, and tittle-tattle. I wasn't sure if their attention was focused on me, the four other stallions going around the arena, or the couple standing in its center. Nuno led me straight toward them, and my nostrils flared.

The woman, diminutive in stature and with tiny, hooded eyes to match, wore a faded velvet cap and an anachronistic pair of puffy riding breeches. What century did she think it was? The closer we got, the more excited she became. She latched onto the arm of her pinguid companion, yanking on him like a petulant child in want of a pony ride. I wondered if she needed a bathroom, especially when her nervous knee jitters transformed into off-the-ground hops. Up and down she popped, waving at us like a village drunk.

Nuno did not wave back.

I stared at her partner. While I doubted many, if any, would describe Senhor Matos as healthy, he was, by comparison to this man, able-bodied. This odd creature resembled a grain bag—that is, if grain bags were mounted on two sticks and had arms that hung to either side like limp carrots. I considered bolting.

"He's the prettiest of them all. A unicorn. I want him. Mine. Mine. Mine!" she prattled on.

Nuno cupped my ear and whispered, "*Isso será rápido.*" This will be quick.

I practically held my breath as he helped the micro-tyrant onto my back. He kept hold of the reins for a few steps before asking if she was comfortable to walk on by herself.

"Of course. Give him to me." She yanked at the loose reins, walked me a few paces, and started to squeal. "Take a photo! Take a photo!"

She giggled and wiggled and flopped around on my back with a seat so unsteady I had no idea what she wanted me to do. Should I walk? Trot? Give up and wait for it all to be over as Nuno had promised? Without knowing what else to do, I started a nervous jig. It was a mistake, as I felt another harsh jolt to my mouth. The naive slack she'd left in the reins made her reaction to pull on them severe and painful. I tossed my head in search of relief, but she paid no attention and blasted another command at Grain Bag.

"Action shot. I want an action shot. No, not like that. Wait. Stop. Just hand me my selfie stick."

Grain Bag lumbered toward me, brandishing a crop-like stick, while she lurched halfway off the saddle to grab it. Using my mouth as leverage, she pulled herself back up and thrust the thing in my face. A sudden, sharp flash blinded me as she dug spurs into my sides and hollered, "Giddyup!"

Other horses may have spooked and bounced sideways, but I stopped dead. Bent deep through my hind legs. And leapt into a spectacular capriole. Like scattershot from a cannon, her camera and selfie stick flew one way, she another. Straight over my head and onto Grain Bag's. His girth helped break her fall and, for that matter, his own. But before Nuno could think to grab me, my ears went back flat against my neck, and I lunged toward them.

Turns out, falling was the easy part for them. Getting up was another, more difficult story. Replete with flailing, stumbling, and more squealing.

The other riders had stopped their horses, and everyone—horses, riders, grooms—stood staring. I thought, *How's that for an action shot?* I imagined the photo capturing the thin vapor rising from my nostrils like steam from a kettle. Fueled by the dragon fire that burned hot within my belly. Lest anyone forget, I was born to fight bulls.

It was my first true protest, and needless to say, a purchase, at least by them, was not likely. The worry, of course, was that a purchase by anyone would be less likely, especially considering the number of bystanders who walked away shaking their heads, aghast at my wild side.

The next two riders canceled their appointments, and Nuno walked me back to the barn. Calm as ever, he told me I'd done well.

"*Vai ficar tudo bem. Não se preocupa.*" Everything will be fine. Don't worry.

I'll never know for sure, but I think he was a smidge proud of the display. Perhaps even hoped it would mean he could bring me back home. I sure got to hoping so. And that's just about the time Boots showed up at my stall, accompanied by a beautiful woman whose legs were practically as long as Nuno was tall.

25

1985: Fort Meade, Maryland

"Don't worry. Everything's going to be okay." That's what the nice people were telling me. But I didn't want to hear it.

Within a week of starting at Severna Park High, I knew I would not be participating in any high school sports or clubs. *Nein, danke.* But after further consideration on the horse front, I realized how much I missed riding (and more so, horses) and decided to check out some local barns. My first stop was Fort Meade. The base had stables that offered lessons and trail rides. I signed up for one of the latter. Figured it'd be a good way to dip my toes (or lower my heels) again, so to speak.

A member of the barn staff led a small group of us out on an easy two-hour ride, mainly on wooded paths and across a few open fields. We did cross one small creek, where we let loose the reins for our horses to have a guzzle on the hot day.

The ride was super chill, and I'd already been daydreaming about coming back, maybe even for lessons, when the guide pointed ahead. "This is the only place where there will be any cars. But most people are pretty good about slowing down for us. Plus, the horses don't care much about the cars."

"Just be sure to walk, not trot across the parking lot," he added. "The asphalt can be slippery."

The asphalt we had to cross accounted for about thirty feet of what in total was about a five-mile ride. There were no cars coming or going from the lot. Not even any cars on the road. But as soon as I was smack-dab in the middle of those thirty feet, my horse started to trot, and then, *pop*!

Out of nowhere, a shot rang out loud and crisp. In short order, I learned the parking lot was for the Meade Rifle and Pistol Club. A firing range.

My horse spooked, slid, and flipped over sideways. I'm not sure how, but I managed to jump out of the way before he could roll on top of me. I scraped up my left arm pretty good, but it's not what stung the most. My horse was bleeding.

Whether on his panicked way down or scramble to get up, he'd scraped the fur and skin off both front cannon bones. His eyes were white with fear. Rushing over, the guide made fast work to ensure I was okay and, checking the horse, said, "It's okay. It looks superficial. We're almost to the creek again. We can let him cool his legs off there."

No one in the group tried to do anything but make me feel better. But the more they tried to comfort and reassure me he was going to be fine, the worse I felt. I know now, maybe even then, it hadn't been my fault. Accidents happen. But at the time, I felt like the worst rider, the worst person. I was a monster who'd hurt a horse. And nothing was going to convince me to return to that place.

That single gunshot shattered my confidence and changed the trajectory of my horse riding. It would be six years before I got on a horse again.

26

2009: Wellington, Florida

In a way, the hard part seemed over. I'd had one final, covert session with Boots and Legs, but they'd been so relaxed and kind it hardly felt like work. Nuno had agreed to meet them at an arena on the other side of the property after everyone else had dispersed for dinner, drinks, massages, or all three back at the Palm Beach Ritz-Carlton.

"A bit too hoity-toity for me," Boots said. "I'd have preferred to stay at a motel and save them some cash. But oh, no."

"Don't be so gauche," Legs joked before quickly changing the subject. She told Nuno she'd visited Brazil once and wasn't shy about giving her limited Portuguese a whirl. Nuno appreciated the effort, and I liked when she said, "*Ele é um cavalo bom e bonito.*" He is a good and handsome horse.

It seemed these women, regardless of their preference in hotels, weren't here to outsparkle the other guests. They were interested in knowing more about my relationship with Nuno. They wanted to know what I liked and didn't like. They listened with intent, and when Boots asked one unexpected question—Had I been weaned early?—Nuno did a double take.

"*Separado da mãe cedo?*" Legs offered a translation. Separated from mother early?

"*Sim.*" Nuno had already understood. "Was little early. Much sad. Much stress."

He explained the best he could how Mother had saved my life but lost her own.

It was hard to hear, but I don't think he could have described her courage any better.

"Much sad is right," Boots said.

"But," Nuno added while flexing his arm to make a muscle, "*Artilheiro é corajoso e forte.*"

"Brave and strong," Legs translated.

"Well, I'd like to have known her," Boots said.

And I would have liked to have known her for longer. So much longer.

"*Sim. Como o filho dela, ela era boa e bonita.*" Nuno turned to Legs to translate.

"Like her son, she was good and beautiful."

Boots gave Nuno a pat on the shoulder. "I'm glad you were there for him. It's obvious he trusts you. We'll be mindful."

As the sun began to drop and the women led me around the arena, Nuno leaned against a white fence to watch. The fading light made the palm trees lining the property's edge look like giant black dandelions against an orange sky. Something about them reminded me of home, and I wondered if I took a deep breath and blew hard enough, if I could blow their tops off, create magic, and make my biggest wish—to go home—come true. But oddly enough, I didn't try, finding myself instead drawn to what the women said next.

"That young man gives a shit, but some of these other people . . . I don't know what they're expecting from these horses," Boots said. "Most are green broke. All of them have been flown halfway around the world and are only just out of weeks of quarantine. They're not goddamn carousel ponies for wannabe princess prima donnas. They're bullfighters."

Yes, finally! Someone who sees me.

"And this one," she continued. "Sure, he's awful pretty and I like the way he moves. But today, he sold me on his spunk. This horse is resilient and he's not gonna take crap from no one. But I'd bet money he'd do anything for his person."

Yes, for Nuno, I will do anything.

"Wouldn't they all?" Legs asked.

"Well, that depends."

"On?"

"The person."

"Is that a challenge?"

"Damn straight it is."

Turns out I'd been in Boots's top-five picks from the start. She'd been pushing Legs to take a closer look. So Legs hopped up and after a short, uneventful ride, she gave me a pat, looked down at Boots, and said, "Let me talk to Frank."

Done for the night, they handed the reins back to Nuno and headed in one direction as we went the other. About halfway back to the barn, we ran into Cowboy.

"Out disciplining that boy?" he said.

"No, no, no," Nuno said. "Just a short ride."

"I see. Well, you have a good night."

"And you."

Cowboy started to walk away but turned back. "I'll be interested to see you two together at the showcase tomorrow."

"Yes. Yes, of course," Nuno said. "*Boa noite.*" Good night.

The showcase was planned for the evening, when temperatures dipped slightly below sweltering. That morning, I saw that a large white tent had been erected in a corner of the enormous covered arena. Later, crystal chandeliers hanging from its ceiling cast a warm glow over white tables and chairs, meticulously arranged to offer the clientele an optimal view of the imminent spectacle.

We were thirty-five Lusitanos. The showcase was our time to shine and the guests' time to watch, scrutinize, and choose favorites. While Boots may have questioned others' expectations of us, to me, they were clear: These were competitive people who expected the best. They were as eager for a last look as they were for the evening's passed hors d'oeuvres and rum cocktails.

As the grooms scrambled to finish prepping and primping every horse, Senhor Matos strolled into the barn. His socks were pulled up to his knees over his breeches, as if he were preparing to ride. Yet, a cocktail already sloshed in his hand, soon to be quaffed in full, no doubt.

Spotting me in the crossties, he summoned Nuno and delivered his version of a pep talk.

"*Ontem não foi muito bom. Certifique-se de que este aqui se comporte hoje à noite.*" Yesterday was not so good. Make sure this one behaves tonight. "*Boa sorte. E não nos decepcione.*" Good luck. And don't let us down.

By *us*, I knew he meant Dona and the family, but I cared only about making Mother and Nuno proud. After Senhor Matos walked away, Nuno looked me in the eye and said, "*Nós vamos mostrar a ele.*" We'll show him.

Shortly thereafter, the parade of horses began.

A man in a beige linen suit and pink tie stood at a podium. He praised everyone for traveling from far and wide to attend this most auspicious occasion.

"Welcome! Welcome! Welcome! We're excited to get started and present to you our finest collection ever. So grab yourselves a beverage, sit back, and get ready to enjoy the ride!"

From every direction there was chatter, laughter, clanking glasses. But also, music.

A lone guitarist, dressed in a crisp white shirt, dark pants, and suspenders, sat on a squat stage amid the meandering guests and bustling waitstaff. Above the din of conversation, he casually strummed and sang what felt like songs only he could have written. Beautiful, soulful, Portuguese fados. I doubted many understood the words, which spoke of everyday hardships, but it didn't matter. The rhythm of the music and its unfeigned delivery set a mood whose intent, perhaps, was to subconsciously plant seeds of loss and longing. Tempting potential buyers to dig deep, bid high, or forever miss the opportunity to bring home the horse of their dreams.

At the gate, a groom gave Nuno a leg up into the saddle, and after the sole palomino walked out of the arena, we walked in. My ears flicked back. Despite the charged atmosphere and a woman providing commentary over a loudspeaker—"To ride him is a unique experience"—my focus remained on Nuno. I was ready to respond to his familiar, gentle aids. When he asked, I answered. I collected my trot, taking shorter but higher steps. I extended my trot, lengthening my stride to cover more ground. I picked up a powerful, expressive canter in both directions. I did everything without a toss of the head or a root on the reins. No fussing at all. Nuno's sigh upon our exit told me all I needed to know.

I went back to the barn and for the rest of the evening enjoyed the cooling air, the *clip-clop* comings and goings of the other horses, and the lingering satisfaction of a job well done. By morning, I held fast to the sense of accomplishment, more certain than ever I had redeemed myself. Not only in Nuno's eyes but also the family's. Maybe, just maybe, I was that much closer to getting my wish of going home.

The auction, later that day, brought a different energy. Seats had been assigned; bidding forms and paddles had been handed out. Grapes, strawberries, and cheese wedges had been plated and placed in the middle of each table, along with glasses for water and wine. A sit-down dinner was scheduled, but beforehand, servers walked among the guests, offering lamb meatball lollipops, hummus, and various other mystery canapés. All very civilized, save for the fact everything felt a bit off-kilter and more than a bit amplified.

The entertainment was louder, saucier. Bikini-clad samba dancers with sky-high feather headdresses bounced to a raucous drumbeat. An inordinate number of fat men in fedoras smoked stinky cigars, sweating in seersucker and spritzing their neighbors with spittle as they drank too much and laughed too hard at their own jokes. With so many horses to present, everything moved at a wild pace. No dillydallying. The auctioneer picked up his microphone and got to work.

"Everybody, grab your paddles and get set. Auctions move fast and furious, and we're ready to go!" Unintelligible babble. "Let's hear some noise for this first great horse! What a stunner!" Unintelligible babble. "And sold!"

In no time, it was my turn, and as soon as Nuno and I entered the arena, I saw her. She was wearing a white silk blouse tucked into high-waisted linen trousers. The look accentuated her long legs as she glided across the room. Boots walked beside her, in bootcut jeans and a pressed western shirt, while every other lady skittered about in flashy, floral prints. Legs was a swan among parrots. Behind them, a much shorter man followed. He was not wearing a fedora.

As during the showcase, our image appeared on a giant video screen that hung above one of the long sides of the arena. The auctioneer started the bidding.

"And what do you hear? Can I get $40,000?"

Cutlery clinked against flatware, but no one raised a paddle. He dropped the price. Still nothing. He went even lower, saying, "Don't let someone walk out of here with the horse of your dreams."

A man in a fedora (go figure) raised his paddle. Nuno's head spun to see who it was. The paddle was Safari's; the smug grin next to him, Cowboy's.

The auctioneer repeated the bid and started to say "Going . . ." but abruptly halted. The man who had followed and was now seated next to Legs and Boots had given his paddle a blasé lift. Safari countered. The mystery man did not submit. Paddles flipped back and forth, faster and faster, like a frantic game of Ping-Pong. Again, the auctioneer's words became unintelligible until I heard, "Going once, going twice . . . Sold!"

Two days later, Nuno led me into another trailer. It was the biggest one yet, with a roomy stall and a giant net of hay. There had been so many trailers and stalls and new places I had no way of knowing where I was headed, but something felt different. And it hit me. Maybe it was home! I didn't care if it meant another trailer ride. Another plane ride. I didn't care if I had to put up with Senhor Matos now and again. I wanted to be home, back to my old routine.

I allowed myself a moment to daydream as Nuno tied my lead rope to a ring on the wall. I could almost hear the Old Man's voice, shaped by all of Nuno's stories, "*Para casa, vamos nós.*" To home, we go. But before I could settle in for even a bite of hay, Nuno took hold of my halter and nudged my head down so he could whisper into my ear.

"*Seja bom, valente. Para Shangri-La, você vai.*" Be good, brave one. To Shangri-La, you go.

He wrapped his arms around my neck, stuck his nose into my mane, and took a deep breath. He stayed there, very still for a minute before cupping my cheek, kissing my nose, and walking down the ramp and out of the trailer. From a short distance, he turned to look back at me, made the sign of the cross, kissed his thumb.

Someone else hopped up on the trailer to heave its wide door shut. *Whoosh, clang, snap.* Just like that, one door closed . . . and Nuno disappeared from my life.

27

1988: Severna Park, Maryland

They say when one door closes, another opens. I'm not so sure. Sometimes, when one door closes, all it does is hit you in the face.

If places were doors, Maryland was a saloon door. And saloon doors don't open so much as say, *Hey, push me!* Only so they can come back swinging at you like an angry drunk outside a dive bar. From its snotty cliques to football dicks, Maryland's hits kept coming. One of the worst of which landed square on my jaw. And boy, did it sting.

"They don't offer German at your new school," my folks told me. "It's French or Spanish."

At first blush, this may seem a small thing. But remember, I was fifteen and had spent the past four pivotal, identity-forming years of my life studying a vocabulary and grammar, not to mention a way of life. Overnight, all of it was made irrelevant. I may not have been fluent, but I would have been placed into an advanced German class. So not only was I denied a foothold, an advantage, but I was also relegated. Once again, I'd have to start over. *Do not pass Go. Do not collect $200. Go directly to jail.* A part of me felt like the world was trying to disappear me. Then again, disappearing was easy when no one saw you anyway.

I chose French. Partly because my heart leaned that way. Mostly because I'd taken rudimentary lessons in elementary school at West Point and knew how to count, sing "Sur le Pont d'Avignon," and say things like "*Je n'aime pas le Maryland. Le Maryland me fait mal à la tête.*" I don't like Maryland. Maryland gives me a headache.

Fast-forward to when I graduated. With three years of French under my *ceinture*, I knew how to say more than *I don't like Maryland.* Though, I still didn't like Maryland. I'd also learned, for example, "La Marseillaise." My nutbag of a French teacher made it, and by *it*, I mean the memorization and singing of the anthem in front of class, worth five percentage points of our final exam. Despite having memorized the song, I was neither comfortable nor willing to humiliate myself publicly and *donc* told her to go to hell. No, of course I didn't say that. I said I'd take a zero on the song and my chances on the rest. I scored a ninety-five (just saying), but I still feel I deserved at least five bonus points for having to suffer through every other poor kid's cringeworthy rendition.

Looking back, I realize what a *Sliding Doors* moment it had been. Not the song avoidance, but the German door closing and my choice of the French door over the Spanish one.

When I got to college that fall, getting back to Europe still topped my want list. At that point, I had gained momentum with French, not German. And I learned if I took enough French classes, I could get into the junior-year-abroad program in Strasbourg (only a short train ride away from my beloved Heidelberg). And if I took enough French classes, why not just declare French as my major. Sitting at cafés, sipping on wine, and demolishing cheese didn't sound so bad.

Allons enfants de la patrie. Let's go, children of the fatherland.

Le jour de gloire est arrivé! The day of glory has arrived!

Well, almost. It would be two more years in America, but I finally felt like I was back on the path toward doing what I wanted.

28

2009: Somewhere in middle America

The miles between Florida and "who knows where" droned on. I repeated to myself, "Be brave." Over and over again. "Be brave." That's what Nuno had asked of me, what Mother would have expected, what she would have been.

But as days blurred together, I started to doubt my ability to keep dread at bay. The view from the trailer window offered nothing but monotonous highways. The wheels hummed their tiresome tune, and I attempted to distract myself with hay, but even food lost its appeal amid the stench of truck exhaust, manure, and urine. I hated relieving myself where I stood, but what choice did I have? The only thing I knew for sure at that point: Gustavo's wife, *la diabla*, would have been in hell.

Every few hours, our driver and his partner would stop to check on and water me and the five other horses I was traveling with. Their routine also included refueling at gas stations and replenishing vital provisions at mini-marts. Not to disparage—they were nice-enough men—but their conversations revolved endlessly around Slurpees, jerkies, and dollar dogs, with nary a word about a final destination. I wondered each night after arriving at a new facility, *Is this it? The end of the road?* . . . until the next morning when they loaded us back into the trailer, once again on our way to somewhere.

Well, not all of us.

One by one, our numbers dwindled. After five days, only three of us remained: me, a beautiful buckskin mare, and a hulking gray Andrade stallion.

The day they loaded just the three of us onto the trailer, everything seemed as usual. More tiresome hours on the road. More standing in manure and urine. More wondering, *Where are we going?*

At some point, storm clouds gathered, the temperature dropped, and raindrops began to tap on the trailer roof. As the sky darkened, the truck slowed and left the highway. Instead of the expected gas station stop, we continued down a narrow rural road flanked by long stretches of farm fields. Amid the rain, I caught a sharp, pungent smell.

Before long, we took a sharp turn, winding our way up a tree-lined lane until it dead-ended at a curlicue of a wrought iron gate. The driver hopped out, punched a few buttons on an intercom, then rushed back into the cab to escape the worsening downpour. Meanwhile, feeling increasingly confined in my tight quarters, I banged my front hoof against the trailer wall. *Let me out!*

The gate swung inward, and the trailer lurched forward.

Without a moon or stars, it was hard to see, so I listened as the gravel squelched and popped beneath the treads and the rain pelted the roof. Suddenly, a red barn loomed before us like a jack-o'-lantern. We came to a stop in front of its warm yellow eyes, and from its mouth emerged the melodic strains of classical strings and a tall man in a black cowboy hat and dark oilskin duster. He hurried to the cab, greeting our driver with a hearty handshake.

"Welcome to sunny California!"

Together, they hustled to the middle of the trailer, opened the doors, and lowered the ramp. Black Hat climbed aboard and went directly to the buckskin.

"Ladies first."

She followed him without a fuss, and they disappeared into the barn.

A few minutes later, Black Hat was haltering the stoic gray and telling our driver to take me and follow.

"Just not too close!"

The four of us passed the red barn and continued up another tree-lined lane. A large fenced pasture was to our right and a large covered arena to our left. Up ahead, lights from another barn switched on. Once inside, we were met by four other horses, two cats, and one pair of very long and very familiar legs. Or should I say, Legs.

She stood in the middle of the barn aisle, tall and commanding. When she spoke to the men, it was evident: Here, she was in charge.

"The smaller gray, Artilheiro, he goes here. The big boy, Xeque, he's over there."

Did she just call me small?

"Hold on," she said, staring at me. "Does he look sunk in to you? Has he been drinking enough water?"

"Yes, ma'am," our driver said. "We've stopped every four hours like clockwork to check. Maybe he's just a bit cold from the storm."

He was right. It was brisk.

Her attention back to Black Hat, she said, "Make sure he gets Celtic Sea salt with his feed tonight. In fact, make sure they all do."

Ah, yes, dinner would be good. Now that the smell in the air has dramatically improved. No more ammonia, but almost . . . is that flowers?

Legs approached and the floral scent intensified. "There should be rain sheets to fit both of them. You know where they are, right? And dammit, where the hell is Frank?"

"Right here, my dear." A figure materialized from the shadows.

It took me a second, but I recognized him. He was the same man who had raised the paddle at Boots and Legs's table at the auction. And of course, this was Frank.

"Ready to go?" he said. "We're already late."

He was dressed in a long black trench coat and reached out to hand her a small shiny purse. It was the first time I'd seen him up close. His small, close-set eyes, coupled with a broad forehead and receding hairline, didn't exactly make him stand out in the looks department. To put it mildly, he seemed like background music to Legs's doe-eyed, number-one-hit appeal.

"Maybe I should stay," she said.

"Don't be ridiculous. They're tired. Let them settle in. Let's go."

"He's right. We're all good here," Black Hat said. "I'll feed 'em, put sheets on. Best to just let 'em be."

"And the salt."

"Of course. The sea salt."

"Okay. But call me if—"

"He knows," Frank said as he reached for her hand.

"I'm serious," she said to them both.

"We know!"

She thanked Black Hat and the driver, bid the barn good night, and headed out into the rain, hand in hand with Frank. Within another half hour, Black Hat had fed and blanketed us. Just as he switched off the lights and pulled the barn doors shut, a colorful bantam rooster half shuffled, half flew into my stall from the adjoining run. I could only guess it was an attempt to escape the deluge. He steadied himself right before colliding with my front legs and showed no concern when I stretched down to give him a quick sniff. Rather, it was I who spooked when he flapped his wings.

"*Mi scusi!*" he said, again shaking his wings as if they were an umbrella and he, an old friend stopping in for a spot of tea.

"*Boa noite,*" I said.

"*Ah, sim, português. Você fala inglês?*" he asked. Ah yes, Portuguese. Do you speak English?

My ears stood to attention!

". . . because that's about the extent of my Portuguese."

"*Que pena.*" Too bad. *What a tease.*

"Come again?" he asked.

"Yes, I know some English. I learned in quarantine."

"Quarantine. How dreadful."

"It was not optimal."

"Not optimal. I see. Well, I'm sure you'll find this place much more optimal. I mean, they don't call it Shangri-La for nothing."

"Shangri-La?" My mind flashed to Nuno's parting words.

"It means paradise. And yes, I'll concede, today was a bit dreary. But mark my words, the sun will come out in the morning and stay for months. Back to bliss!"

"So you like?" I asked.

"Like?! I was going to be someone's dinner before landing here!"

"How dreadful."

"Ah, quick study. You're a smart Lusitano." He paused. "Or is that redundant to say?"

I'd never easily liked anyone, or anything really, but this bird, he was already growing on me. I took a step toward him and introduced myself.

"My name is Artilheiro."

"Pleased to meet you Archie-lay-roo. They call me Napoleon. And no, the irony has not escaped me."

Of all the stalls, I thought, *another Napoleon had found his way into mine.*

"I hope you don't mind if I crash here for the night. Seems all the commotion with the weather and your arrival, someone miscounted at the chicken house tonight."

"My pleasure. I welcome the company. Perhaps you'll tell me a thing or two about Shangri-La."

That was all the loquacious Shangri-La lobbyist needed to hear.

His oration began with the dietary delights of the ranch. "Oh, the food. Everything's clean, fresh, organic. Blueberries, raspberries . . ." My mind drifted until I heard, "I bet I eat better than the family who'd've eaten me had the First Lady not stepped in."

Not to belittle his almost beheading, but it was the last part of the sentence I wanted to know more about.

"First Lady?" I asked.

"Don't tell me you missed the tall pretty one?"

"The buckskin?"

He was quick, that tiny rooster. "Don't even think about it. The mares are off-limits. And yet, I'm intrigued. I shall explore the foaling barn tomorrow. But I digress, the First Lady. She no doubt has a thing for you fancy-dancing lot, but most in her care have come from less fortunate circumstances. *Compassion* is her middle name."

"And Frank, does he have a middle name?" I asked.

"Oh, Frank. He's a curious one, isn't he?"

"Is he? I wouldn't know."

Napoleon's eyes twinkled at my subtle hint for gossip.

"Frank," he began, "is the First Lady's husband."

That much I had figured. The rest, well, Napoleon's storytelling demonstrated his fine ear for detail.

Born Norman Franklin, he hadn't been called Norman by anyone but his parents since the first day of first grade when he told his teacher her breath smelled like hyena feces and counseled her on the merits of flossing. That same day, when his kind, elderly neighbor asked him how school had gone, he'd said, "It stunk. Like you." In his defense, Norman did suffer from hyperosmia. Then again, anyone with a nose would have agreed with him on the double-funk factor; it was simple manners that prevented them from saying anything.

So everyone took to calling him Frank on account of his inability to tell a lie, not even for the sake of politesse. And as was his nature, rather than take offense, he embraced the sobriquet, dubbing himself Frank Franklin. He thought it had a nice ring and would be easy for people to remember. But Frank was memorable for reasons beyond his name and straight talk.

A self-made man, he'd always had a quick and curious mind for numbers and problem-solving. He also had an uncanny ability to predict the future, and eventually his combined talents led him to a career in venture capital. He had good instincts, made consistently good bets, and perhaps of most importance, he was fair and honest. People didn't necessarily feel the pull to be his best pal, but they trusted him. And in doing so, they'd made small fortunes. But if you were to ask Frank about his greatest coup, he'd tell you it was Legs. A hundred percent, Legs.

Frank had spent the majority of his lifetime filterless and free. He couldn't care less about what most people thought of him, and it seemed to have worked out well for him. By the time he met Legs—a decade ago, they'd been seated beside one another at a mutual friend's dinner party—he was more than financially secure and had nothing to prove to anyone. He said what he felt and did what he wanted and there was no telling him otherwise. The moment they met, he knew they'd end up together. She, not so much.

Their mutual friend was named Ralph, and he loved to throw lavish theme parties in the backyard of his Atherton estate. This particular party's theme: the Jazz Age. A long table had been set with crisp white linen and giant silver candelabra. A seven-piece band played beneath an old oak whose Medusa-like branches draped around them in a perfect frame. Champagne flowed. And a seance had been promised to those who opted to stay late and misbehave.

The dinner bell rang and Frank locked eyes with Legs; she'd been assigned to sit next to him. Unlike the others, all beaded and flapper-fringed, she wore a tuxedo, and, as per usual, its cut accentuated the length of her lower limbs.

"Wow, you are obscenely tall," he'd said to her.

She stared down at him and then pointed to the other end of the table, asking another guest, "Is that seat over there taken?"

Fortunately for both of them, it was. That night, they wound up discovering they shared similar tastes in art and cars and music and animals. By the end of the evening—and yes, they stayed to meet a phantom spirit or two—he'd scored her number. And by the end of the month, they were off to Spain to rescue and bring home a handful of Galgos, an ancient breed of hunting dogs who are tortured and slain en masse every year. It was the start of what would become one of their most meaningful shared passions. And what eventually led to marriage, a ranch-retreat-rescue called Shangri-La, and a love affair with the majestic Lusitano breed.

"Majestic, eh?" I said.

"Ah, you were listening."

"My mother taught me well."

"Good on her. And good on you. And besides, it's true. There's no denying you are a majestic, handsome lot."

"As are you."

He proudly shook his smaragdine sickles, dug a small hole in the fluffy pine shavings, and said, "To be continued. Now, lest you regret it later, get some rest."

29

1991: Saintes-Maries-de-la-Mer, France

Innocence is doing what you want. Problem is, so is regret.

I had zero regrets choosing to spend my junior year abroad in Strasbourg, France, rather than staying on at Pennsylvania State University's main campus in State College. Or as one of my somewhat condescending but not altogether wrong Université de Strasbourg professors liked to call it, "Pennsyltucky."

Classes abroad had been fine. Okay, maybe more than fine. But the real education, which was nothing short of magic, had come from meeting new people, making new friends. Sitting in corner cafés, drinking at hole-in-the-wall bars. Eurailing here, Eurailing there. Most of the time with friends. Occasionally, solo.

I was, dare I say, happy.

Even if, by that spring, I was not yet fully fluent in French, I was edging closer to becoming fully full of myself. This budding confidence allowed me to act more as I pleased, heedless of potential consequences. Is that innocence? Or just foolishness?

All I know for sure is that when I kissed a certain French boy (and no, not the one who would later become my dressage trainer), I was doing what I wanted. Completely. Utterly. I didn't give a thought to anything else in that moment. Not to the date I'd come with. Not to the fact my best friend had a crush on him. A boy we'd known peripherally for some time, courtesy of his more sociable older brother, who happened to be one of our closest French friends.

The night started out fine. Vincent, my date, was another French guy I'd met about a week or so earlier at the basement "night club" of La Gallia, my all-girls dormitory. We'd had coffee some other afternoon and he'd invited me to this shindig: the Soirée de Médecine. From what I gathered after arriving, it was a not-so-normal and thus big-deal night out for medical students. Lots of sleek black dresses. Lots of booze. My jeans, leather moto jacket, and Doc Martens made me feel out of place. The booze made that feeling disappear.

Malheureusement, the more I drank, the more boring Vincent became. I considered a French exit but also had to pee. Between the bathroom and the front doors was the dance floor. I have a hard time resisting dance floors. Besides, what could it hurt? Maybe intrigue would find me.

What I hadn't expected was to run into anyone I knew, let alone that French boy. But there he was, standing mere feet from me as if Moses had parted the Red Sea and pointed a spotlight on him. Beautiful. Irresistible. And when he caught my eye, I caught his grin of recognition.

I was toast.

We met in the middle of that dance floor like two magnets snapping together. No words. No hesitation. Just started kissing. Like we had no other choice. To this day, that first kiss goes unrivaled. It was perfection.

Unfortunately, Moses didn't drown the other partygoers. My friend saw the whole thing, and when she confronted us in the women's bathroom—no idea why I thought a bathroom stall was a good place to continue kissing—I did the only mature thing I could think to do. I turned tail like Cinderella and ran. Only, this Cinderella grabbed the young prince to come with. Outside the dance hall, he slowed me down, made sure I didn't lose a shoe, and convinced me to go to his and his brother's apartment. It was much closer than mine and upon arrival, I promptly fell asleep.

I woke early. Embarrassed, my head spinning. Without so much as an adieu, I quietly snuck out and ran all the way back to La Gallia. I packed a bag, grabbed my Eurail pass, and headed to the train station. Head still pounding, I boarded a train bound for the south of France. Specifically, Arles.

The Camargue had been on my wish list for ages. Yet convincing anyone to join me proved futile. Where was their sense of adventure and romance? How could the promise of pink flamingos and wild white horses not entice? I suppose everyone has their own preferences and priorities.

This time, it was just me and a pitcher called Life. She'd thrown me a curveball, and I had a choice to make, and fast. Fuggit, I swung for the fences.

On the seemingly endless train ride down, my yellow Sony Sports Walkman got a workout playing Yaz's "Midnight" on repeat. Play, rewind, play. I don't know why I did her wrong. It's too late. I'm an asshole. I mean, it hadn't been that long since all I wanted was a friend. And then I had to go and plant a Judas kiss. A kiss that was also on repeat in my head, but for a completely different reason.

My hope was that a bit of time and distance, but most of all, a ride on a pony, could be a salve. *But wait, this far? The youth hostel can't be this far, can it?*

Exiting the train, I had followed the guidebook's directions, but something didn't seem right. *Where the hell is this place? And could this backpack be any more uncomfortable? And oh my God, is this another town?! Did I just walk all the way to another town?!*

It felt like I'd been walking for miles. It was hot. I was anxious. But so far, there was no sign of a youth hostel. As the sun began to set, I got more and more chickenshit with every step. Sure, I could pop into a café to ask for help or directions. But could I really? Despite moments of boldness, usually fueled by alcohol, deep down, I still felt like that timid little girl who ate gravel rather than ask for an extra marshmallow. Plus, what if someone noticed I was traveling alone? Would I become an easy target? Was this place safe? Was any?

I decided to turn around and head back to the train station. I remembered there was a hotel next to it. Hold that thought. Upon further inspection, it was more of a motel. Note to self: From now on, no matter the city, always get at least half a mile from the train station before seeking food, drink, or a place to lay one's head.

The room had a toilet and a shower, but not together. The toilet was behind a door. The shower, on the other hand, stood in the center of the room like a vertical glass coffin or a portal ready to beam me up. It was as if a work crew had come in, set it down, realized it was lunchtime, and just left, never to return. Sharing this room with anyone but a lover (which, ew, why would you do that?) would require some creative draping or eye aversion. And I gotta say, it would have been hard to look away from that train wreck.

The bright side? The motel door had a lock. And I kept telling myself, *Tomorrow, you'll be on a horse.*

But that night, I needed something to eat. So, once again, I ventured into town. I could have dined at Café van Gogh. It was only a fifteen-minute walk from the motel and is perhaps better known as the restaurant in Vincent van Gogh's painting *Café Terrace at Night.* On the canvas, he chose to paint the sky blue instead of black, saying, "Now, there's a painting of night without black. With nothing but beautiful blue, violet, and green . . ."

I wasn't feeling beautiful blue, just blue. So I wimped out, worried someone might talk to me. Or worse, nobody would. Instead of taking a chance on a prix fixe menu at a famous café, I really took a chance, swinging into a poorly lit commercial supermarket. I bought plastic-wrapped cheese and a stale roll before heading back to my time-portal boudoir. Early to bed, early to rise. That was the better idea. Right.

The next morning, I was true to my word. I rose early, ate more tasteless cheese and by then petrified bread, and headed for the bus stop. Luckily, I didn't break a tooth, and there were plenty of buses headed to Saintes-Maries-de-la-Mer, the capital of the Camargue. Within forty minutes, I found myself strolling the streets of what felt like a postapocalyptic seaside trailer park.

The town had been touted as a destination but felt more like a final destination. Most of the buildings were white, or at least had been at some point. When that was, I couldn't say. Perhaps I needed to consult my time portal. More than anything, their flaking exteriors gave off a feeling of abandonment or a sad *meh, who cares?* Like old, dry skin not worth the effort of a sunscreen application.

There were two, maybe three cafés open and serving the few odd tourists at that hour. I walked past but not into several touristy shops. I had no need for trinkets or postcards. And while, years later, I would regret not buying a wide-brimmed felt *gardian* hat, that day, my mission was singular. Finally, I spotted an A-frame sign advertising horseback rides.

"C'mon, Erin, you can do this," I urged myself. "Remember, horses heal."

I took a deep breath and approached the zombie seated on a plastic folding chair next to the sign.

"*Bonjour, monsieur,*" I said. "*J'aimerais bien faire de l'équitation, s'il vous plaît. C'est possible?*" Hello, sir. I would very much like to go horseback riding, please. Is that possible?

"*Mais, bien sûr,*" he said, swiping a mosquito from his face. But of course.

"Cool," I said before adding, "*Comment ça marche?*" How does it work?

"*Vous avez déjà monté à cheval?*" he asked. You've ridden horses before?

"*Oui, mais ça fait quelques—*" Yes, but it's been several—

"*Très bien. Vous aimez galoper?*" All right. You like to gallop?

"*Galoper?*" I asked. "*C'est possible?*" Gallop? That's possible?

"*Mais, bien sûr!*" But of course!

I nodded.

"*Prenez cette rue.*" He pointed to the road leading back out of town. Take this road. "*Suivez-la pendant un demi-kilomètre et vous verrez les écuries.*" Follow it for half a kilometer, and you will see the stables.

"*Il y a quelque chose* à *signer?*" Is there something to sign?

"À *signer?*" He looked confused. To sign?

I aped scribbling my signature.

"*Mais non.*" He laughed. "*C'est bon. Allez!*" No, it's good. Go!

I was pretty sure when he said *gallop* I wasn't in Kansas anymore, but no paperwork, no need to sign all liability away? That sealed the deal. Definitely not Kansas or anywhere else in the United States of Lawsuits. When I found the stables, the attendant offered me a nylon hairnet and a helmet and, once again, asked if I knew how to gallop. I really started to think maybe these folks were serious.

After about twenty minutes of traversing brackish marshes and spotting a flamboyance of pink flamingos (check!), my small group—three clients and one guide—reached the beach. The moment we did, it was game on, with a full-out, hold-on-for-dear-life gallop. These Camargue horses may have been small, but they knew their job. When they kicked it into high gear, the floor dropped, and we were off like a shot.

Like a shot.

It was my first time back in the saddle after the firing range. They say it's like riding a bike, but that's a load of horseshit. I was well out of practice and probably did that horse's back no favors, bouncing around on him like a rag doll. But my God, I couldn't remember the last time I felt so free and alive. A horse beneath me, the sea breeze in my face. Now *this* was *living*.

I barely remember the bus ride back to my motel. I do remember needing a shower. I had sand in my hair, mud on my face and clothes. I'm sure I looked like a street urchin, but so what? I stripped down, body aching, bruises on my inner thighs already starting to appear. Voice of the Beehive's "I Say Nothing" rang in my ears. Holy shit. That ride left me "black and blue."

Washed and dressed in clean clothes, I didn't want to let the momentum of the day go to waste. I had one more night in Arles and intended to make the most of it. After a quick bite of more subpar cheese, I chose to spare my teeth from the bread and set off to explore the town and visit its renowned amphitheater before sundown. Though I didn't enter, I walked around its iron-fenced perimeter, gazing up at its stone walls and arches, imagining the chariot races and bullfights they'd seen. I couldn't help but wonder if Vincent van Gogh had once stood in that very spot, or if he had strolled down to the Rhône as I did.

Standing at the river's edge, I vowed to myself, *One day, I'll come back, and I won't be alone. That way, I'll be more inclined to dine at that damn Café van Gogh.* But for now, no Prince Charming would be riding in on a white horse to save the day. It was just me. Myself. And one giant inner-thigh bruise.

But you know what? It wasn't midnight. It wasn't raining. And I was proud of myself for having the guts to travel solo. That meant something.

As for what awaited me back in Strasbourg . . .

I think it's important to say my friend and I made up. She had a boyfriend, albeit a long-distance one, and my peccadillo helped her realize she wasn't ready to let him go. In the end, the whole thing made our friendship better and stronger than ever.

And the French boy?

When I got home, I had waiting for me the first of what would be many letters to come. In beautiful script, the envelope read:

Erin ??? Chambre 100
Cité Universitaire
GALLIA 1 bd Victoire
67000 STRASBOURG

Either he thought I was the Riddler or didn't know my last name, but with the letter, it seemed he wanted to find out. He invited me to join him and a group of our mutual friends at his family home outside of town. He also said he had questions about *that* night. I found his honesty endearing, compelling.

In addition to the more formal letter, he included this note (poem?). I've translated it from his original French version. Not to assume you can't read French or use Google translate, but the latter isn't always the best with nuance. At least not French nuance. I wouldn't know about other languages.

She was top class
an upscale girl,
a good upbringing
plus a good education
She had so much charm
all grace and ease
with refined manners and sophisticated tastes
She was a distinguished girl,
Me, I was . . . le pouilleux. (the louse)

One evening I met her
disheveled like a pute
staggering like a drunk
and in her haggard gaze,
I was the distinguished young man,
She was . . . la pouilleuse.

She taught me about her life,
but at the time, I didn't understand.
I taught her my life, my world of trash,
Then, I tried to approach her extra-terrestrial heart.
And I received that night the slap of my life.
That's what made me understand
that I was trying to become what she was looking to destroy in herself at all costs.

She fell asleep at my house,
then without saying a word, she left,
That's when I realized I will never see her again.
She was a distinguished young girl.

Me, I was le pouilleux.

Oh, how I miss handwritten correspondence. And man, oh man . . . words. The power they hold. Even thirty years later.

All the old letters, photos, and mishmash of memories are like scars, reminding me I dared to care, loved and lost, but also lived to tell a tale or two of more than two cities.

Even if I'm still restless from time to time, I have no regrets.

30

2009: Gilroy, California

I heard Xeque restlessly pacing in his stall. I understood. I'd also decided not to partake in the fine bedding on offer. Not because the sea of pine shavings didn't entice. So thick, so fluffy, and without a stalk of rough straw in sight, they beckoned, *Come. Rest your weary legs.* But I couldn't do it, couldn't shake my unease.

The quarantine, the auction, the road. Together, they'd drained my confidence and tarnished my trust. I couldn't relax and wasn't about to let my guard down or, perhaps more important, take a chance on crushing my newfound avian friend whose shrill crow now marked the dawn of my first official day at Shangri-La.

In all his imperial glory, Napoleon sat perched on a fence post at the end of my run, howling at the sun and delivering on his promise. The clouds had parted, and what had once been still and quiet in the night was now coming to life.

I noticed the air first. It smelled different than Miami. Here, it was thinner, fresher. I was keen to take in my new view when the barn doors swooshed open behind me. A short, stocky man in droopy jeans and a sun-bleached baseball cap pulled low over his eyes heaved a wide hay cart into the aisleway. The other horses whinnied greetings as he moved quickly down the row, doling out grass and grain.

When he opened my stall door to drop a flake, I wasn't expecting his abrupt move toward me. Startled, I jumped sideways, swung around, and bolted into my run.

"Whoa. Whoa," he said. "*Tranquilo. Está bien.*" Easy. It's okay.

Thankfully, he stopped and took a beat before making another move toward me.

"I just take your blanket," he said.

My ears twitched, but I stood my ground as he walked closer and carefully reached to unhook the blanket's many straps and slide it off. Free, I swung back around, trotting and bucking my way to the far end of the run.

Napoleon, still on his perch, laughed, "Wow. You Lusos. Drama-rama-dinga-donga."

Dinga-donga? I was about to argue his point when the dogs arrived. A bounding, barking, manic pack of mutts. They blew past my run, propelling me into a half pirouette to keep sight and count of them all. One, two, three, there must have been a dozen or more. Little ones. Big ones. A few chased another poor chicken. Napoleon knew to stay high and calm. A couple of wee ones, sibling puppies perhaps, collided with one another and went tumbling in opposite directions. Squeaking balls of white and brown fluff. My head followed the frenzy as they raced around and into the barn.

Curious about their hurry, I turned back toward my stall when another force of energy, a golf cart piloted by Legs, whizzed by and threatened to topple sideways as it rounded the end of the row of runs. She skidded to a stop, and more dogs leapt from her lap like happy fleas.

"Settle down," she said.

Like a miracle, they . . . well, okay, there was no miracle. At least not in obedience to that command. Whether deaf, dumb, untrained, or all the above, not a single dog calmed or changed volume. Yet, something special did happen as they gathered around her in a protective circle, awaiting her next move. In that momentary display of adoration, I realized: She was their savior. They knew it. They would never forget it. And they would help me see her in a new light.

Legs in her element was even more impressive than Legs at the auction. It was as if a spotlight followed her every move, with all eyes in her vicinity drawn to her radiant glow. As Napoleon was keen to point out, while Frank may have funded the ranch with his deep and generous pockets, Legs managed its operation with her profound love and affection for all animals, regardless of size or peculiarity. And no, I was not one of the extra weird. In time, I simply became known as "extra."

On that first day at Shangri-La, it was perhaps this *extra* quality that drew Legs to approach my stall before the others'. Even Xeque's.

"How's it going, Artilheiro?" she said before turning to the man with droopy drawers to ask, "How's he doing, Abel? Did he eat all his food from last night?"

"Yes, ma'am. All his grass," he said. "This morning. When I come to take his blanket. He just a little nervous, but no much trouble. He a good boy."

"Very good," she said. "And Xeque?"

"He more nervous. He no eat his food."

"Let's be sure to give him a bit more salt in his grain this morning. And we'll get them both out for a walk and longe." She stopped to look around. "Where's Rex?"

"*No sé.*" I don't know.

Legs shook her head and rolled her eyes.

"What is it with some people? This is a barn. We start early. We finish late."

"Yes, ma'am."

"Oh, I know you know, Abel. You're a good man. *Gracias.*"

"Yes, ma'am."

"Okay, I'll be back after I feed the dogs. If you could turn out the other horses, just not Xeque or Artilheiro, that'd be great."

"Yes, ma'am."

After Legs and her pack parted, half in the cart, half racing behind it, Abel turned up the country music and began to muck stalls. As he hummed along, my mind flashed to Lucca and Cesar. But only for a moment. I returned to my breakfast, nibbling until full and bored and ready for another look around outside.

My run faced a huge tree-lined outdoor arena, next to which was a viewing gazebo. The gazebo was as big as two stalls put together and furnished with an oversize plush couch, matching side chairs, and towering potted grass plants. To the right of my run, about four stall lengths away, a Wild West covered wagon was parked against a large round pen. The wagon's top had been cut in half and converted to offer both shade and a full view of nearby activities. Much like the gazebo, the wagon sported a plush couch and so many pillows I had to wonder if it was more for show than practical use. To my left, another stall and run stood empty. And finally, in the near distance, beyond another wrought iron fence, was a two-story shingled house.

The view wasn't as vast as it had been in Brazil, but I had a feeling there would be plenty of entertainment from the constant comings and goings. The dogs had been an early indicator. A pig was next. Its snorting and grunting made me turn to look, but its size and color had me do a double take.

"That's Dirty Diana," Napoleon said.

"But she's not dirty," I said.

This pig was remarkably clean, though as pink as a blistering sunburn.

"It's more for her rapscallion ways," he said while attempting to flap his way up and onto my back. It took him several tries, and because I was curious to hear more, I stood still.

At five hundred pounds, Dirty Diana (a.k.a. Dirty D) did what she pleased and was infamous for making her way into Frank and Legs's kitchen for morning, afternoon, evening—whenever, really—snacks of organic blueberry muffins and leafy greens. She'd been "borrowed" from a nearby farm in the hopes her owner would eventually forget about her and the fact she could be turned into bacon.

Napoleon digressed into a history lesson on why pigs, when consumed, are called pork and not pigs. A wave of exhaustion gripped me, and I was only half listening.

"It was a way to disassociate the animal from the meal. It's the same with bulls and beef. Though neither the pigs nor bulls at Shangri-La would ever have to worry about that."

Did he say bulls?

"Interestingly, chicken is still chicken," he added with a feather shudder.

"Wait. There are bulls at Shangri-La?"

"I'm talking about the potential for me to be a meal, and you want to know about the bulls."

"Yes, the bulls. Very much so. Where are they?"

"They're out that way," he said, motioning with his comb as if he couldn't be bothered to point a wing. "In the far pasture. On the other side of the ranch."

I turned and stretched my neck as far as I could to see if I could glimpse them.

"No. No. You can't see them from here."

"Soon though? They will take me there?"

"I have no idea. Why are you so interested in bulls anyway?"

"Because I am a Veiga. Of course this is why."

"A what-a?"

"You don't know?" I asked.

He was attentive, curious. A bird who craved knowledge.

"It is my lineage. I was born to fight bulls."

"Fight them? Are you crazy?"

"I am not crazy. Do not insult me."

"No offense, but those bulls are just for decoration."

"Decoration?"

"Like they *scream*, 'This is a ranch!'" he said. "They're Texas longhorns."

I didn't understand. But he started to.

"In other words, not *toro bravo*. Not fighting bulls."

"How do you know?" I asked.

"My family comes from Mexico. I know some things. Trust me."

My disappointment obvious, he tried to comfort me by changing the subject.

"There's plenty else to keep you busy here. They'll have you out and riding in no time. Over in the upper pasture, through the vineyard. They'll take you on long hacks. You'll see. You'll love it. Maybe you'll even make a friend or two . . . besides me."

"Like the buckskin?" I couldn't help but ask.

"I told you I'd check her out. But seriously, you gotta be careful. I once saw a stallion jump three fences to get to a mare, and she and her mini herd didn't take too kindly to him."

"I don't understand."

Napoleon said it had only been a few weeks since one of the stallions had broken loose and made his way to the mare pasture. Black Hat and a few of the yard crew had gone running, yelling, and waving arms and hats in pursuit. Foals scattered. Mares screamed. But like a creature possessed, that stallion had a singular focus. Nothing was stopping him from trying to mount the closest mare who, by all accounts, wasn't having it. Her first kick landed square and with such force it left a hoofprint on his chest. The next one sliced him open. By the time the workers finally broke up the fight, bite marks and bloodstains covered his neck and flanks.

For days after, they led that poor, confused stallion back and forth to the wash rack for cold hosings. He hobbled along, taking cautious steps on tender, swollen limbs.

"Still," Napoleon added, "he was lucky. It could have been much worse. My advice: Put the buckskin out of your mind."

I wanted to put lots of things out of my mind. But couldn't. And wouldn't. Least of all the bulls and the buckskin. Again, Napoleon read me well and tried his best to distract me with a continued listing of the ranch's different species.

"So, as you've seen, we've got horses and chickens. Cats and dogs." He waited to be sure I was listening before going on. "Soon, once you're turned out in pasture, you'll be sure to see the ducks and cranes and peacocks. Nota bene, the First Lady likes her birds."

I'd never been to a zoo but started to think this place may be one.

"Then there's the camels and zebras. Donkeys and zonkeys. Well, one zonkey. Her name is Daisy and she's a peach. Sort of the beautiful, more exotic better half to her constant companion, Donatello. He's a mini Mediterranean donkey. Not that's there's anything small about him other than his height. Legs found him starving at some horrible place and now, he's practically bursting at his fuzzy gray seams from all the good forage. His problem? He's too cute. Depending on what visitor may work their manipulation magic on the First Lady, I fear he may one day end up at another horrible place. A pawn in some charity fundraising nativity scene."

A pawn? Nativity? My confusion was clear, but before he could explain, Legs returned.

"I can't believe this. What is going on today? Still no Rex?" she asked Abel, who was busy sweeping the aisle.

"No yet."

She threw her hands up in the air.

"Well, thank you for putting out the horses. I tell ya, I don't know what I'm going to do with that man. It's always one thing or another."

Abel shrugged his shoulders but quickly lowered his eyes and got back to sweeping.

Legs looked over at me and grabbed my halter from its hook.

"Hello, handsome. How about we get you out of here?"

We headed to the large round pen. Once inside, with the gate securely closed behind us, she went to remove my halter. But at the click of its throat latch, I jumped back. I didn't make it far. The halter had not fully come off, and I felt a firm tug at my poll when the lead rope reached its limit.

"Easy now," she said. "Easy. No one needs a broken nose here today."

She approached cautiously, but I could barely stand still as she reached up to slip the halter over my ears. Free, I reared up before swiftly dropping to the sandy ground. Rolling. Stretching. Scratching my itchy back. I went back and forth several times before springing upright like a startled armadillo.

"This one's a clown," she said to Abel, who'd come to watch.

Instead of climbing onto the viewing wagon to have a seat on the pillow-covered couch, he hoisted himself up onto the side of the round pen. With his arms draped over its side, he gave a quick clap and whistle. I answered with a whinny, buck, and fart before tearing off around the pen.

"*Muy bonito,*" Abel said. Very beautiful.

"All he needs is a horn and he could be a unicorn, huh?" She chuckled at her own joke.

Abel nodded. "You ride him today?"

"I don't—"

"I'll ride him today," Black Hat interrupted.

"Well, if it isn't Rodeo Rex. Nice of you to grace us with your presence this . . ." Legs checked her watch, "Oh yes, is it still morning."

"My apologies, ma'am, Abel. The missus isn't feeling well, and I had to get Star over to school."

"Is your phone under the weather, too?"

"I honestly didn't think it'd take so long, but traffic was a bear. Some truck had slid off the road, probably going too fast after the rain."

"I hope everyone was all right," Legs said, "but you've got to call. Abel shouldn't be doing everything on his own. Especially with the new horses."

"Well, this one seems spritely," he said in a poor attempt to change the subject. "How 'bout I take him out on a walk around the property. Show him the paradise he's just landed in?"

"Paradise. Good try," she said, unaffected by his obsequiousness. "He's a bit excited, but sure. Maybe that's not a bad idea."

Rodeo Rex (or whatever his name, I preferred Black Hat) ran to open the round pen door for Legs.

"The mares are all out, right?" she asked as they crossed paths.

"In the morning. First thing," Abel confirmed.

"Okay then. You know the routine, Rex. Just a nice quiet walk. I'll see you back here in a bit."

He gave his hat an obliging tip, and once she'd turned back toward the barn, he pulled out a pair of weathered yellow gloves from one back pocket of his crisp inky-blue Wranglers and a stud chain from the other. The chain seemed excessive, but when he attached it to my halter, I chose not to give him the satisfaction of a rear or a bolt. Nothing to give him reason to use it.

Legs had referred to him as a man, but up close and in the light of the sunny day, his face, which I gathered had seen plenty of sunny days, didn't show a wrinkle. I figured him for Nuno's age or younger, but physically, he was Nuno's photo negative. What little showed of his high and tight haircut was white-blond, and his eyes were as opaque as a distant fog. He offered no hello, no pat on the neck, and I could tell two things immediately. One, he was going through the motions, his mind elsewhere; and two, I didn't trust him in that moment and knew I never would.

We walked for maybe a half hour, slowly making our way around the property. As we walked side by side in silence, I noticed that Legs and Frank seemed to have a penchant for pairs. There was two houses: Frank and Legs's main residence, which I'd glimpsed from my run, and a guesthouse. The guesthouse, which sat closer to the property's wrought iron entrance, was as big, if not bigger, than the main residence. Its wraparound porch overlooked a lush lawn that sloped down to two large round ponds. In the center of each pond, cascading fountains seemed to be entertaining a group of yodeling, diving ducks.

In addition to the arena behind my run, there was a covered arena with tall mirrors along one side. Both were enormous and, I soon learned, equipped with sturdy, high-end German sound systems built to withstand not only the elements but also an inordinate amount of country music. In fact, much of the property was wired for music, and on most days, it reverberated with either country or classical melodies from dawn until dusk. It may not have been Maysa, but I grew to enjoy both styles.

There were also two barns. I recognized the big red barn from the night before. The foaling barn, as they called it, was quiet and empty when we passed, save for a couple of fat barn cats, licking their paws and sunning themselves atop a bale of hay. Like at home in Brazil, the stallions and mares were kept apart, with the latter spending nearly all their time out as a herd in a sprawling pasture situated up and over a hill at the opposite end of the property from my barn. I didn't catch sight or scent of any mares that day, but I sensed them. Or maybe it had been wishful thinking as I wondered about the buckskin and how she was faring in this new wonderland.

There was so much to take in on that initial walk, and Napoleon was right about one thing: Legs loved her birds. Chickens, ducks, peacocks. So many peacocks. Their vibrant colors were extraordinary, and since they roamed free, their feathers littered the grounds.

Black Hat bent to pick up some of the fullest, most iridescent ones along the way, and when we reached the guesthouse, he yelled to someone inside. A woman peeked out from behind a curtain before swinging open a set of wide French doors and sauntering out in a pink satin robe with matching heeled slippers. A mess of jumbo golden Os sat at odd angles atop her head, quivering as she walked toward us.

"More feathers?" she twanged through large, painted lips. "More feathers ain't what I need. Or want."

"I thought they'd cheer you up. Kinda like flowers, but better. These'd cost a pretty penny to buy."

"Well, I don't care none about pennies. And you can keep your damn bird flowers. What I want is to go back home. This place is boring."

"Darlin', you really gotta give it more of a try."

"How? Ain't hardly nobody round here even speaks proper English. You expect me to learn *español*?"

"That's not fair. And that's not true. You're just a bit too quick to judge."

"Excuse me?"

"Now hold on. Before you go and get all upset, how about this? How about we plan to drive on up to the city sometime soon?"

"Tonight! I wanna go tonight."

"Well, not tonight. I mean, we've got Star. And, well, I'm gonna have to work—"

Before he could finish his sentence, she'd flown inside and slammed the doors shut so hard a potted plant fell from a ledge and startled me. I felt the stud chain come down hard on my nose as he barked, "Now, I don't need any guff from you, too."

Later, after telling Napoleon about my tour, I could see the wheels turning in his neuron-packed bird brain.

"Mark my words," he said. "He'll rue the day. It's never a good idea to underestimate a rooster and a Luso."

31

"Paris is always a good idea."

—Audrey Hepburn

Why, Audrey, I couldn't agree with you more.

These days, people often wonder where my love of horses came from. But if given a glimpse into my past, they also wonder about my love affair with the City of Lights and how it all began. Not that you would ever guess if you saw me on a regular day now, more often than not dressed in a drool-stained sweatshirt or dirty riding breeches, but fashion has long held a special place in my heart.

According to my mom, my love for horses and Paris manifested early on. As evidence, I present another letter she wrote to her mother when I was two years old.

November 8, 1972
Erin just came walking out with her pocketbook over her arm and said she's going on a plane to Paris but then changed her mind and is going to see Mom-Mom (you). So Eddie said he was going too. Eddie's even wrapped up a cookie to take with him on the plane. I wish we could fly home anytime we felt like it. Eddie and Erin are two little characters.

I wish I could fly anywhere anytime, too. Especially to Paris.

My first trip to this old but forever flame was in September 1972—two months before my mom wrote that letter but obviously a memory that held fast in my toddler brain. Based on silent Super 8 footage from that trip, I was dressed in white-and-navy-blue plaid pants, a navy-blue top with a white collar, and a pink Swiss-dot swing coat. The coat had a matching bonnet that tied at my chin with a satin ribbon. Brown curls framed my face as I tippy-toed my way through the streets of gay Paris in my black patent leather Mary Janes.

Audrey, eat your heart out.

Though fashionably styled by my mom, the outfit was not the standout memory of the trip. That, instead, was the balloon. The goddamn blue balloon. Of course it matched my outfit. My mom wouldn't have had it any other way.

She'd tied it to my tiny wrist. And as I shook my arm up and down, it bounced around like an upside-down yo-yo. I can only imagine the giggling (wee-hee!) followed by the tears (boo-hoo!) when the string slowly unraveled and my blue balloon floated up, up, and away into a beautiful, blue Parisian sky. By all eye-witness accounts, it was as if my arm had floated off with it.

Oh, well. *Tant pis*, kid.

Now, balloons are a thing I can do without. (Horses *hate* them.) But there was a time when Paris itself had become this big, bright, beautiful balloon I was chasing. I didn't think I could live without it. To this day, the thought of it still lifts me. And yet, I'll likely never live there *again*. I say *again* because I did end up living there. Twice.

After college, I moved back to Severna Park, Maryland, to live with my parents so I could save money for grad school (my first Paris move). That year home was not a fun one. I got three dumb jobs and had no time or gumption to do much of anything else. I repeat, it was not a fun year.

The first gig was a dreadful nine-to-five number at a management consulting firm. I mostly answered phones, made photocopies, and, despite having zero experience in the field, interviewed people to see if they were a good match for open consulting positions. On a couple of occasions, I had to go to the airport to interview job hopefuls in a terminal, at some arrival/departure gate. Keep in mind, this was 1992. Keep in mind, even at the time, this was weird.

Imagine me stationed at a vinyl airport chair, inviting someone to "take a seat" beside me. Two strangers sat side by side, with only a metal armrest between us. Oh, and with my "superior" only a few chairs away, conducting her own interviews while silently judging me.

Later, she called me out for wearing a skirt that was too short.

"We don't want to give these candidates the wrong impression," she said.

Looking around the janky-ass terminal, I considered saying, "Oh no, we wouldn't want to do that." I also considered adding, "And just for your information, this is a skort, not a skirt." But I didn't want to get fired for insubordination. So I took a deep breath and swallowed those thoughts.

Wait, I take that back. Not the fact I took a deep breath. That's probably true. But not wanting to get fired? I totally wanted to get fired and never have to conduct another shitty interview between "Last call for Toledo!" and "Can Phil McCracken please come to the podium?"

Truth be told, I didn't speak my mind because I was chickenshit and needed the money. Instead, I said a wimpy-ass "sorry" and tried to adjust my skort to look longer. The skort, however, was not made of pliable pizza dough, and instead of improving its length, the only thing I likely succeeded in doing was making the rest of the domestic travelers think I was picking my butt. Or worse, had a yeast infection.

Believe it or not, those interviews weren't the worst part of that job. What was, you ask? Why, the firm's owner.

Rumor had it he was having an affair with one of the out-of-town consultants. They say there's someone for everyone. In his case, maybe two or more someones because he was married and not to the out-of-town consultant. Still, I couldn't wrap my head around it. This pock-faced womanizing pudge of a man was unattractive to the point of revulsion.

Small graces, he was rarely in the office. But when he was, he kept the curtains drawn in an already-dark room while he sat behind a huge mahogany desk, polluting the air with cigar smoke, bourbon breath, and dirty jokes.

"That's a good one," I never once said.

But what I did once experience while in that man cave with my anti-skort superior was *her* arrival. I'll never forget it. She walked in like a nightmarish amalgamation of half of Snow White's dwarfs rolled into one. Frumpy, Lumpy, Dumpy, Grumpy, Unhappy . . . all giving me an if-you-touch-my-man look that could have curdled milk. Suddenly, everything made sense. What a perfectly imperfect match . . . from hell.

My second job was better by a smidge, and that smidge was the fact it was only two days a week instead of five. I worked as the weekend receptionist at a real estate agency and found it to be both dreadfully boring and socially taxing. If I had to talk to another stranger . . . Oh, that's right. I did.

Job three, which I'm sure you're dying to hear about, was as a salesperson at Victoria's Secret in the Owings Mills Fashion Mall. Don't let the name fool you. It was no height of fashion. My best guess is someone simply, perhaps innocently, transposed two words. In my experience, Owings Mills Mall Fashion made much more sense. And though it's a tough call, and the opposite of how Dorothy felt about the Scarecrow, I think I hated this position most of all.

I worked the evening shift a couple of times a week. I folded bras and panties while doing my damnedest to avoid awkward conversations with mostly men seeking advice on what lingerie to buy their honey bunnies. How the *f* would I know? I only work here.

The year passed about as fast as molasses through cheesecloth, but the following summer, after confirming enrollment to the program I'd deferred, my folks kindly drove me up and dropped me off at the charming campus of Middlebury College in Middlebury, Vermont. *Laissez les bons temps rouler.* Let the good times roll.

I spent eight weeks in Vermont for the summer "language immersion" graduate program before leaving for a year of academic study in Paris. I could write a novel about the entire experience, but for now, I'll say it was well worth every dirty joke I heard, every stranger I spoke to, every piece of underwear I folded. At Middlebury, I found my people, who, by the end of the year, included a boyfriend.

I was in heaven.

32

2009: Gilroy, California

Shangri-La was meant to be a magical place, a little slice of heaven on earth inhabited by beautiful creatures living in peace and harmony. To some degree, that's exactly what it was. By almost any standard, life at Shangri-La was a charmed one. Especially from an outside-in perspective. People came to visit, by the droves, full of oohs and aahs and naive wonder. In so many ways, like the ranch in Brazil. In so many ways, not at all like Brazil.

"Oh, you and Frank are so lucky to have all this," they'd say. "It's just magic!"

"*Lucky,*" Legs would repeat. "That's an interesting word. But you know what's really interesting? When you live at Disneyland 24-7, it tends to lose some of its magic."

I didn't know what she meant by *Disneyland,* but I was counting on a little magic as I tried to settle in. Well, as much as I could, not knowing what life was going to throw at me next.

As on the first day and every morning thereafter, Legs arrived early to the barn. I grew accustomed to the whiz, screech, and slam of her golf cart, accompanied by the yips and yaps of her pack of crazies. Seeing Black Hat's casual approach to punctuality, it was easy to see why she felt the need to be on the scene as much as possible.

She seemed to lack faith in others, never fully trusting anyone, especially Black Hat. It was next to impossible to meet her high standards in operations management and, most important, ranch safety. She didn't miss a detail and was always quick to assist when problems arose, without fail, on a daily and often last-minute basis. Whether it was someone running late, equipment breaking down, animals getting loose, or vendors needing payment, she addressed it all. Not to mention the frequent arrival of new creatures on the ranch's doorstep, more often than not malnourished, flea-infested, and suffering from severe mange.

Around these parts, normalcy was about as easy to find as a fighting bull.

It wasn't that issues stemmed from ill intent but rather inattention to detail, ignorance, or ineptitude. None of which, I might add, should get a pass. Some mistakes were frustrating but ultimately innocuous. Like the gardeners cutting down the wrong tree or planting shrubbery in the wrong place. Others may have seemed small but had the potential for great harm. Like a rusty nail left in the middle of the aisleway. And sadly, like what happened with Stanley and Iris.

I learned their story on my second night at Shangri-La, when Napoleon purposely missed lights-out. Black Hat had called for him but didn't have the patience to go on a bird hunt. Not even a little one.

"Damn bird," he said under his breath before shouting, "If you get eaten by a coyote, that's on you."

Napoleon, who was a fan of neither Black Hat nor, apparently, curfews, had hidden himself in a corner of my sea of shavings.

"I like that you pee outside," he said. "Such a tidy stallion."

"Should you have gone to your roost?" I asked.

"Well, I won't say he doesn't have a point, but I know how to get up high when I sense trouble. And I'll not soon forget what Stanley and Iris taught me."

"Stanley and Iris?"

They were a bonded pair of East African cranes who'd arrived several months before I had and, according to Napoleon, were a striking, long-legged couple. Atop downy black heads, they proudly wore bristled crowns of gold. Their ice-blue eyes seductive centerpieces framed by snow-white cheeks and scarlet wattles. When they faced one another, their long gray necks arched to form a perfect heart.

It had been such a pity when, one evening, someone forgot to secure the latch to their enclosure. After the coyotes killed Iris that night, Stanley was left with little will to live.

"I don't think I've ever seen a sadder bird in my life," said Napoleon. "Not even a Thanksgiving turkey."

"A what?" I asked.

"Never mind. Sore subject," he said. "My point is Stanley had lost his partner, his special someone."

I thought of Mother and Nuno and imagined the poor bird's heartache. "How's he doing?"

"Not so well," he said. "Coyote got him the next night. And really no fault of any human. Abel had put him away, swore he'd double-checked and secured the gate. Best guess is Stanley found a way to slip under the chicken wire, desperate to reunite with his Iris. Only thing they ever found was a smattering of feathers."

"I don't like this story," I said.

"I'm sorry. You're right. That wasn't very pleasant," he said. "Life is full of ups and downs. I promise, there's way more good here than bad. You'll see."

As usual, Napoleon had a point.

At Shangri-La, horses were kings, and Legs spared no expense on us. Our timothy hay was delivered from Oregon because, as per her research, its quality was superior to anything local. Our oats were mixed with Celtic Sea salt, whose broad mineral mix aided digestion and heightened the gloss of our coats. Our carrots were cored and filled with specially formulated homeopathic remedies, each based on analyses of our mane hair, and in my case, intended to help soothe my sensitive lumbar region while also tempering my sometimes mare-like moods.

The perks extended beyond high-quality specialized diets. We also had a chiropractor, an acupuncturist, a masseuse, and a very special vibrating floor, which was meant to increase blood circulation and speed rehabilitation. After a workout, they'd walk me onto this odd, slightly raised piece of rectangular floor, set an alarm, and for twenty minutes, I stood without fretting or even thinking to move, which was not at all like me. A body- and mind-numbing sort of goodness.

Our chiropractor lived in Colorado but Legs flew him in once a month because of, again, his superior reputation. As a bonus, he was an incredible chef and loved to cook and entertain at the main house after a long day of healing. Our acupuncturist and masseuse came from the next town over (how prosaic!), but their needles and fingers must have been blessed with some of that residual Disneyland magic, as they carried me to another place, if only temporarily, as did the vibrating floor.

Though the sun was a near constant in the sky, if the weather did take a turn, out came the sheets and blankets in all different thicknesses and textures for varying purposes. Stable sheets, rain sheets, fly sheets. One horse even had his own Belly Dickie. Talk about a contraption. It looked more like a hoist than a blanket, but its custom-made intent was to protect his sensitive nether regions, which had suffered severely from a relentless barrage of bugbites. Horse flies, Legs would say, had a particular lust for his blood.

That horse was Xairel, Legs's Grand Prix dressage hopeful. He was also a Lusitano, and I'd heard more than once about his most incredible bloodlines. Oof. In one way, I thought, he could keep his blood. In another, I was envious.

For some reason, I thought Legs would be my rider, my only rider.

But with half a dozen stallions, who knows how many mares and geldings, and all her responsibilities overseeing ranch operations, including managing the barn, her workers, and social outings, she barely had time to eat and sleep, let alone ride. So, when she did ride, it was most often on Xairel.

So, there it was. Whatever I could possibly desire, I had at Shangri-La. With one exception. I did not have my Iris, and I was powerless to choose who would open my stall door, tack me up, and hop on up. And to be clear, if I had a choice, Black Hat wouldn't have been that person.

Besides my talks with Napoleon, my favorite time of the day was turnout. Our pastures were ample, one acre per stallion, and shaded along the edges with tall white birch trees. A minor complaint: The grass had quickly turned from a moist green to a brittle brown. Without much to graze on, I spent most of those hours watching the comings and goings of the ranch.

Some days were busier than others, but most afternoons, I could count on seeing Black Hat's wife. The Missus liked to take leisurely strolls around the property with their daughter, Star, a devilish child of five or six years. Star was never without her pink glittery boots and matching cowgirl hat. She ran and squealed more than seemed normal, always chasing birds, throwing rocks, or picking flowers she had no business picking. Her mother either ignored or encouraged her bad behavior.

"Oh look, Star, there's another peacock. Go get him!" The Missus would say.

Or like the first time the two of them stopped at my pasture fence . . . The Missus held a large bag of carrots as her young wildling leaned through the fence rail, frantically waving a couple of orange sticks in an attempt to get my attention.

"Come here, horsey," Star said. "Come here."

Instinct told me to keep my distance.

"Mama! He won't come, Mama!"

"Well, that's not nice."

"Bad horsey! Bad horsey!" Star chided.

Instinct was right. This kid had less patience than Senhor Matos. Two "come heres," two "bad horseys," and there it came. The fit. The breakdown. She snapped into slinging those carrots as far as her chubby little arms could manage. So, a weak two feet at best.

The Missus stood laughing, even as Abel appeared at my gate, grabbing my halter to bring me in for the night. He said nothing to them, but as he put the halter over my ears, he looked me in the eye and gave me a pat.

"*Ignóra eles.*" Ignore them. He said it ever so softly to me, but the Missus overheard.

"Did you just call me ignorant?"

Abel shook his head.

"No," she said. "I think you did. Do you think I'm deaf? Or stupid?"

She came toward us shaking her plastic bag of carrots.

Abel kept walking, even as I startled and began to prance and snort.

"Don't you walk away from me," she shrieked, now running to confront us. Still shaking that noisy plastic bag.

Again, instinct took over. I swung my haunches around before going up. My front hooves clicked above their heads.

"Get back!" I heard Black Hat yell as he ran toward us, dragging another stallion by a lead rope.

No sooner had my feet hit the ground than I went up again, the relative peace of a few moments ago gone and me, whipped into a fight-or-flight frenzy. Black Hat's stallion lurched sideways, trying to pull away and bolt in the other direction. The other stallions in the surrounding turnouts started to spook and run. Hooves pounded the ground. Dust flew. Horses screamed.

"Whoa! Whoa!" Abel and Black Hat called in unison as I snapped back tight on my lead rope.

I wanted loose, but as Abel started to repeat, "*Tranquilo. Tranquilo,*" I came back to the ground, my neck high and arched but feet planted. We stood together for a few seconds, waiting on Black Hat to calm his own stallion.

Everyone but the Missus took a collective sigh of relief. And when she started in again about Abel's disrespect, Black Hat shut her down.

"Back to the house. Just please. Take Star and go back to the house."

"But—"

"No. Not now. Please."

"I want to ride that horsey." Star stomped her feet and pointed at me.

"Not now, sweetie," he said, and then again, to the Missus, "Please."

It was the first time I thought I saw a spark of something upstanding in Black Hat. After the Missus walked off, he apologized to Abel. But it was a glimmer of hope soon enough snuffed out. The next evening, his true colors were again on vivid, self-serving display.

A few things to know about Black Hat. Number one: On the outside, he was your basic wannabe cowboy. Tight jeans, big belt, and a long-sleeve button-down shirt, no matter the weather. Number two: He loved to stretch the truth. To hear him tell it, he'd grown up driving cattle along the Chisholm Trail, and his rodeo days had come to an end only because he had a family to look after. But the Missus took odd pleasure in stripping him down a notch or two when it suited her whim. Her version of the story didn't quite match his.

In reality, he'd been born and raised in suburban Redwood City, the only child of two techie geeks whose horse knowledge extended to *The Black Stallion* and My Little Pony. His first ride, she teased, hadn't come till he was thirteen, when a friend's birthday party took him to Half Moon Bay's Sea Horse Ranch. There, he was offered a dead-broke horse named Cinnamon. A better name would have been Weak Sauce. No spice left.

At that same party, Black Hat met a gal named Emily Lou Logan. Anytime Emily Lou's name was mentioned, the Missus stuck a finger in her mouth and pretended to gag. Emily Lou had apparently claimed to love horses even more than she loved some teen heartthrob named Rider Strong. She fast became Black Hat's first crush. Dead set on impressing her, he convinced his parents to spring for a few lessons at Stanford Red Barn, which eventually led to a horse lease and an obsession with old spaghetti westerns. To give him some credit, he'd been blessed with good balance and a certain necessary fearlessness. But also, and unfortunately, that enormous ego.

Much to his parents' chagrin, he opted to skip college to pursue the rodeo. And women. Many women. By the time I met Black Hat, he'd "settled down," but he was still convinced he knew all there was to know about horses. He wasn't keen on taking advice from anyone. Not even his employer.

Legs was generous in arranging and paying for him to ride with a variety of trainers, but Black Hat had his own ideas on just about everything. Take, for example, a straightforward request like what tack to use. Legs wanted us ridden in dressage or Portuguese saddles. Black Hat called them prissy, and whenever an opportunity arose, like Legs and Frank heading out of town, he'd pull out and heave upon us his heavy, squeaky Western saddle. Its extra weight was one thing, but the way it dug into my back and endlessly rocked to and fro didn't seem to concern Black Hat. He liked how it fit his butt and that was that. Legs's request and my comfort be damned. He was basic all right. Basically full of shit.

But back to that particular evening . . . Frank and Legs were about to head out for a long weekend at their Pebble Beach home. There'd been much ado about getting all the dogs loaded into two cars. One car would not have fit that circus. From my run, I watched as the two of them swapped kennels back and forth, working hard to complete the transit puzzle.

Black Hat walked over from the round pen as they snapped the final crate into place.

"Well done," he said.

Legs feigned wiping her brow. "Only took an hour."

"Wanted to make sure we take off just in time to hit rush-hour traffic," Frank added.

Ignoring him, Legs turned to Black Hat. "It's gonna be a hot one. Maybe just stick to some light longeing. Or see if they'll go for a swim in the pond."

"Yes, ma'am. Not a problem. Don't you worry about a thing."

Famous last words. Not an hour after Legs, Frank, and their pack of pooches had hit the road, Black Hat stood in the same spot, directing a steady influx of guests on where to park. Soon, the road from our barn to the pond house was lined with cars and trucks, and strange people were wandering the property. They carried towels and coolers and inflatable pool floats. A few made their way into the barn, where the Missus was giving her idea of a tour.

Her finger slipped on the volume dial of the barn's speaker, and the sudden blast of loud music sent horses rushing out of their stalls.

"Whoops!" She took a swig from her red Solo cup before adding, "So, this here's the stallion barn."

A man in the group peered out into Xeque's run. "Aw, dude. Check out the size of those balls!"

"Don't be gross," said a woman in a stars-and-stripes bikini and cowboy boots. "No one wants to look at horse testicles."

"Says you," said another woman as she approached my stall. "I like this one. What breed?"

"Oh, he's like from Florida," said the Missus.

Dear God, I thought. One question and the Missus was already out of her depth.

Black Hat gently corrected her. "Well originally, he's from Brazil. And he's a Lusitano. They're all Lusitanos. Working horses, bullfighters. The owners—"

"Oh no, not another *Lusi this, Lusi that* lesson. No one's interested," the Missus said, stealing back the spotlight by shoving a bag of carrots in her audience's faces. "Here, y'all. Grab some carrots. Feed 'em if you want, but let's get going. It's hot, and I'm itchin' for a swim."

Poor Xairel had come in from his run, curious about the carrots. Just as he stretched his head over his stall door to reach for one, Miss Short Shorts got a fright and spun around so fast her bottled brew went flying. It hit the bars of my stall and exploded. Minuscule shards of glass went everywhere, and both Xairel and I jumped back.

While everyone else stood laughing, Abel rushed into the barn and reached for a broom. Without a word, he started to clean up the mess.

"Watch your step, folks," Black Hat said. "Let's get out of here so he can clean."

Turning to Abel, he said, "Thanks, man. And hey, if you wanna come down for a beer and a hot dog later . . ."

"No, *gracias*."

"Okay, suit yourself."

It was the last I saw of the revelers until the wee hours of the morning when they noisily stumbled to their cars and blinded us with their headlights. The bright side: At least they were leaving.

The next morning, Abel did a good job cleaning, leaving no trace of the party for Legs and Frank to find. Well, almost no trace. Oddly, I hadn't noticed it until the following morning when Legs and Frank returned, but a stars-and-stripes bikini top was dangling from the post at the end of my run. Later that day, it was gone.

Two weeks later, Frank and Legs went away again. Only this time, as the party cars started to arrive, Frank's was among them. He said he'd forgotten his briefcase but then pulled out that bikini top and asked the crowd, including Black Hat, if anyone had seen its owner.

Later that evening, Napoleon amused himself by quipping, "Take that, Rodeo Rex! And oh yes, don't let the door hit ya where the good Lord split ya."

33

1995: Menlo Park, California

Thank you to whatever Egyptian invented the door. For doors, they are important. Sometimes they bring closure. Sometimes they spell opportunity. Sometimes they are the thing you can slam in someone's face or, simply, opt to close for a bit of privacy. Sometimes.

After my grad-school Paris year and a short stint in what-the-fuck-was-I-thinking Cambridge, Massachusetts, I landed in Northern California. Admittedly, because of the grad-school boyfriend, who'd first been finishing his undergrad studies at a school whose mascot is an elephant and next decided to get his master's at a school whose mascot is a tree.

He lived on campus. I found a house share in Menlo Park.

My housemates were four humans, a cat, and a ball python. The humans were a bit of an odd bunch, especially the one who not once, but twice, came to me scratching her crotch and complaining about having "yet another yeast infection." Henceforth, Sourdough Starter. I've never been able to look at white jeans in the same way again. And I certainly declined offers to share her popcorn or potato chips. Another housemate, Heather, owned the cat and the snake and could have easily doubled for Kim Basinger. The cat was named Madame Jambonette and, yeah, she was a fat cat. She mostly lived outside, which was fine with me since she made me sneeze. The snake, whose real name I can't recall, I dubbed Maneater. He only came out at night.

After a late shift at work, I'd open the front door, and Maneater would be slithering across the living room floor, reveling in giving me a heart attack and lording over the pathway to my bedroom like a border patrol agent. And by *bedroom*, I really mean *nook*. Like a stage, it had three walls and a curtain, and with Maneater making the rounds, I slept with one eye open and one hand over my throat.

But hey, the place was cheap. And it was all Bob Cratchit—err, I—could afford.

My master's degree in French had secured me, let's see, a bicycle and a job working the cheese station at Oakville Grocery at the Stanford Shopping Center. At the end of every shift, I'd load up as many free leftover bagels as my bicycle baskets could fit, switch on my headlamp, headlight, and flashing rear light, and pedal home as fast as I could. On a good night, Heather was home; most nights, she was bartending.

The house had three official bedrooms, but she, like me, had a curtained-off nook. We bonded over that oddity and our love for animals. In addition to Madame Jambonette and Maneater, she owned a quarter horse named Bijou. And, yes, you may have noticed the French influence. Her ex-husband had been a Frenchman. But no, not either of *those* Frenchmen.

I learned about Bijou and her Frenchman the first night we ever got drunk together. Not long after I moved in, Sourdough Starter gifted us a bottle of Benedictine & Brandy. And when I say bottle, I don't mean a tiny airplane bottle, but one large enough to have us nursing wicked hangovers for the next two days. Live and never learn. Seems to be my motto.

We started off having a wee nip. But as we got talking and

laughing, one drink led to another and at some point, another one of our housemates came home. Let's call her the Cyclist.

Every night, she clippety-clopped into the house in her cycling shoes, disrobed behind her closed bedroom door (yes, she was one of the privileged few), and headed straight for the washing machine to do a load of laundry comprised of one pair of biking shorts, a top, and maybe a pair of socks. She then returned to her bedroom, generally without saying a word, and closed that door again.

The noise from the machine didn't bother her, but it bothered Heather. A lot.

That night, Heather got it into her head it would be funny to stick every pair of tennis shoes she owned into the dryer. She wanted to see if she could make it loud enough to annoy the Cyclist. I agreed it would be funny until the dryer got going. *BUMP BUMP BUMP!* That shit was loud. I panicked.

For some reason (that's right, Benedictine & Brandy), I had the brilliant idea of stripping down to my skivvies and throwing my clothes into the dryer to somehow muffle the noise. I didn't want to ruin Heather's fun, but I also didn't want the Cyclist to get us kicked out of the house. Unfortunately, the Cyclist appeared a few moments later to find me standing there like a jaybird and Heather like a ravenous rat, her face deep in the fridge taking a bite out of a chunk of cheddar.

"Hey," I said, giving a nonchalant wave before racing past her and into my nook, which was all of ten feet away and where I could have easily grabbed other clothes, pillows, any number of noise-muffling options. I attempted to slam my curtains shut. Imagine the menacing *shhhh* of wooden curtain rings sliding over a wooden curtain rod. *Take that!* I couldn't stop laughing after I heard Heather laughing so hard she nearly choked on her cheddar.

My room in that house may not have had a door, but that night opened one of the most important doors of my life as Heather turned out to be the person who would, one day, bring horses back into my life.

But first, I had some unsettled business abroad.

34

2009: Gilroy, California

The whole Black Hat business was bizarre. The battle to boot him had been won, but I was still trying to figure out how.

At first, I was sure Abel had cracked, no longer willing to tolerate their disrespect, clean up their messes, or keep their secrets. Yet when Legs questioned him about the bikini, Abel held up his hands and repeated, "*No sé. No sé.*" I don't know. I don't know.

He was convincing, but regardless, the winds of change had begun to blow. Frank had given Black Hat and his pink ladies enough time to find new accommodations but not enough to worm their way back into his good graces. It simply wasn't a good match.

"Trust," Napoleon said after that first party, "is a tricky thing to win back."

"Bird, lest you forget . . . you're talking to a Lusitano."

"Touché, pony, touché."

Fortunately, Frank and Legs made fast work of finding a replacement. Or at minimum, a stopgap. What couldn't be done before was somehow arranged for the moment. Napoleon and I were heads down in my bowl of morning oats discussing the heat—boy, the summer days could be scorchers—when I heard a familiar cackle. I jerked up, swiveled my ears forward, and whinnied a greeting loud enough to shake my entire body.

More leathered than ever, Boots in the aisleway was a vision.

"Well, hello to you, too, Artilheiro."

She was my hope. My hope of finding my mate for the bullfight. Not because she was a bullfighter but because she had moxie, and I believed she believed in me. I stood tall and proud as she peered into my stall to give me the once-over.

"Eating well, I see."

Is she calling me fat?

"Are you calling him fat?" From behind Boots, Legs leaned over to have a look for herself. "He's not fat."

"He could use a little work."

"Well, that's what you're here for."

"Oh no, no, no. I'm here for the food and entertainment, and to make sure you don't bring in anymore goddamn Rodeo Rexes!" Boots shook her head. "I told you. Just 'cause that boy'd hop up on any ol' thing didn't mean he was the right man for the job. Least of all for these horses."

"Well, I asked you first, and you said no."

"I believe I said I was busy. And that maybe you ought to wait a year."

They both looked at one another and laughed.

"Live, learn, and get burned," Legs said. "But I wouldn't have had it any other way."

"Oh, I know, honey, I know. No use crying over spilled milk. Plus, day's about to get hotter than a jalapeño's armpit. Time to get going." Out of habit, she touched her left breast pocket, patted the pack of cigarettes, and turned back around to me. "Let's start with Artilheiro."

"You mean Dra-GŌN?" Legs said in her best baritone.

Nothing escaped hypocorism at Shangri-La. Though I preferred *Artilheiro*, which had also already been shortened to *Arty* ("Ar-tee" and not "Ar-chee"), I suppose it could have been worse. I mean, Eins, Zwei, und Drie were the golf carts. Precise, but uninspired. And then just as I thought it, Boots said it aloud.

"Well, at least that's better than Electric Pea."

E-Pea was Frank's commuter car and his guaranteed ticket to "rock star parking." His words. I don't know much about cars or rock star parking, but I do have a certain aesthetic, and Pea was about the ugliest contraption I'd ever seen. And thank goodness, not Frank's only mode of transportation. Legs was getting me out of my stall when Frank drove up in Oh Cherry, a bulbous-nosed antique pickup truck that wore a permanent bright-white gap-toothed grin.

"T-bone or New York strip?" he yelled above the rumble of the engine.

"Well, if you're asking, I'll take a nice big juicy rib eye, thank you," Boots said.

"Whatever looks good. Just don't forget the Aperol," Legs added as she hitched me to the crossties and went over to rattle off a list of other items for Frank not to forget while he was out.

Boots didn't wait for Legs. She unhooked me and walked me to the arena. Despite the heat, I had plenty of energy. Perhaps some of it nerves. I snorted and pranced the entire way. If they wanted a dragon, they'd get a fire-breathing one. Boots, however, was unfazed by my huffing and puffing. It wasn't until I moved my shoulders into her space that she snapped my halter and asked me to step away.

"My space."

From arm's length, she jiggled the lead rope until I took another step back. Immediately, the jiggling ceased.

"Good boy."

Perhaps because of the heat, she stuck to basic groundwork. Leading, bending, yielding. Move your haunches, now your shoulders. A few steps this way, a few steps the other way. If I started to get stuck and lose my balance or forward momentum, she stopped, reset, and started over until, ever so slowly, I began to calm down, relax, even enjoy myself and our improvised dance. I reached and lowered my head so I could feel the stretch all the way through and down my back. I licked my lips. Sighed. Farted.

"Yup, that's what I like to hear," she said. "Good boy."

And that was that. We'd been working for only twenty minutes, but Boots called it good. As a reward for my exemplary behavior—I am a quick study—she led me straight to my pasture. I spent the rest of the morning beneath the shade of a tall birch, watching her and Legs work the other stallions.

I liked that Boots was clear in what she wanted, clear in how she asked for it, and careful to never ask for too much. Instead of feeling pushed too far too fast, as was often the case with many of the other "here today, gone tomorrow" trainers of the Black Hat era, time with Boots and Legs felt more like play.

Later that evening, I heard them laughing on the back patio of the main house. The mood of the ranch had changed.

Over the course of the week, the weather cooled, and Boots spent more time in the saddle, even setting up small jumps and obstacles and, finally, suggesting a trail ride through the vineyard to stave off the monotony of riding in endless dressage circles.

The vineyard stretched out across fifty rambling acres on the property. Though Frank and Legs harvested and sold its pinot noir crop to various winemakers each year, they weren't, per se, in the wine business. As Frank saw it, "Wine people are flaky. I don't need that pain in the ass in my life."

I sure as heck didn't care about the wine business either but I missed the trail and pawed at my stall door to signal, *Me! Take me!*

It worked! As Boots saddled me and Legs saddled Xeque, the smell of oiled leather, earthy and sweet, drifted from the tack room to the grooming station. Inside the tack room, rows of saddles hung neatly on one wall, while countless bridles adorned another. In a corner, an ornate gape-mouthed wooden carousel horse glared at us, frozen in a perpetual high-stepping trot beside an oak armoire whose doors barely contained an abundance of monogrammed saddle pads. At the room's center, a large round wooden table, bookended by high-backed chairs draped in sheepskins, sat atop a sprawling cowhide rug. It was a beautiful room, and a beautiful evening.

We rode out past the ponds and guesthouse. The camels lazed under a huge oak in the middle of their pasture while the nearby pigs grunted and headed for dinner in their pens. A few peacocks followed us, almost in a procession, until we reached a wrought iron gate that led to the rows of grapevines.

Shutting the gate from atop my saddle, Boots looked over at Legs and asked, "Have I ever told you why I love horses so much?"

"Because they aren't people?"

"Because they call us on our bullshit. Each and every day. They will not lie to us. And they will not refuse what they understand."

"And?"

"Start trusting your intuition. Build a foundation of comfort and balance. And don't let anyone tell you what's what with your horses. Not even me. Well, maybe me."

"Oh, definitely not you."

"These boys don't have a choice. So make the right choices and protect them. Because everything they were bred to do and be depends on trust. And if Rex was lying to you, he was lying to these horses. And they deserve better."

"I know."

"You deserve better."

"I know."

"Well, all right then."

With that, Boots leaned forward, gave with the reins, and let me go. Xeque was quick to follow my lead, and the four of us rode tantivy toward the setting sun, cresting a hill and running smack into the middle of a herd of grazing cattle. Boots gently pulled up on the reins, coaxing me into a slow jog and then a halt. Before me, for the first time: longhorns. Except for a few small calves, who hopped and bucked and skittered off, the rest barely registered our dusty arrival. They paused only briefly to moo and give us a meandering glance before returning to their grazing.

I started to canter in place.

"Easy, boy. Easy," Boots said, taking a firmer hold of the reins as I spun in a circle and nearly sideswiped Legs and a snorting Xeque.

Boots laughed. "Fire-breathing! This dragon likes to fly."

But it was more than that. I was ready to rumble.

I couldn't wait to tell Napoleon about the ride, but when I returned to my stall, he had already been safely locked away for the night. The only thing awaiting me was a stray riding glove atop my sea of shavings. The next night, it was a bell boot at the end of my run. Then a polo wrap draped over a fence rail. Until finally, it was Napoleon, desperately trying to drag an enormous empty feed bag through the slats of my fence.

"What are you doing?"

He laughed. "Caught in the act."

"The act? Wait . . ."

And that's when it hit me. Abel hadn't been lying about the bikini—Napoleon had been the one leaving things all along.

In that moment, I couldn't help but love that crazy, clever rooster even more.

Bird brain = mind-blowing.

35

1996: Paris, France

After less than a year in California, I couldn't shake Paris, that seductive city, from my mind. As it happened, neither could my boyfriend. We had friends who had stayed or returned, and by some miracle, we had saved enough money to make our way back and stay for at least a few months if we didn't find jobs. As fate would have it, I did find a job.

In the months leading up to that Paris return, I'd sent cover letters to nearly every English-language publication I could find in the city. I still had no clear career path, but if I could do anything, I wanted to find a job that involved writing, in some capacity. Miraculously, within the first couple of weeks of arriving, I landed two interviews. And more miraculously, two offers. The first was with *Time Out*; the second was with *Harper's Bazaar* (technically, also *Marie Claire*, *Town & Country*, and *Cosmopolitan*).

Which one do you think I went for?

After I popped up out of the Franklin D. Roosevelt Métro station and walked down avenue Montaigne and into the building that housed the *Harper's Bazaar* office, as well as Chanel, I thought I was dreaming. The two women I met that day were beyond beautiful and oh so chic, cool, and kind. To them, I was sure I looked like all the seven dwarfs rolled up into one and I could have barely dreamed of being offered the position save for one tiny, funny detail.

Though I was only twenty-six years old, I had a streak of gray in my hair. Just like the younger of the two women. We had both begun to gray prematurely and joked about how mature it made us. At least on the outside.

The initial offer was for a six-week internship, assisting with the autumn ready-to-wear shows. This entailed dealing with French press and fashion houses, securing tickets to a gazillion different shows for a gazillion different fashion editors, coordinating photo shoots, getting all the right looks to the right places at the right time via crazy Paris couriers, and a million other tasks and details I never could have imagined were part of publishing a monthly magazine. It was both terrifying and exhilarating. The hours were long, the pay was shit, and I absolutely loved it. So much so that when I was offered a full-time position, I . . .

For context, at the same time, my boyfriend, who had not found a job and, quite frankly, hadn't made much effort in that department, told me he didn't want to stay in Paris. He was going to return to San Francisco.

I had a choice to make.

I spent so much of my life shy and quiet that sometimes I wonder why I chose to study another language in school. It meant I would actually have to speak. Out loud. To strangers. But I'll tell you what. It also helped me grow a pair and, in a way, find my voice. Especially after I decided (duh) to stay in Paris. On my own.

Accepting the offer to work at a renowned fashion magazine had its perks—the pay, I repeat, wasn't one of them—but Paris wasn't all Tour Eiffel photo shoots and Versace runway shows at the Ritz. Paris was also a series of hassles, from finding an apartment and securing my *carte de séjour* to arguing with taxi drivers, designer houses, couriers, retailers, museum security guards, and, my personal favorite, the dreaded RATP ticket booth agent. Shall we start with him?

There I am, realizing it's the first day of the month and shit, *merde*, mother f'er, I forgot to buy my *carte orange* in advance. Of course, this hits me only after I've descended the urine-glazed Métro stairwell and turned a corner to see an already-dozen-deep line at the ticket counter. Because I'm late, I bet everyone's paying with their *cartes bleue*, which will require precious extra time for punching in personal codes and waiting on bank-confirmation slips.

Deep breath. *At least I have cash.* But tick tock, tick tock. *C'mon, people.* Punch. Wait. Punch. Wait. *Okay, phew, my turn.*

I hand 300 FF (one 200 FF note and one 100 FF note) to the attendant, who looks down at but does not touch the bills. To be clear, a *carte orange* costs 243 FF.

"*Vous n'avez pas la monnaie exacte?*" he asks. You don't have exact change?

I shake my head.

"*J'ai pas de monnaie*," he adds. I don't have change.

"*Pardon?*" I say, thinking I may not have heard him right.

"*J'ai. Pas. De monnaie*," he repeats *m o r e s l o w l y*, before looking back at two of his cronies, who are doing what? Do they work here? Why are they just standing around?

"*C'est tout ce que j'ai.*" That's all I have. Those are the words that come out of my mouth, but the thought in my head is how much I wish I had 243 FF in dirty centimes to dump over this smug bastard's head. *Espèce de connard.* Dick.

"*Allez à la boulangerie, madame*," he suggests. Go to the bakery, ma'am.

Did he just call me ma'am? And tell me to go to a bakery? So I could what? Pay for a 2 FF demi-baguette with my 100 FF note to get change for him?

"*C'est le debut du mois et vous n'avez pas de monnaie? C'est curieux ça,*" I say, my volume starting to rise. It's the first of the month and you don't have change? That's curious. "*Et d'être clair, vous me disez qu'il faut que j'aille à une boulangerie?*" And to be clear, you're telling me I have to go to a bakery?

He hunches his shoulders, throws his hands up in resignation, smirks back at his coworkers (though "workers" was a stretch) before adding a throwaway "*Desolée.*" Sorry.

Not that his disingenuous "apology" doesn't rub me the wrong way—along with everything else about this interaction—but his next move, which is him trying to wave me away like a bad smell, flips a switch. Like a sprung fire hydrant, words, mainly expletives, fly from my mouth. English, French, doesn't matter.

Pointing to him, I say, "You're a dick. *Et non. Je. Ne. Bouge. Pas.*" No. I'm. Not. Moving. Then, pointing to the growing line behind me, I add, "*J'ai toute la journée*, you little cocksucker." I have all day. "*Vous pouvez faire de la monnaie à la boulangerie.*" You can go get change at a bakery. "*C'est votre boulot, pas le mien.*" It's your job, not mine.

A second later, a 50 FF note miraculously appears from his cash register drawer. I see there are loads of them, and that's when something else hits me. This is just a game for him.

The devil doesn't wear Prada; he wears an RATP uniform.

"*Merci,*" I say, taking my change before adding, "*Vous avez des problèmes.*" You have problems.

He did have problems, but as I alluded to before and despite this minor, ballsy victory, so did I.

During what turned into weeks and weeks of apartment hunting (at the time, there was no internet, no email, just newspaper ads and too many people searching for something affordable in a completely unaffordable city), I learned a thing or two, including how to translate real estate ads. "*Charmant*" meant miniscule. "*Unique*" meant freaky. "*Moderne*" meant cold, gray, and grim. Some of the places I saw I wish I could have unseen.

Take, for example, the eighth-floor walk-up. The ad raved about a skylight as if it were a portal to the heavens, claiming it drenched the apartment in a warm, one-of-a-kind glow (caveat emptor: one-of-a-kind = unique = freaky). I'm here to tell you, it was anything but. Still, I understood why they were plugging it so hard. That skylight, more porthole than portal, was the only window in the place, which could have been more accurately described as a prison cell or torture chamber. Its energy screamed straitjackets and electroshock therapy. I'm not even sure I managed a "thanks for the tour of chez no fucking way!" before rushing out the door.

Then there was the "you can do it all at once" apartment. I was pleasantly surprised when I arrived at the building. There was a park across the street and plenty of bustling neighborhood shops and cafés. Even upon entering the apartment, I maintained hope. The living room was small but bright, with a high ceiling and a lovely view onto the park. *Okay*, I thought, mentally rubbing my hands together, *let's see what else we've got*. The living room fed into the kitchen, and wait, what? What was a shower and a toilet doing in the kitchen? Like *in* the kitchen, not a separate room off to the side with, perhaps, a door.

Was this Saintes-Maries-de-la-Mer all over again?

I joked with the real estate agent about it being a multitasking kitchen, where you could simultaneously take a dump, shower, and flip pancakes for brekkie. He did not laugh but instead called it *très pratique*. Practical? I called it unsafe, unsanitary, and un-fucking-viable. I didn't even bother to ask about the bedroom, afraid he might pull out a Murphy bed from a kitchen cabinet with a Houdini ta-da! Wait. I forgot. He had no sense of humor.

When I arrived in Paris, I initially stayed with an old friend, who, to be fair, was closer to my boyfriend than to me. So when my boyfriend left, this friend arranged for me to temporarily stay at one of his friend's vacant apartments until I could find my own place.

The apartment was in a Paris suburb, roughly an hour away by metro. Given that I typically worked till 7:00 p.m., it was always late and dark by the time I got there. I'd rush to unlock the apartment's *three* door locks, but once inside, I wondered if locking myself in was a good or bad thing.

The place was eerily big, bleak, and empty. It had two levels and a million light switches that sometimes worked, sometimes didn't. I could never quite figure out the *rez de chaussée*–level lights and so would race upstairs to do nothing more than scarf down my convenience-store dinner, often a luscious can of tuna and maybe a bag of pretzels, before hurrying to bed. From beneath the covers, I prayed no ghouls, goblins, or serial killers would come for me in the middle of the night.

After a couple weeks of combined apartment-hunting lunch breaks and creepy banlieue nights, I started to wonder if I'd made the right choice to stay in Paris. The dream was becoming a nightmare . . . until one of my work colleagues offered to put me up at her charming Marais apartment.

It was nearing Christmas, and she was heading home to England for a couple of weeks to celebrate the holidays. She said, "Make yourself at home." And she meant it. Not only for those initial two weeks but the several more it took me to finally find my own digs. God bless you, Birdie—and your goat's milk tea—to this day and beyond.

During that couch-surfing time, I also learned that to secure an apartment, you needed a French bank account. But to get a French bank account, you needed an address in France. If you didn't have a French bank account, there was one workaround. You could enlist a guarantor, someone who would accept financial responsibility should you fall down on your obligation. But! That guarantor couldn't be my parents in the United States. It had to be someone in France.

I found out about these glitches after I'd finally found an acceptable (cute even!) one-bedroom apartment. And after I'd already borrowed first and last months' rent plus the security deposit from my folks. And after I'd hurriedly carried the cash to the real estate agency during yet another lunch break to sign the paperwork. They told me no, without a French-based guarantor, their hands were tied. When I got back to the office, my whole team waiting to congratulate me, I'm not sure I got a single word out before breaking down in tears.

Had it not been for my boss, who stepped in and up, agreeing right then and there to be my guarantor, I'd have surely lost the apartment. And almost as surely, my nerve to stay. So God bless you, too, Jane.

Fast forward eight months . . .

The news flashed across a TV screen in JFK Airport.

"Princess Diana has been in a car crash."

I was just boarding a flight back to Paris after a week's vacation at home with my family. A flashbulb memory, I can still see that TV screen. The same way, years later on the morning of 9/11, I would remember my then boyfriend screaming, "America is under attack!"

By the time my flight landed the next morning, there was an update. Diana had died.

The site of the crash, the Pont de l'Alma underpass, happened to be right by my work bus stop. Returning to work the following day, I couldn't believe the shrine of flowers and photos people had already left. They were incredible, and the crowds that gathered were somber.

Maybe a week later, I started to notice a different type of crowd and a different mood. The site had become a photo op, with tourists huddling in front of the tunnel, smiling and saying cheese for the camera. It creeped me out. What a wicked species we are.

Not long after, our team began work on the *Harper's Bazaar* Diana tribute issue. It was to be one of the last issues I worked on as I'd also made the heartrending decision to give my three months' notice. Not because of the icky tourists, but more so because the romantic Paris I'd imagined never quite panned out. I'd landed a job. I'd found an apartment. I'd made amazing friends. In some ways, I'd never been more fulfilled, and I was damned proud of myself for going it alone. In other ways, I'd never been lonelier.

The long-distance relationship I'd tried to maintain had miserably and irreversibly failed. *Quelle surprise.* And though a dalliance with another expat proved fun and distracting, it wasn't long before he, too, had to return to the States. I found myself feeling like something profound was missing, and for better or for worse, I lacked the perspective, patience, and maybe most of all, the roots to stay put.

In addition to the gig and my friends, it broke my heart to give up that hard-won apartment on rue Gassendi in the fourteenth arrondissement, not far from Cimetière du Montparnasse. It sat above a quiet Indian restaurant and faced, if you can believe it, a quiet elementary school. It had a small living room I furnished with a table and a chair and not much more (remember, my pay was shit); a bathroom with a bathtub (a rarity in Paris); and a tiny kitchen I outfitted with a tiny table and chair (yes, just one chair), a tiny stove, a tiny fridge, and a tiny washing machine that, with each use, never failed to give me a shock. But hey, it beat going to a laundromat. Screw that.

It wasn't fancy, but it was cute, clean, safe, and, best of all, mine. And maybe that was the biggest lesson I learned. I had pluck enough to take care of myself. Where there's a will, there's a way! And maybe this time leaving would prove to be less about running away from something and more about running toward something.

I got home around Thanksgiving but only stayed for a quick visit. I didn't want to lose momentum or let my feet turn cold.

36

2009: Gilroy, California

The cold had taken Napoleon.

No, not to the grave, but to the big house. A few days prior, he'd begun to wheeze and cough so badly I wondered if he'd swallowed a rattle. Vets were called, arrangements were made, and off Napoleon went in Electric Pea to the Gilroy Veterinary Hospital.

Upon his return the following day, the rattle had dulled, but before he could finish telling me about a magical chamber filled with the most delicious air, Legs whisked him away again. An unusual cold spell had set in, and she and Frank wouldn't have it any other way. Napoleon was to continue his convalescence in the comfort of their heated garage. I missed him. I was worried about him. But at least the music that evening, a lyrical version of Pachelbel's *Canon in D Major* performed by the Trans-Siberian Orchestra, was a comfort. Even the holiday radio disc jockey acknowledged its perfection.

The soft sounds of a piano joined by plaintive violins and a children's choir echoed through the barn. Even as the temperature continued to dip, I was warm inside and out, enjoying listening to them sing of Christmas night. And on this very Christmas night, the air held no scent other than the crisp clean of the cold. Abel had soaked our grain in warm water, and after touching my ears (Legs's barometer for warmth), he swapped out my turnout sheet for a puffy new stable blanket.

Christmas stockings hung from all the stall doors, and after Abel had adjusted and secured all the buckles and straps on my new blanket, he reached inside mine and pulled out a small wrapped object. It crackled in his hand as he worked to open it and offer me the treat within. Without hesitation, I cleeked it from his hand, only to abruptly spit it out.

"No, no. You take."

He picked up the skinny red-and-white candy from off my stall floor, brushed off stuck shavings, and held it to my nose. I was hesitant to open my mouth, nuzzling Abel's fingers with my lips until, finally, I gave in. On the second try, I fell in love and promptly mugged him for more. I'm not sure about the other horses, but I got two peppermint candy canes that night. A rare sugar treat.

As Abel hurried to close up for the night, a sudden wind picked up, swirling shavings around my legs like a tiny tempest. I thought of Mother and our one and only Christmas together. I was just ten days old, and while there were no candy canes or warm blankets, I needed neither. On that evening, a gentle breeze blew, and Mother's milk was sweeter than any other treat. Her words of encouragement came back to me: "You are your own horse, Artilheiro. You can be whatever you want to be."

Despite it being Christmas—a time to believe in magic and fairy-tales—I wasn't so sure anymore. Could I really be whatever I wanted to be? I lived where there were no fighting bulls, and riders came and went like the wind. Here today and gone the next. How could I become a bull-fighter without bulls, without my one true *cavaleiro*? Maybe what I wanted most was impossible.

And then, as if he were standing next to me, Napoleon's voice popped into my head: *Quit with the melodrama and enjoy your imported grass and sea of shavings.*

37

1997: Palo Alto, California

I am haunted by Waters.

I know that's Norman Maclean's line. But since my Waters has a capital *W*—because it's a proper noun, a last name, Carlton's last name—I'm hoping it's okay to borrow. Frankly, whether it's permissible or not, I can't help myself, especially considering Carlton lives in Missoula. From what I gather, the town lured him away from Palo Alto with its big sky, sweeping landscapes, riffled Clark Fork River, and, of course, dearth of bastards.

He's lived there for years now. And for years, he's invited me to come and visit his ten-acre slice of heaven. And for some reason, I still haven't gone.

Maybe it's inertia. Maybe it's envy. More likely, it's because I know as soon as we're together, we'll open up some beautiful, bold red. (Carlton drinks only fine wine.) Slice into a warm and tender, red-centered cut of beef. And eventually, find ourselves on Memory Lane.

The first two aren't so bad.

But no. I kid. I obviously don't mind reminiscing about old times. I'm a sentimental sucker. But depending on the time, I have to be careful in how I navigate around what I sometimes consider mistakes and bad choices made along the way. Those can quickly and easily kill a bold, red buzz. But here we are, or, should I say, back. Back in Palo Alto when the bubble was still bubbling, and people left and right around us were becoming millionaires. Back when I was still trying to figure out how to get a job that didn't involve submitting a time sheet and worrying about what temporary hell the next week might bring.

At least by then I'd traded in my bicycle for a red and reliable (well, sort of) Subaru Legacy I'd bought for $700 from my parents' next-door neighbor in Maryland. It felt so right, and so wrong, to drive that baby solo halfway across the country, where at certain stops—Alabama and Louisiana, I'm looking at you—I had a harder time understanding folks than when I was conversing in a foreign language abroad. I never thought I'd say it, but I was relieved to reach Houston, where I met up with my expat divertissement. He may have left Paris, but not my life, and he'd kindly volunteered to drive me the rest of the way to California.

As you know, I had left California for love and in pursuit of adventure, not necessarily because I'd tired of it. Once I'd firmly closed the Paris chapter, I decided to return to a place I knew—at least a little—and a few people I could count on, including Maneater Heather. She and some other girlfriends had moved into a house in San Carlos, and as luck would have it, a room had become available for me to rent. A legit bedroom. Door and all.

Not long after my arrival, but long enough for the expat to have left, Heather told me about an opportunity. A friend of hers was producing a weekly public-service TV program and he needed an extra cameraman.

"Does it pay?" I asked, completely ignoring the fact I had no relevant experience.

"No, silly. It's public-service TV. But it would be a great way for you to meet new people," she pitched, before scribbling a number on a piece of paper and handing it to me.

"The producer's name is Carlton. He's a good guy. Give him a call."

I'm not sure what possessed me to make that call, but before I knew it, I was in a studio behind a camera, filming a doctor and her brother take calls and answer medical questions live on the air. After the second show, or maybe it was the third, Carlton asked if I'd like to join him for a drink at Rudy's, where Heather tended bar and he was meeting friends.

"Sure, why not?" I said.

Oh, hindsight, hindsight, why didn't you stop me?

That night, the first of many to follow at Rudy's, Carlton introduced me to . . . let's call him Sour Cherry. At first glance, I won't lie, I found the guy's appearance peculiar. It was something about his deep-set eyes; they seemed off-kilter. I wondered if his nerdy wire-rimmed glasses were the issue until he took them off to clean them with a wrinkled cocktail napkin. Nope. The glasses were his friend and so, too, it seemed, were the two young women seated at his table.

They were drinking sparkling wine, not from a big bottle but from two of those piccolo numbers that could make anyone look like Lemuel Gulliver. It was a detail I noted as cute (as were they) though somewhat incongruous in what was, for all intents and purposes, a dive bar. When Carlton asked what I'd like to drink, I said I'd love a Guinness before taking the empty seat next to Sour Cherry. Sensing the women weren't thrilled with my presence, I did the one thing I could think of to try to curry favor. I yelled to Carlton, "And two champagnes! Ask Heather if she wouldn't mind starting a tab for me."

Starting a tab can be a dangerous thing at a bar. Guinness and bubbly flowed like, well, Guinness and bubbly, and at some point, someone mentioned Germany. That word, that place, was the spark. By the end of the night, I saw Sour Cherry in a different light altogether.

Not only did his father live in the same small town in Bavaria my parents were set to move to a few months later, but Sour Cherry had also lived in Heidelberg while growing up. Though he was a few years younger than me, it turned out we'd both had the same eighth-grade English teacher, Mr. White. We'd both been to Hinterbrand and shuddered at the thought of the "run and dip" (a mile run, a backward plunge into an icy stream, and a mile run back). He may not have been an army brat (his father worked for the American school system overseas), but he understood what it meant to be one.

My, how small the world can be. It felt as if we were destined to meet. Heather giving me that number. Me volunteering to man a camera for a public-service TV program. The producer inviting me out for a drink and introducing me to not only Sour Cherry but also Bubbles—that's just what I'll call her for now.

But first, Sour Cherry. He marked the debut of my problem with serial monogamy, where I'd jump from one relationship to the next, never giving myself the space to breathe and just be on my own.

Less than a year after our introduction, Sour Cherry and I were living together in a tiny studio apartment in Mountain View. It had a balcony, which we never used, and a brown vinyl accordion divider for when we wanted to make both the living room and bedroom spaces feel even more claustrophobic. That's right. You heard correctly. Another bedroom without a door.

But wait, it gets better.

There was a swimming pool. It was warm, but not because it was heated, more because it was stale. I went in once and itched for days afterward.

Still, it gets better. The pièce de résistance? The upstairs neighbor and her vibrating bed. She ran that contraption for hours a day, purportedly for "health" reasons. She said physical; I guessed mental.

I'd seen her car in the carport. A behemoth of a Plymouth covered in grime, it looked like it hadn't seen a road since the eighties. And based on the number of stuffed animals crammed onto its parcel shelf, that was probably a good thing for humanity. After Sour Cherry and I complained to management about the bed, she took to shoving manifesto-length letters under our door (she refused to ever meet with us in person) to tell us what wicked, selfish people we were. I took to leaving black pots at her door. No, I'm kidding. I didn't go near that door.

In the end, the pool was avoidable. The accordion was comical. But that vibrating bed, that fucking vibrating bed made us want to pull our hair out. It felt like an unending earthquake and only exacerbated our already-volcanic relationship, which flipped between idle and explosive, idle and explosive. Sour Cherry was funny as fuck and smart as hell. But for every reason it made sense for us to be together, there were a dozen more that screamed we couldn't have been more mismatched. We shouldn't have lasted three months together, let alone the three years it took to pull the plug, once and for all.

And still, in hindsight, oh hindsight, I give those disasters credit for pushing me to find something else, something different to do with my time and energy.

When I say I am haunted by Waters, I mean it in the best of ways. Life is a tortuous road of ups and downs, twists and turns. The night I met Sour Cherry, which, in its way, was orchestrated by Maneater Heather, started me down a new path that initially felt fun and exciting. But eventually, like Peggy Lee, I found myself asking, "Is that all there is?"

1999: Half Moon Bay, California

After the Camargue, the next time I rode a horse was in California.

Sarah, an old friend from the East Coast, suggested the idea. She had ridden saddlebred horses as a kid, albeit not very well (her words, not mine). Nevertheless, she was always game to try. Knowing I was a hippophile, she suggested we meet one afternoon in Half Moon Bay at Sea Horse Ranch to go for a relaxing ride on the beach.

Upon arrival, I saw a rather sad establishment. Horses stood in a line, tied to metal posts, already tacked up. Their tails swished to fend off flies, while their heads drooped in resignation. It was as if they were waiting for their cowboys to stumble out of a saloon or come running from a bank robbery. Only, no. I take that back. These horses didn't have the spunk a bank robber's horse would need.

These poor creatures were probably hoping strangers wouldn't arrive to get on their backs at all, even if, according to the establishment's rules, rides were walk-only. Under no circumstances were riders allowed to do anything that might cause these horses to break a sweat.

"Sarah," I said, "are you sure about this? I feel kinda bad for these horses."

"Yeah, c'mon, we're here. It'll be fun."

"All right. If you say so," I said before signing my life away.

Unlike in the south of France, we had to fill out liability and experience-level forms. I debated, should I claim to have experience? I wanted to say I did but also thought, would that prompt them to give me a spicier horse and if so, would he get rowdy and, God forbid, move fast enough to break a sweat? As a rule follower, I started to sweat just thinking about making a horse sweat.

But looking again at the lineup of horses, I realized spicy was probably not on the menu.

We were handed janky helmets and led to our horses. I honestly don't remember a thing about mine. Sarah probably would; her mind is a steel trap. But Sarah's horse was another story. I'll never forget Sarah's horse, who, I'd like to point out, was white.

Before hopping up on her sad, pale steed, Sarah asked the ranch hand what his name was.

"*Es* Snow," the hand responded.

"Essno?" Sarah asked, wanting to be sure.

"*Es* Snow," he repeated.

"Essno," Sarah said again. "That's so pretty."

"*Sí*," he nodded.

"What does it mean?" Sarah asked.

The hand looked at me. I nodded, then turned to Sarah.

"Sarah," I said, putting my hand on her shoulder before pointing to her horse. "Your horse is white. His name is Snow. It means snow."

Sarah started laughing in that way only she laughs. Half giggle, half snort. God love her for always finding a way to make me laugh, on purpose or not.

Once mounted, we made for the beach, where we did not gallop but really only did our best to keep our horses from diving for grass and, after turning around at the halfway point, from racing back—and breaking a sweat—to the barn. These horses were barn sour!

The sun had been shining, and the horses were good not to spook at the *ding-ding* of a bazillion bicycle bells and lurching children on the pathway to the beach, but I hadn't enjoyed the ride and, once dismounted, felt about as forlorn as the ramshackle barn before us. That day, I realized I was no longer a rider. That day, I'd been nothing more than a hack out for a hack.

It didn't sit well with me.

Soon after, I contacted Stanford Red Barn and enrolled in riding lessons, determined to find out what more there could be.

38

2009: Gilroy, California

Boots preached consistency but couldn't commit to it. After our vineyard ride, her presence waxed and waned over the next six months. She had her own barn to manage, her own business to run. That took precedence over any temptation of Frank's cash. Consequently, our relationship fell into a repetitive cycle: a lovely long weekend at Shangri-La, followed by the ambiguous promise of "See you in a month." Or two.

I was always glad to see Boots but increasingly confused each time she left. Her disappearing act disappointed me because I enjoyed her visits. They were always fun, always filled with new exercises, games, and challenges. Despite having settled into a semi-regular routine between her visits, contentedness eluded me. My Christmas doubts, like unwanted guests, lingered. I'd grown weary of wanting and found myself succumbing to a creeping sense of lassitude and bitterness.

My fondness for Boots differed from my appreciation of Legs and her dedication. Legs was a thoughtful owner and a polished, sensitive rider. She always gave it her all, especially when Boots went away. But time was never on her side. There was simply too much for one person to do and something needed to change, again.

To start, she and Frank hired an extra full-time ranch hand named Jorge. He was thin as an organic carrot and quiet and efficient as Abel. I liked him. And the hardworking, trustworthy pair gave Legs a certain sense of comfort and relief.

On a second change, I was more dubious. Rumblings were that Legs had put a plan in motion. She'd taken to heart what Boots had said in the vineyard about trusting her instinct and building a foundation. For Legs, the time had come to bring a long-term dream to life. She wanted to start her own riding program. Nay, riding academy.

Her idea was simple in theory, less so in execution. The academy aimed to bring young female riders (a.k.a. "the girls") to the ranch to work in exchange for room and board, a modest stipend, and the opportunity to train with world-class equestrians on a unique breed of horse. The girls would come from Europe only. And only from Germany, Austria, or Switzerland. Legs had previously tried to work with Americans and failed. Or rather, they had failed. In her view, they were "difficult," always thinking they knew better, deserved more.

"From what I've seen," Legs said, "young American women are far more interested in boys than ponies."

She may have been biased. You couldn't have guessed from her accent, but Legs was Swiss, and German was her native tongue. Raised in a quaint village near Zurich, she'd enjoyed an idyllic childhood filled with fond memories of mountain hikes, Bircher muesli, and a doting grandfather who preached the value of hard work. Opa, as she called him, had prospered during the Second World War, selling munitions and, perhaps, a bit of his soul (Oh, Switzerland, not so neutral after all?). Though generous with gifts and affection, he firmly believed in earning one's keep.

As Opa had told Legs, and Legs repeated to Boots, "Inheritance is a curse. It'll steal your initiative and make you dull."

She said life becomes truly interesting and rewarding only when you have to work hard for something, when you have to fight for it, when you test your grit. And that's what Legs wanted for her academy: girls with fight, girls with grit, girls like herself.

When she was sixteen, her fairy-tale youth ended with her parents' acrimonious divorce. Following the split, her Swiss father remained in Switzerland, while her American mother moved her to Saratoga, California. Her mother believed in Opa's doctrine, but also . . . what is it they say about pride and noses? She refused to accept any financial support and thus arrived with nary a cent to her name.

While Legs's classmates cruised around town in their brand-new Mercedes and BMWs, she rode a secondhand scooter to the Fotomat, where she developed other people's vacation photos after school. On weekends, she had a second job at Garrett Stables, mucking out stalls in exchange for the chance to ride green horses no one else dared sit on.

The idea for establishing her academy was a return to youth. A chance to give back, in a sense, to like-minded young women who might not otherwise get such an opportunity. The only real holdup was orchestrating her preference for European riders. First, she had to find suitable applicants from afar. Next, she had to sort out visas. But more work brings more rewards, no?

Her resolve firm, she was eager to begin but also knew she needed help in the interim. She started trying out new trainers and inviting more friends to ride us until her program was in full swing. To be fair, the plan made a certain amount of sense. Why else have all these horses if not to share us? It wasn't as if we were feral and untrained. Even as her youngest stallion, I was far from green and, as Legs described me, had a canter to die for. That's not to say I was necessarily easy, trusting, or forgiving, which, come to think of it, could have given new meaning to the "to die for" descriptor.

Some of the trainers were better than others. The same could be said of the friends. But one person caught my attention. I liked her smile. It was genuine. And I liked what she had to say about white horses. It was bang on.

The day she arrived, the chilly weather had subsided, and the skies were a picture-perfect blue. In other words, back to an average Northern California day. Abel had just brought me in from pasture and I was enjoying a long, cool drink when I heard footsteps and . . . was that a nervous giggle?

I looked up to see three backlit figures standing outside the barn.

"Wait here," one said to the others before walking in. The voice was unmistakable. And so, too, was the six-foot slender silhouette.

Legs stopped Abel on his way from my stall. "One at a time, please."

"Artilheiro first?" he asked.

She nodded, and Abel returned to halter me. I had just grabbed a bite of my imported timothy. None too pleased by the interruption, I stomped my feet and let out a high-pitched scream as he led me past Xairel's stall on the way out of the barn. Xairel ignored me, not so much as pinning an ear.

In the sunlight, the mystery figures came into view. One was Dany, the comely French trainer who'd visited several times before. He had a vague connection to the Cadre Noir of Saumur and often ended our sessions with a few steps of Spanish walk. Sometimes Spanish trot. I liked working on "tricks" like those.

As was his custom, he wore snug tan breeches that accentuated his trim figure, brown leather half chaps that showed he wasn't your average black-booted Joe, and a billowy white shirt that Legs had teased him about on his first visit, saying, "Nice blouse."

"Sank you," he'd responded sincerely. "My mozzer sent eet to me from France."

Legs never again referred to his shirts as blouses. But . . . they were blouses.

Next to him was a slender, ponytailed blonde. She wore a huge smile across a faintly freckled face and, unlike the sartorial Frenchman, an untucked shirt, dusty jeans breeches, and well-worn paddock boots.

"This is our youngest stallion," Legs said. "His name is Artilheiro. But we call him Dragon."

I arched my neck, let out another loud whinny, and took several elevated trot steps. *I'll show you a dragon.*

"Okay, Abel. That's fine," she said. "Could you bring out Xeque next?"

Following the procession of stallions, which also included Xairel and Zap, Legs invited Dany and the blonde into the barn for a closer look.

"They're beautiful," she said.

My ears pricked. I appreciated her choice of *beautiful* over *cute*. Bullfighters are not cute. Ever. I was also drawn to the lightness, the brightness about her. Like a little ray of sunshine.

"Will they fade to white?"

"Eventually," Legs said. "But rather than fade, I'd say they'll glow."

"There's just something so special, so regal about a white horse. Like they harken back to another time. The Rolls-Royce of the Renaissance."

"Rolls-Royce?"

"You probably know this. That white horses were a symbol of divinity, nobility, and luxury. And while no doubt noblemen chose them for many reasons, there was one rather odd, seemingly nonsensical reason."

"And what was that?" Legs asked.

"They're harder to keep clean."

"You 'aven't seen Artay's stall yet," Dany chimed in. "Vairy clean stallion."

"You're right. That doesn't make sense," Legs said, raising an eyebrow.

"Well, it's because only the elite had the means to adequately care for them. They had stables. They had grooms. A clean white horse was a status symbol. Like a Rolls-Royce, if you will."

"Aha," Legs said.

"You know, le Grim Reepair also rides a white 'airse."

Sunny, as I decided to call her, punched Dany in the arm. "Don't say that. It's bad juju."

"Oh, it's fine," Legs said. "But what about you? Would you like to ride a white horse?"

"Me? Oh no, no. I just came to watch. And of course, nothing against the Grim Reaper," Sunny said, looking over both shoulders.

"But you're here and you'd have fun. Plus, Dany tells me you have soft hands. That you're his best student."

"She eez," he confirmed.

"You're both kind, but no. I'm not that good. And these are stallions. I've never ridden a stallion. And I don't know these horses. I might upset them."

"'And. And.' It'll be fine. You'll be fine," Legs said. "These horses will be unlike any you've ever ridden."

I could hear Legs's pride in us. She wanted to show us off, and it made me stand a little taller. I snorted and pawed at my stall door.

"See, look," Dany said. "Ahrty eez ready to go."

Well, what I really want is a treat, but . . .

"Here's an idea," Legs said. "Let's grab Leonidas first. He's my Selle Français schoolmaster. You can warm up with him. Then, we'll see about Arty."

Leonidas lived at the opposite end of the barn. His nickname was Opa, after Legs's grandfather, and everyone referred to him as the Cary Grant of the barn. A perfect gentleman and a perfect sixteen hands. Not only had he been Legs's first Grand Prix horse, but he was now her go-to "test drive" mount thanks to his gentle and protective nature and status as the epitome of good manners. Age and arthritis were catching up with him a bit, but he was always happy to offer an amateur rider a chance to experience the high-level movements.

I busied myself picking at my hay until I heard them head to the arena, at which point I moseyed to the end of my run to see what entertainment may be on offer. Even from a distance, I sensed Sunny's nerves.

"Are you sure this is okay?" she asked. "It's really not necessary. I can just watch."

She protested, but her smile never faded. It was clear the opportunity to sit on Opa was an honor.

"I help you up?" Jorge asked.

"Thank you, but I think I'm good."

Sunny took Opa's reins and led him to the mounting block. The old man knew his job and patiently waited as she settled into the saddle. One deep breath later, she asked him to walk on with a soft rein.

Legs called to her from the viewing platform, where she and Dany had settled themselves onto the giant couch to watch. "Don't be afraid to trot or canter. Test him out. Find his buttons. He's a really good boy."

Sunny walked him around the arena twice in each direction before she asked him to pick up the trot. With each step, she relaxed a little more, especially as Opa showed no signs of doing anything other than taking care of her.

"Try his canter. It's like a rocking chair!" Legs called out again.

Sunny abided, and she and Opa loped around the arena like two old friends out for a gambol.

"Do you know how to passage?" Legs yelled next.

"Sorry?" Sunny trotted Opa over to the viewing platform, bringing a cloud of dust with them. "Sorry, I couldn't hear you."

"Do you know how to passage?"

"Oh, no. I've never done that. I'm sorry."

"No need to be sorry." Legs went into full teaching mode. "Okay. Keep your legs at the girth and lightly tap his sides with alternating calves as you trot. Don't forget half halts. And think, lift, lift, fluff, fluff."

"Lift, lift, fluff, fluff," Sunny repeated. "Okay, let me give this a go. Opa, you ready?"

"He's always ready," Legs said.

Following Legs's instructions, Sunny asked Opa to passage.

"Holy crap!" she said with childlike delight. "It's like I'm riding a cloud! What a superstar! Oh, good boy!"

Had her giddiness been a wildfire, it would have caught and spread across the entire ranch, through the vineyard, up the hill, and straight to the moon. The innocence of it intrigued me. I wanted to know more and wondered if I would be next up. Or if I'd be chosen at all. Legs wasn't always keen to let anyone other than the trainers work with me. Too sensitive, she would say.

But somehow today felt different. To those who appreciated and respected horses, she was incredibly generous. Her horses were special gifts to be shared—like Vovó Karla's cooking—so long as the moment and the recipient were, respectively, right and deserving. And in that moment, I saw a shared giddiness in Legs herself. She was having fun, which only amplified her generosity.

Looking at Dany, she said, "Okay, I think it's time for a Lusitano."

Sunny dismounted Opa like a cat from a shelf and walked to the viewing platform.

"Thank you so much," she said.

"A piece of cake, non?" Dany said.

"Well, he's very well trained."

"Fun, no?" Legs asked.

"So fun. Opa's incredible. What a blast."

"I think it's time we bring out the Lusitanos you saw earlier."

Jorge had returned to take Leonidas, and Legs asked, "Do you know if Abel's finished longeing Xairel?"

Precious Xairel. I knew she'd pick him to go next.

"Now," Legs said, "Xairel's a big, strong boy, but don't let that worry you. He's very sweet. I think you'll enjoy him. He's got lovely movement."

"Are you sure this is all okay?" Sunny asked again. "I really hadn't expected this. It's so nice of you."

"Of course!" Legs said, and called again to Jorge as he was walking away with Leonidas. "And would you please longe and tack Xeque next? Then maybe Zap?"

Then Xeque? Then Zap?

I headed back into my stall to escape the sun, the heat, and the humiliation of not being chosen.

"She's saving the best for last," Napoleon said. He was perched on my water bowl, dipping his beak.

"I appreciate the vote of confidence, but must you stick your dirty feet in my water?"

"Why, yes. Why, yes, I must." He dipped a claw, lost balance, and toppled to the ground. In a mad flutter, he proclaimed, "I'm okay! I'm okay!"

"Are you sure?!" I didn't need Napoleon back in the hospital.

"I'm fine, and I'm serious. Mark my words. You're next. So buck up."

As usual, the damn bird was right.

Jorge came to get me a half hour later. *Here we go!*

He gave me a quick if slightly excited longe around the round pen, saddled me up, and led me to the arena. I passed Xeque on his way out. We exchanged flattened ears, and I arched my neck and gave a warning squeal.

"Don't let them pass that close to one another!" Legs yelled over to Jorge and Abel, and the two gave their own exchange of lifted eyebrows and rolled eyes.

But Legs was right. It was too close, and I swung my hips around fast, kicking out at Xeque and nearly knocking Jorge to the ground. He held fast to my reins, accidentally snapping the bit hard against the roof of my mouth, which caused me to pull back harder.

Legs and Dany jumped to their feet, and everyone called out, "Whoa. Whoa."

Catching his balance, Jorge reached over to stroke my neck. "*Está bien. Está bien.*" It's okay. It's okay.

I stopped pulling but started to snort and prance in place around him.

Rather than reprimand anyone, Legs said, "That's stallions for you." She looked at Sunny and added, "Ready to ride?"

"Yup," Sunny said before touching Jorge on the shoulder. "You good?"

"Yes, no worries."

She checked my legs. "You didn't hurt yourself, did you?"

My legs were fine. My mouth was just a little sore.

"That probably didn't feel too good on your mouth, huh?"

Aha! She'd noticed.

"Needless to say," Legs told her, "he's a little different than Opa and even the other Lusitanos. A little more, shall we say—"

"Dragon," Sunny finished her sentence before turning to me. "Do you breathe fire?"

Did she think I was going to take off and fly through the air? I mean, I hadn't truly acted up since Florida, and that lady deserved it.

"*Dragone* eez heez bullfighting name," Dany called out from the couch, which he'd settled back into after the minor display of stallion posturing. "I could come et pretend I ahm zee bull," he offered while making horns with his fingers the way Nuno used to do.

I couldn't believe my eyes and ears. *Yes, let's play bull!*

"Maybe another time," Legs suggested.

"Yeah, maybe another time." Sunny suddenly looked nervous again.

"You'll be fine," Legs said.

"Famous last words."

Sunny took the reins from Jorge and placed her hand on my neck, running it down its length and giving me a gentle scratch at my withers. My ears came forward and I lowered my head and curled my lips. She'd found the spot. It was a moment of knowing and transmission.

"I think I'll walk him around a little bit first."

While I mightn't have been the biggest or zippiest or most advanced, I had presence, personality, and, as you know, a canter to die for. Once Sunny eventually did head for the mounting block and set herself in the saddle, I answered every question she asked: walk, trot, and, yes, even canter.

Legs and Dany refrained from giving too much advice and allowed us to ride in relative autonomy. Perhaps they were holding their breath, waiting for the dragon to appear. He never did. Not even a flared nostril. I was so good, they ought to have started calling me Cary Grant, Jr.

Before leaving, Sunny returned to the barn to say thank you to each of the horses she'd ridden. She lingered at my stall a bit longer than the rest, waiting for me to come in from my run. Curiosity got the best of me, and I walked in and up to my stall door.

"Thank you, Dragon." She paused, stared hard at me, and added, "Do you like that name?"

My ears went back a smidge.

"Ha! You're funny. And you may be young, but I bet you've seen some things. Are you an old soul, Artilheiro?"

I wished I could tell her what I'd seen, what I liked, including how much I liked that she was asking.

"But I suppose I'm interrupting your dinner and should shut up."

Dany appeared next to her and asked what I considered a rhetorical question. "Your favoreet?"

"I hate that word. I don't play favorites," she said. "But if I had to choose . . . yes. There's just something about him. Something, I dunno, ethereal . . . otherworldly."

"He is a character," he said. "Maybe you come back wiv me anozair day."

"I'd like that very much."

"Okay. But now, we go."

As soon as they left, Napoleon reappeared. "Aw, she likes you. She likes you. Favoreet! Favoreet!"

"Stop that!" I said, half wanting to admit he'd nailed the accent.

"I shall not," he said. "And besides, she seemed nice."

"Yes," I agreed. "She was nice. And not too terrible a rider."

"That sounds promising."

"She probably won't be back. And also, like all the others, she's not—"

"A bullfighter."

"No. That, she is not."

"Oh, well, that's very bad, I suppose," Napoleon said.

"You know how I feel. You know what I want."

"Arty, my friend." Napoleon flapped his wings before continuing. "What I know is that sometimes, the things we were born to be aren't always the things we are meant to be."

"I'm meant to be a bullfighter."

"And I was meant to be someone's dinner."

39

2000: Palo Alto, California

I have no idea what I was born to be, but without a doubt, I was born loving horses.

Though I'd been riding since I was a child and finally, as an adult, had once again dipped my feet back into the horse-world waters with my lessons at Stanford, I'd never fully considered taking the plunge to become a horse *owner.* Mostly because it hadn't been in the budget and those same feet got itchy every couple of years, but also because I had a near-paralyzing fear of not knowing enough to properly care for one.

I italicized the word *owner* because words matter, and when it comes to animals, I've never been a fan of that one. It's always felt a little wrong and maybe more than a little imprecise. The Hawaiian word *kahu*, on the other hand, hits the nail on the head. It means honored guardian or protector. And as a *kahu*, it means you are responsible for the physical and spiritual well-being of your animal. In short, I wanted to be a *kahu*, not an owner, and I was terrified of not being up to the task.

In early 2000, Maneater Heather finally set me straight when she said, "The only way to learn is to do." She suggested I lease a horse, a sort of test drive to the "lifestyle." Because it is a lifestyle. "You need to find out if this is something you can commit to, day in, day out, year after year."

So that's what I did. I found myself a horse to lease. His name was Buddy, and he had what I would call an inner beauty. A mottled Appaloosa, he had a white face, pink nose, and black eyes framed by spotted pink sockets. At times, he looked more swine than equine. His owner was a deaf woman, a fact that may seem of little consequence, but she read lips and had an attentiveness about her that made me feel more heard than I did with most hearing people.

There have been few moments when I haven't felt completely alone in this world. Most of those I credit to animals, not humans. But when this woman entrusted the care of her horse to me, it was the two of them who helped me feel needed and lucky. I was with Buddy for six months. Leasing him changed the course of my life. Though I kept him at arm's length from my heart—he was never going to be mine—our time together gave me the experience and, dare I say, courage to confront two of my biggest fears: falling in love and making a commitment to stay.

Permanence, even semipermanence, had always made me uncomfortable. Call it a side effect of my army brat upbringing, but the constant moving from place to place planted a seed of ever-present discontent and kindled a dangerous curiosity: *Is the grass greener elsewhere?* The more I saw, the more I wanted to see. Motion had become a drug. And like Newton's first law hypothesizes, there was no stopping me or my addiction . . . until an external force hit me like a freight train.

Buying a horse changed my life. Not only did it make me stay put—a tough ask for a commitment-phobe and habitual runaway—but it opened my eyes and mind in ways I'd never imagined.

Since 1985, when I watched Etienne Navarre ride across the big screen atop Goliath in *Ladyhawke*, I'd fantasized about one day having a Friesian. But Friesians, like unicorns, were rare. I'd never even seen one in real life and really only knew they came at a hefty price (a.k.a. out of my budget).

Alas, when my search began in earnest, I modified my dream horse criteria to: a gelding, sixteen-plus hands, black, and around seven years old. That is, until I read the ad for a horse named Quantrill. He was priced at twice my budget, but in addition to mentioning everything on my list, the ad said: Friesian cross. I called the number immediately. Not because I had the money but because I'm prone to rash and emotionally led decisions.

The woman I bought Quantrill from—because yes, of course I bought him—had found him at a horse auction. He hadn't been up for auction. He hadn't been for sale at all. She'd simply happened upon him while wandering around the premises, slightly bored, between bidding rounds. He was in a dark back stall, looking underweight, out of condition, and decidedly unhappy. When she peered to have a closer look, he lunged at her, crashing against the stall's metal bars.

"Get back!" some old cowboy squawked. "That horse attacks people! He's the devil!"

To her credit, she looked beyond the visible ribs, dirty coat, and, most exceptionally, devilishness and instead noted his desirable height, sloping croup, and ample feathering. I don't know how much she offered to pay for him, but that cowboy agreed to the sale and, one could only imagine, possibly muttered, "Good luck and good riddance."

Quantrill was purchased as a husband horse. In this case, as a last-ditch effort to save a failing marriage. But much like deciding to have a baby to save a marriage is a bad idea, so is buying a horse. Especially for a man with little interest in the animal and no aptitude for the sport. Quantrill was no cure for what ailed their union. A year and a half after landing at this new home, he'd been ridden only twice, the couple's divorce was pending, and back on the market he went. No fault of his own. And without so much as a neigh in the matter.

The buying and selling is always left up to us humans. My say. The woman's say. The cowboy's say. God knows how many other people's say. We'd all chosen what would happen to this horse, this singular sensation. But what about him? What did he want?

To try to find out, I hired the only person I could think of who might be able to help.

"He doesn't like the name Quantrill. He prefers you call him Q." Or so said the animal communicator.

With her hand placed flat across his forehead, covering the white star in its middle, she also said something about a mean man in a big hat, possibly in Arizona. Not sure what made her think it was Arizona. I didn't ask. I figured whatever she was sensing and sharing, I could choose to take or leave. There wasn't going to be much I could do about some mean man from his past, possibly in Arizona, but I could do something about the name. *My* horse's name. Or at least, the one he'd come with.

His previous owner had named him after William Clarke Quantrill. You can look him up if you haven't heard of him, but suffice it to say, he and his raiders, including Frank and Jesse James, were also mean men. Not from Arizona, but of the ilk that no horse need bear the name, especially if he chooses otherwise. Plus, Quantrill wasn't a familiar name, and people often heard it wrong.

More than once, I got, "Oh, like the liqueur."

"No. Not Cointreau. It's Quantrill. Like the Civil War bushwhacker."

"Oh, wait! Is that because he's black?"

Honestly, I couldn't make this shit up.

Yes, he was black. Head to tail except for that white star and a hint of a white snip. But no, that's not why he was named Quantrill. But yes, partly why Quantrill would become Q. Or occasionally, Q-tip or Q-nicorn when, in winter, his star would grow out thicker than a cotton ball. Or Q-cifer when he'd decide to nip, kick, or take off with me. He wasn't a devil, but he also wasn't always an angel. I'd never been thrown from a horse so many times. Never been bitten so hard. One of his chomps, on my inner left thigh, left a bruise for three years. Discernible bite marks included.

But I loved this boy. He was my first son, a gift to myself for my thirtieth birthday.

Once again, the animal communicator closed her eyes, placed her hand across his brow, and asked me what I wanted to know. As if on cue, Q once again stopped fidgeting and dropped his head to half-mast. He looked ready to fall asleep.

"Is he happy? I want to know if he's happy."

Because really, that's all that mattered.

40

2010: Gilroy, California

"Are we cursed?" she asked. "Is the universe trying to tell us something? That's what I'd really like to know."

"Sometimes bad things just happen," Frank tried to reassure her. "No rhyme, no reason. It's just life. Or in this case. Well, you know what I mean."

A series of odd events began to unfold a few weeks before the academy's first students were set to arrive.

On a normal afternoon, Jorge was moving the mares and zebras back into the lower barn from their pasture, just as he did every afternoon. Only this time, he didn't see that the newborn baby zebra had fallen a few paces behind the herd and didn't make it through the gate before it clicked shut in front of him. As the baby watched his mother walk farther and farther away down the road that led to the barn, panic set in. He darted back and forth, back and forth, and, not noticing or caring about the iron gate, ran full force into it. The impact snapped his neck, killing him instantly. His mama—and Jorge—never quite recovered from the loss.

"*Debería haberlo notado,*" he said again and again. I should have noticed. "¿Cómo no me di cuenta?" How did I not notice?

"You don't have eyes in the back of your head," Legs told Jorge. "It's not your fault. For some reason, it was his time."

The following week, a pig (thank goodness, not Dirty D) was found drowned in one of the guesthouse ponds. A few days later, Luigi, one of the oldest, happiest, and yappiest of the rescue dogs, went missing;

the coyotes howled extra loud that night while the rest of the ranch fell silent after hours of fruitless searching for the "love bug." Much like the zebra mama, Legs couldn't settle. She kept coming in and out of the barn, opening and closing the same doors, calling out his name, hoping he'd suddenly appear, safe and whole. But Luigi never appeared that night. Or any other.

All the while, Frank did his best to console her in the only way he knew how.

"We must think logically, rationally. There's no curse. No hexes or hobgoblins," he said. "It's a numbers game."

"It's not a game, Frank. And they aren't numbers."

"You know what I mean. The more animals we have, the more we'll lose. They can't all live forever. And the best we can do is accept that fact."

"Here's another fact, Frank. I'm sad. Can you just let me be sad?"

For the third night in a row, he took the flashlight from her hand and led her to sit down on the trunk in front of my stall.

"Of course you can be sad. All I'm saying is maybe it will help to focus on other things. Like your academy. We can't be all doom and gloom when those young women get here."

She let out a long breath as she rubbed her temples before sliding her fingers through her hair, releasing a musty yet sweet odor. I saw no tears, but her voice sounded strained. "Of course, you're right."

"And who knows," Frank said, "we never know what tomorrow will bring."

Which, in this case, was more bad news. This time, from France. Dany's mother had taken a hard tumble down a flight of stone stairs, breaking her hip. He had no choice but to return home immediately.

"I need to 'elp hair," Dany said when he stopped to pick up his final paycheck.

Legs was gutted, and she wasn't alone. I, too, felt the sting. Just as she'd been counting on him to help kick off the academy, I'd been counting on him to play the bull. While I understood—of course, no one can question the importance of helping one's mother—I also began to think maybe there was something to Legs's portentous intuition.

"Maybe this whole thing was a bad idea," she told Frank.

"What whole thing?"

"The academy. The girls. Hell, the ranch—"

"Stop. Stop right there. This isn't anything but a curveball. And I know you well enough to know whatever's thrown at you, you'll find a way to knock it out of the park."

"I'm so tired of curveballs. I don't know why I thought all of this would be easier."

"Easy? Since when have you ever wanted easy? I mean, look around. We've got a veritable zoo!"

Her lip curled sideways into a smirk.

"Have faith, my darling." He took a seat beside her, draped an arm around her shoulder, and whispered into her ear, "All will be well."

And for another blip, it was. Calls were made. People were persuaded—or at least the only one who mattered was. I saw Frank take center stage and nail it. He was no longer background music but loud and clear and adamant about the answers he needed. Once again, Boots found herself saying yes, found herself saving the day. Perhaps she'd been expecting his call. Perhaps she liked playing the hero. Regardless, Boots set to work on rearranging her schedule to accommodate his plea. In the meanwhile, she asked for only one thing: "Set a good precedent and put those girls to work as soon as they arrive."

Unfortunately, Frank and Legs did no such thing. They were terrible with boundaries and from day one welcomed those girls like family, settling them into the cozy guesthouse, inviting them for dinner, even hosting a wine-tasting soirée so they could make a few local acquaintances and practice their English. Had I not known better, I'd have guessed they'd arrived for a vacation and not a job.

Their names were Elsie and Hilda, and though strangers to one another upon arrival, they were quick to bond, latching on to their many commonalities. At nineteen, neither had set foot outside of continental Europe, but if anything were to so move them to travel halfway across the world for an extended stay, it was horses. They'd both been riding for more than a decade and considered their barns second homes. Elsie was tall and skinny with a wild mess of long blond ringlets that framed a pale, blue-eyed face. Hilda was also tall, skinny, and blue-eyed, but by contrast, her blond mane ran straight as straw down the length of her back. With their hair pulled back and helmets on, they could have passed for sisters, if not twins.

When Boots turned up early to the barn the following week, she concurred. "Well geez, what do we have here? The Bobbsey Twins?"

The girls didn't answer but looked to Legs for guidance.

"*Berühmte Zwillinge. Sie denkt, du siehst gleich aus.*" Famous twins. She thinks you look alike.

They looked at one another, each raising a single eyebrow and shrugging their shoulders in unison. When Legs spoke German, they were quick to respond, but when pushed to converse in English, they tended toward the demure, unsure of what to say. Who could blame them? The expectation of understanding a new language was intense. Then again, if I could be expected to learn . . .

Boots asked them to show her their routine, whatever they'd established since arriving or whatever they used to do back home. She wanted to see how they warmed up a horse, how they chose to work with each of us, if and how they made adjustments for each horse.

Legs translated before adding, "To be fair, they haven't had much time to ride."

"At all?"

"No, no. They've ridden Opa and Xairel."

"And Xeque," Elsie added.

"Any of the mares?" Boots asked.

"I've decided not to include the mares in the program. Not right away anyway."

"We rode also Falke and Fin," Hilda chimed in.

"Okay, no mares, but Friesians. And Arty? What about Arty?"

"Yes, he's in the program. They just haven't ridden him yet."

From the end of the aisleway, Boots looked over at me. "Well, no time like the present. Who wants to be the first to ride Arty?"

Nervous, the girls pointed at one another and giggled.

"He doesn't bite," Boots said. "Well, not always."

Elsie stepped forward, showing a bit more confidence. "I vill ride him."

I didn't know whether to feel pride or concern for being singled out, but I didn't have much time to contemplate.

"Chop, chop then. Get that boy saddled!" Boots turned to Hilda. "And you, how about we start you on Xairel. Just keep those two horses clear of one another in the arena. Capiche?"

The girls made haste, quickly picking our hooves, brushing our backs, and strapping on brushing boots. Within ten minutes, we were down at the covered arena with Elsie gently easing herself onto my back. At first, her seat was light and well-balanced, but then, rather suddenly, she gave a swift kick that caused me to tense, swerve sideways, and lose balance as my hind legs got caught up in a dangerous dance with the mounting block.

"Easy there," Boots said. "Give him his head." Elsie released the reins, and I found my footing. "Good. Good job. These horses don't need much prodding. He'll follow your weight."

Elsie shifted, but too much, and I veered sharply in the other direction.

"Millimeters! Think millimeters."

I felt her turn her head so she could better hear Boots.

"That's it. Nice and easy. Less is more. Especially with Arty."

Per Legs, Elsie and Hilda were jumpers, accustomed to riding and working bigger, heavier horses that needed more leg to advance, more hand to contain.

"I see. They're fearless things," Boots said. "But maybe a bit too rigid."

"Well, and maybe still young enough to not know any better," Legs added.

"And young enough to mold."

"Precisely. They've come to Shangri-La to learn a different kind of riding on a different kind of horse."

"These horses will be good teachers," Boots said to Legs before turning her attention back to Elsie and Hilda. "Okay, ladies, let's get started."

For the next hour, we walked. In fact, for the next two weekly lessons, we walked.

"If you don't have a relaxed horse, there's no reason to move to another gait," Boots said. "When we practice, it's not about getting somewhere fast. We aren't in a rush, and these horses are young."

"*Ja, ja,*" the girls agreed. Yes, yes.

"It's also not about perfect," Boots added. "Practice doesn't make perfect. It makes . . . what?"

"Permanent," they said.

"And why is this distinction important, ladies?"

"Because ve do not vant to practice der wrong sings."

"Exactly. Because then those wrong things, those bad habits, will become permanent. And no one wants to have to undo incorrect. Understood?"

"*Ja.*"

"Just to be sure. I'll say it again. If you teach a horse the wrong way, for example, with tension and force, and then don't bother to course correct— Do you know what I mean by 'course correct'?"

"*Ja.*"

"Okay, so if you don't bother to course correct, the horse's brain and muscles will settle back into bad habits. From the start, take the time to teach things the right way, in a calm way, and you'll save yourself and these beautiful horses years of frustration in the long run."

"*Ja.*"

It all seemed a good, agreeable start, but as time passed, Boots noticed a trend, even as they advanced beyond the walk exercises. The girls never questioned anything she asked them to do. They simply nodded and said, "*Ja, ja.*"

"After the half halt, you have to release and take again."

"*Ja, ja.*"

"No, your other left!"

"*Ja, ja.*"

"Not like this." On the ground, Boots pretended to be on a horse, spreading her legs and hunching forward. "But like this." She straightened her position and cantered herself in a circle like a bowlegged cowboy at a square dance.

"*Ja, ja.*"

"Elsie, you're clenching again. You have to stop clenching!" Boots turned to Legs. "How do you say *clenching* in German?"

"*Zusammenpressen.*"

"Zoo. Sam. Oh heck! Can you ask her to stop clenching? Arty's about to go through the roof."

"*Du musst aufhören, dich zusammenzupressen. Entspanne deine Beine.*" You have to stop clenching. Relax your legs.

"*Ja, ja.*"

Boots was right. I wasn't enjoying this ride. Even with the translation, nothing changed. Elsie continued to clench, which caused me to tighten my back, which caused her to pull on the reins, which caused me to curl my neck and go behind the bit, which caused her to kick my sides, which caused me to jolt forward, which caused her to clench again. It was a perpetual cycle of tension. And unfortunately, no matter who was speaking, there was a disconnect.

"I can see someone is thinking hard," Boots said. "There's steam coming out of those ears. And I don't mean yours. Elsie. I need you to stop."

Again, no change.

"Elsie! Stop!"

Frustrated, Elsie yanked the reins hard and fast.

"No, no, no. Never like that. Never take your frustration out on the horse. Take the time to ask and let him answer. Gently."

I pulled the reins back, equally quick and hard from her hands.

"Don't fight him. Let him have his head. It's okay." Boots walked over and patted my neck. "Now, Elsie, I need you to breathe. And I need you to sit and listen to your horse. What is he telling you?"

"I don't know."

"Well, I appreciate an honest answer."

"He's angry?"

"Well, okay, maybe. But let's think about that a minute because *angry's* a loaded word. And I'm not so sure that he's angry. Because I can see him trying. I think he's more confused. He's trying to tell you he doesn't understand what you're asking."

Elsie let out an exasperated sigh. "He hates me."

"He doesn't hate you."

Yet, I thought.

"I don't want you to get down on yourself. This is what lessons are for. Right?"

"*Ja.*"

"I think maybe you're thinking too hard, which is making you react too strongly. Arty is different than even the other Lusitanos here."

"*Ja.* For sure. I prefer Xairel."

My heart sank.

"He needs you to start riding from here." Boots pointed toward Elsie's heart. "Get out of your head. This is supposed to be fun. If you're not having fun, you think the horse is having fun?"

"I don't think Arty is ever having fun."

"Well, that's just not true." Boots looked me in the eye. "He's just trying to find his way as much as all of us. Isn't that right, Artilheiro?"

I looked back, wanting so much for her to know what I wanted, wanting her to see I didn't belong in this arena, wanting her to take me back out on the trail, wanting Dany to show up with the bull. I had no idea what was true anymore. But at least Boots was trying, and she always saw so much potential.

Herr Otto, on the other hand, and like too many others, only ever saw shortcomings. He was the trainer who replaced Boots when she eventually had to get back to "reality." And yes, the irony of hiring a German trainer did not escape me—Legs had built her entire program around the lightness and harmony of classical dressage, with the intention of breaking from the modern German system, which was all about competition, precision, and control. But he was available and now, look at me. I speak English. *Eu falo português. Yo hablo español. Je parle français. Und ich spreche Deutsch.* And here's what I have to say: *Ich hasse Herr Otto.* I hate Herr Otto.

On his first day, a tiny sports car careened to a stop in front of the barn, startling the birds, spooking us horses, and sending the dogs into a crazed barking fit. Luckily, the girls were able to quickly corral the pack into the tack room, allowing the rather large driver to lumber from the car, a coffee in one hand, a pastry in the other, and a belly dangling over his breeches like a sack of rolled oats. A shudder rippled down the length of me. Not only was the physical resemblance uncanny but perhaps worse, so too was the air-sucking mien of superiority. This was Herr Otto, the German Senhor Matos.

Legs drove up to show him around, but Herr Otto wasn't so interested in a tour, making a point to repeat he had only a couple of hours that day, so best to get to work. I hoped that meant they wouldn't get to me, but like most of my wishes, this one didn't come true either. I was first on the list, and within five minutes in the arena with Elsie, his criticisms began.

"Oh ja," he said to Legs, "ziss one does not vant to accept zhe leg."

This was true if he meant I did not appreciate a strong kick into a restraining hand. More than offending me, it made me feel boxed in and claustrophobic.

"His name is Arty," Legs interjected, "not 'this one.'"

Take that, jackass.

"He is also very crooked."

"He's very young." Legs continued to defend me. "And very flexible."

"Ja, but zere is much verk to do."

"Well, that's why I'm paying you."

Zing. You tell him who's boss.

To be sure, I wasn't the only one he picked on, just the one he picked apart most. I thought Legs would be quick to decide he wasn't the man for the job, but he was back a few days later and then every other week or so.

With Herr Otto, there was never room for discussion. No room for compromise. No room for expression. It was his way, or it was his way. He didn't prefer me, and his influence carried. Even when he wasn't around, my rides got shorter and shorter. The girls were fast to tack me up, fast to put me back into my stall. On weekends, they did not take me on rides through the vineyard and back pastures. They did not take me to swim in the ponds. Instead, they put me in the hot walker and joked, saying it would be better in my case to call it a "hothead" walker.

This went on for months. Six of them to be exact. At that time, Elsie and Hilda's visas were set to expire, and so they returned to the fatherland, replaced at the ranch by the next pair of girls, Sabine and Ursula. I thought things might change with their arrival, but on their first lesson day, Herr Otto asked them to draw straws to determine who would be each horse's primary rider. Sabine drew the short straw. She looked at Herr Otto, who looked at me.

"You lose, Sabine," he said. "You ride Arty."

She loses? Is this man serious? This is how he begins his first lesson with new riders? Where is Legs?

But before a "*ja, ja*" could fall from Sabine's lips, another hand reached over to pluck the straw from her hand.

"How about I take that 'short' straw?"

Herr Otto's eyes widened as he turned to confront this interloper.

"Seems pretty rotten to make these girls draw straws," she said. "And Arty? Really? The short straw for the best in the barn?"

My eyes grew wide, too, and I stuck my head out and over my stall door to get a better view. It had been a while, and I'd worried she had gone the way so many others had. But there Sunny was, back, looking at me and singing my praises.

"It vas a joke!" Herr Otto attempted to defend himself.

"So why isn't anyone laughing?" Sunny pointed to the girls, who stood stock-still.

"Excuse me, but who are you?" he asked.

"She's my friend," Legs said, coming out from the adjacent feed room. "I invited her to audit today, but perhaps she'd prefer to ride."

"Oh no, I'd much prefer to watch." Sunny turned to Sabine, handed her back the straw. "Consider this your lucky straw. And earn it. He's the one. Number one."

Later that day, one of the Friesians cow-kicked Herr Otto in the chest, stopping his heart. Unfortunately, it restarted a minute later. But his time at Shangri-La was done. And not because of the kick, but because Legs fired him.

And so began—or should I say, continued—the revolving door of trainers and riders.

Maybe I'm the one who's cursed.

41

2006: Mountain View, California

I heart dive bars. So when my friend Fred told me there was a dive bar called Fred's within walking distance from the apartment I'd been living in for about a year, I was baffled (*How had I not known?*) and intrigued (*I must check it out!*).

Like cowboys, dive bars are a weakness of mine. I love me a good dive bar. Great thing about 'em: the endless characters. I've met some strange cats at dive bars. I've listened to life stories, love stories, ghost stories. I've even shared a tale or two of my own. I've bought rounds. I've had rounds bought for me. I've laughed. I've cried. I've danced.

But the best thing about a dive bar? Most of the characters you meet, you never see again.

Unfortunately, there was one character I did see again. I met him on my first visit to Fred's.

That evening, I'd hosted a small dinner party. Fred's hadn't been on the agenda, but after enough wine, I suggested it to my friends and, surprise, surprise, they were game. For some reason (wine), it sounded like an adventure.

From the outside, it had all the markings of a good dive bar. A huge neon sign sat atop the one-story building. In bold, bright red, the word *Fred's* flashed over a tilted turquoise martini glass, olive included. In contrast to the neon was a small, dark, creepy parking lot. In it, I spotted two PT Cruisers. Part-time cruiser, full-time loser. Oh, Fred's. I *see* you. One hundred percent *not* where I'd want to order a martini. Or anything else that called for an olive, lime, lemon, anything that couldn't be wiped down and disinfected. And still, my kind of place.

Once inside, I was not disappointed. I quickly clocked a pool table, a jukebox, and a sign that read YOU LOOK LIKE I NEED A DRINK. I certainly didn't need a drink, but I headed straight to the bar while my friends grabbed a table.

"Four Guinnesses, please," I said to the bartender. "Oh, and a shot of Jäger."

"Thirsty, eh?" said a voice to my right.

"The Jäger's for a friend," I said before turning to see the voice belonged to a cute-enough young man with a serious shiner.

"Whoa!" I pointed to his eye. "How'd you get that?"

"Ah, this?" he said, smirking and touching his cheek. "Soccer game."

"Ouch, and that?" I pointed to a cut on his lip.

"Same game."

"Bullshit. That's totally herpes."

"Oh, is it?" He laughed. "And how would you know about that?"

Touché, I thought but didn't say. Instead, I said, "And that's also the worst fake Scottish accent I've ever heard."

He smiled again and I noticed his slightly crooked teeth. In addition to cowboys and dive bars, I have a thing for wonky chompers. Don't get me wrong. I'm not into *Hee-Haw* gaps or Bucky Beavers, but take, for example, Ethan Hawke's smile. It's perfectly imperfect. And dead sexy.

I'm not sure what made me think he was putting on a phony accent. Turns out I was wrong about the herpes and that. He was, in fact, from Scotland—Dunfermline, to be exact—and he did, in fact, not only play but also coached soccer. Or as he preferred to call it, football. Aha! Maybe his previous use of the word *soccer* was what had set off my phony-accent Spidey-sense.

He set the record straight later that evening when he and his friends—a Swede, a Lithuanian, and a South Carolinian—challenged me and my friends—three Americans, including one named America—to a game of pool.

I'm not much for pool, so I drank my Guinness and watched and cheered and, at some point, managed to knock my phone onto the sticky floor, where it broke into several pieces. Before I could hop off my stool to fetch and fix it, the young Scot rushed over and said, "Allow me."

Unlike all the king's horses and all the king's men, he easily put my Humpty Dumpty phone back together again. Little did I know, he also used the opportunity to call his phone from mine. I had to give him credit. It was a clever, if sneaky, way to get my number.

He called and left me a message much later that night, after the bar had closed and our two groups had gone our separate ways, likely never to meet again. In short, the average goodbye at a dive bar. I've often wondered, what if I hadn't dropped my phone? Or what if I hadn't responded?

One year and two weeks later (kids, don't do this at home), on December 22, 2007, we said, "I do."

Something I never thought I'd do: get married.

And unfortunately, something I never should have done.

His name was Simon.

42

2013: Gilroy, California

Swoosh! The door swung round once again, and in blew another student rider.

She arrived from Europe, of course. But she was nothing like her predecessors. The moment she entered the barn, I knew something was off. Her sour, tangy odor, as if she'd filled her pockets with rancid fruit, made my nose curl. This was no residual airplane funk. I knew better. I'd been on a plane. And I hadn't come off smelling like a rotten apple.

The sharp scent matched her sharp features. Her nose protruded like a jagged perch from a gaunt, ashen cliff. Her eyes, like crevices, were set deep behind puffy purple bags. Some of the other students had arrived jet-lagged, but theirs was a sleepy giddiness, a simmering excitement. This was different. This was profound exhaustion. This girl's bones ached to rest.

She moved like a wraith through a graveyard, hovering at each stall door, scrutinizing us through those sunken eyes. She did not cluck or coo. Her dark, empty stare unnerved me, and I turned to escape into my run. Thankfully, she walked away.

Her footsteps shrank into a faint, distant shuffle. Then, silence.

I returned to my stall to resume my evening meal when suddenly a clamorous scraping startled me. I looked over to see her pale face and lopsided smile pressed against the stall bars.

"*Du bist süß. Wie heißt du?*" You're cute. What's your name? The sweet words did not match her voice, which was rough as a farrier's rasp.

She peered down at my nameplate and tried to sound it out. "Ar . . . til . . ."

"Ar-chee-LAY-roo," Legs said. "It's Portuguese for 'gunner.' *Kanonier.* But we call him Arty."

"Vhat lefel training?" the Wraith asked.

"Oh, this boy can do many things. Huge canter. Piaffe. Passage."

"I vould like to ride him first."

"I was thinking maybe we'd work up to Arty. I generally like to start folks out on Opa."

"*Opa? Ein altes Pferd?*" Opa? An old horse? She rolled her eyes before turning to face Legs. "Is it necessary?" At once, she exuded insolence and confidence.

"He's twenty-five, yes, but I assure you"—Legs wasn't taking the bait—"there is nothing old about him. He was my first Grand Prix horse, and he is who we start with. Who you will start with."

For a second, the Wraith's grimace relaxed.

"But before any of that," Legs added, "you should get some rest, settle in. Dinner will be ready in about an hour."

"*Ich hab' kein' Hunger.*" I'm not hungry.

"Oh, you ate at the airport?"

"*Nein, aber ich bin nicht hungrig.*" No, but I'm not hungry.

"You've got to eat."

"I vill hafe some coffee in zhe morning. I sink I prefer to rest az you said."

"Suit yourself."

"*Was?*" What?

"Just whatever makes you comfortable. I can take you down to the guesthouse and then we'll just get started tomorrow morning."

"*Ah, ja. Danke.*" Ah, yes, thanks. She may have said thanks, but she didn't appear overly thankful—which I was, once again, when she left for the evening.

I dipped my head back into my feed bowl but kept an ear twisted sideways toward the front of my stall. Napoleon fluttered in from the other side.

"That woman needs a Happy Meal," he said.

"You saw her?"

"Well, what there was to see. A rake of a girl."

"I don't have a good feeling."

"I wish I could disagree with you, but she's left me with a chill." Napoleon flapped his wings before proceeding to peck at the oats in my feeder.

"But what choice do I have?"

"Perhaps more than you know, Arty."

I wasn't quite sure what he meant. By that time, I'd seen many riders, trainers, and, more and more often, clinicians come and go. There had been the Spaniard. His specialty was in-hand work, and though based halfway around the world, he never left home without his big stick—which sounds both odd and dreadful but was neither. Well, maybe a little odd, but the way he used it was much like a conductor would a baton, gently guiding us with minor signals. The goal was better balance. And trust.

"If his mind is tense," he said, "his body will be tense. You cannot sculpt his body into a shape with pressure. But if you establish trust, you can shape his mind, which will allow you to shape his body."

Within one session with him, I freely offered a light, fluid, forward passage on the longe line. Within two, I showed the bold, even steps of the Spanish trot. If I had a choice, I would have very much liked for him to stay, but he was wanted elsewhere, and his visit was one of the briefest. After he left, the students employed their sticks, less elegantly, for maybe a week before they settled back into their old ways, too impatient to persist with the "boring" in-hand work.

There had also been another German. A woman. Unlike Herr Otto, she swept into the barn like a warm summer breeze, soft-spoken, calm, and full of admiration for the Lusitano breed. During her also-too-short stay, she taught both from the saddle and the ground and spoke of classical equestrianism. She began with a story from more than two thousand years ago about a Greek soldier and carried us through the centuries with snippets about an underrated English duke, a misunderstood French circus performer, and a modern-day Portuguese artist. What stood out to me was a goal of minimalism. I would have also very much liked for her to stay, but like Big Stick and Boots, she had other obligations.

After, there had been a "trainer" from Austria, who was apparently so wealthy she didn't need to work but seemed keen to lecture on classical riding or, more accurately, look down her nose at everyone. Shangri-La was far from an average barn, but when the Austrian arrived, she practically implied it was a hovel. She couldn't believe there was no valet to greet her and bring her luggage in from the limo. Oddly, the only thing she didn't mock was me. In fact, she took such a fancy that at the end of her three-day stay she offered to buy me for twice what Legs had paid. Thank God, Legs declined. The woman was a technically talented rider but also a self-important loon who lacked empathy for horses and humans.

"Yes," Napoleon said. "I remember them all. Characters good and not so good. But in the grand scheme of things . . ."

"Yes, I know. Don't say it."

"Seek—"

"I said don't say it."

"Perspective."

"Always the last word with you."

"*Ja, ja.*"

The next morning, after complying with Legs's requirement to ride Opa first, the Wraith returned to the barn and asked again, "And now Arty?"

If nothing else, she showed focus. Or as Napoleon would later say, "Single-minded creepiness." I had to wonder, why me? She'd not seen me outside of my stall, not seen me worked or even at liberty in pasture. Yet she'd decided she'd wanted something and was not about to be told no again.

Legs relented. "Okay, let's get him—"

Before Legs could finish her sentence, the Wraith had grabbed my halter, slid open my stall door, and was coming at me like a tiny bull. I lurched back, knocking into Jorge, who was coming in from my run with a wheelbarrow and mucking rake.

"Careful!" Legs yelled.

I hopped forward, almost into the Wraith, but, feeling trapped, quickly turned and darted into my run. Luckily, Jorge had pushed the wheelbarrow and himself out of the way to avoid another collision.

"Jorge, *estás bien*?" I heard Legs call out. All okay?

"*Sí, sí.* No problem."

"You have to pay attention," Legs scolded. "You can't just rush into stalls like that."

If the Wraith responded, I didn't hear it. She brushed past Jorge like a cold wind, sending him spinning as he tried to drag the wheelbarrow out of my run.

"*Komm hier*," she said, her eyes wide, the corners of her mouth crimped. Come here.

The temperature dropped with each step she took toward me. I did not want to submit to her command, but what choice did I have?

43

2008: Santa Rosa, California

The sticker read CALL MY SHRINK. I BOUGHT ANOTHER HORSE. A friend gave it to me as a gag gift after I bought Ole, but I stuck it on my laptop like it was a badge of honor.

Yup, I'd bought another horse. And yup, I can't argue with the fact it was pretty crazy. But was it a mistake? Not on your life.

The idea of getting a full-papered Friesian had never left me. And when the timing was right, I cried "YOLO!" and never looked back.

I mean, Ole. The name itself was crying YOLO.

Norwegian for "ancestor's descendant" or "heir," Ole is a short but powerful name. His breeder, Iris, chose it for him, not because he would be short but because she knew he would grow to become very powerful. A pillar of strength, goodness, and vitality.

Ole was born in Friesland, a northern windswept province of the Netherlands, and at the time, Iris had become friends with a young woman named Anneke, who used to ride Ole's mother, Sil. Within hours of Ole's birth, Anneke visited Iris's farm and, as she later told me, knew on sight he was meant to be hers. If you were to look at photos from that day, Ole still blue-eyed from birth and Anneke crouched down beside him on his bed of straw, stroking his ear, I'd dare you to disagree.

Two years later, Ole's eyes had turned a golden brown and Anneke had imported him to the United States, where she'd secured a job as a trainer and rider at a stable in Santa Rosa, California. For another two years, all had been going well until a family emergency required her to fly home to the Netherlands. Fortunately, she didn't have to stay for long. Unfortunately, when she returned to the States, the border authorities promptly deported her for having overstayed her previous visa. It would be years before she could even think of returning, and without the financial means to fly Ole back across the ocean, she had no choice but to list him for sale.

The one thing she did have a choice in was who she would sell him to. Her requirements: He would not go to another trainer or a sale barn. Her hope: She could find him a forever home.

My requirements once I'd begun searching again—thanks to an improved financial situation, a craving for diversity, and the support of my Frenchman trainer, Dany, who'd come around to the idea of a Friesian (his preference may have been an Iberian, but he knew I wasn't budging): Extra tall. Four years old. Not yet under saddle.

For some reason, I was set on getting the tallest Friesian I could find. In fact, so tall it was outside of the breed standard. I also wanted a horse who'd been given the chance to mature before being asked to carry a rider, and one without a ton of training. Because sometimes, more training can initially mean more undoing. And it was better, easier, faster to start from scratch.

When we drove north to meet Ole, to say he was bigger than life would be an understatement. At four years old, he was already seventeen hands. Every hand is four inches and horses are measured at their withers. For reference, I am five feet seven inches and the top of my head still didn't reach his withers. He was also black as night, not a snip of white on him. And those eyes. He had the kindest, softest eyes but also a look that filled me with a sense of sorrow. Since Anneke had left several months before, no one had done much with him, and he stood next to me like a giant puppy in want of love and affection. I wanted to bring him home that very minute. But I also knew a rash decision was no good for anyone, especially the horse.

Because we couldn't ride him (Anneke had been up on him only a couple of times herself), we went to a small round pen where, from a mounting block, Dany simply draped his arms and chest over Ole's back to see how he would react under the weight. Ole didn't seem one bit bothered and walked on like no big deal.

In the car heading home, Dany said, "If I had the money right now, I would buy this horse." That's all I needed to hear. Well, almost.

For good measure, I rang the animal communicator to see if she could get a read on the boy and his situation. I can't say I remember anything else she told me, but one tiny comment sealed the deal for me.

She said, "He liked the way you smelled."

Now, there's no way (or is there?) a horse could have known that's my all-time favorite compliment to receive. In a way, I hope it meant I smelled like a horse. Because that's my all-time favorite smell in the world.

Like Q had done before, Ole ticked every requirement box. And soon, he went on to exceed every expectation I'd ever had for a horse. All while further raising Dany's opinion of Friesians. Those two became partners, with Dany heralding Ole's intelligence, talent, willingness, and kindness. And for me, Ole became my benchmark for goodness.

In temperament, Q may have had a bit of the devil in him, God bless him, but Ole? He was 100 percent pure angel. I won't lie, the thought of introducing those two made me sick to my stomach. What if they didn't get along? What if one of them hurt the other? In the eight years I'd had Q, he'd become a top horse in the herd, but never had I seen him with a horse friend.

Ole became not only Q's first friend, but his best friend. Man, they were something to see together. I couldn't have asked for a better match. If you called for one, both came running. It was like every Christmas, birthday, dandelion wish had finally come true.

44

2013: Gilroy, California

Instinct arrives unclouded by conscious thought and as potent as the smell of a rotten apple, which again and again told me, *Run!*

When I could, I did. Either to the end of my run or to the other side of the pasture. But that's where my choices ended, and there was no real escape from ye olde Wraith, who didn't appreciate my *games*. Her initial interest in me faded into bruised disdain, quick as pigs to their trough at dinnertime. She called me spoiled and tiresome. I called her things better left unrepeated.

Skinny as the rest of her was, she pointed bloated, accusatory fingers at me, casting blame for rigid and explosive rides.

"He's bad. He's dangerous. She should sell him."

She even went so far—too far—as to mock Boots. "Why she choosed him, I don't get."

Luckily for her, not for me, she vented only to Abel, who recommended she keep her opinions to herself.

Oh, Abel. I thought you were a friend.

Like too many humans, the Wraith never stopped to consider her own behavior, her own faults. It was she who was spoiled and tiresome. Living on this beautiful ranch and riding us handsome horses, without a smile but always with the expectation we were to read her mind and understand her wishes. She wasn't a teacher. She was a taskmaster.

Yes, she did put in the hours, very long hours. But like a machine, the effort was sans joy, sans respite. One after the other, she thrust us along her assembly line of brush, tack, push, pull, huff, puff, rinse, repeat. Kind words and gestures were scarce. Nary a "good boy" nor a soft, reassuring stroke. Instead, she displayed her cold, hard edges with a certain sadistic arrogance. If ever she did deign to touch me beyond lifting my legs to pick my hooves or heaving a saddle onto my back, it was to give a swift, flat smack on the neck. Her intent may have been reward for good behavior, but it had the sting of a reprimand.

Her chill poked at the barn staff as well. When Jorge saw or even sensed her arrival, he was sure to pivot and swiftly head off in the opposite direction. Abel was cordial but also never lingered to chat. Perhaps her *eau de mort* offended them, too.

Though only a bit more than a month since my first ride with her, it felt like much longer. I well remember Legs telling her that day to work me solely at the walk and trot for a month. After, they would reassess. Now whether that decision was a punitive measure is debatable, but the Wraith nevertheless abided. She was, after all, a student worker on a generous stipend, and during that month, Legs and Frank spent no long weekends away at Pebble or elsewhere.

A month is a rather arbitrary length of time when it comes to horse training, but at exactly four weeks and without checking with Legs, the Wraith opted to move forward. She was behind schedule that day, and my warm-up was quick. Not even once around the arena at walk and a quick half circle of trot before I felt her outside leg swing back and her hips swing forward. But before I could respond with a lovely canter strike-off, she added a spur jab. She had not given me a chance, and so I changed my answer, pulling my head to the ground to deliver the biggest buck possible before promptly coming to a halt.

Catapulted forward, she clung to my neck like a monkey on a vine

. . . not . . . quite . . . able . . . to hold on. Her bony ass hit the ground. Hard. It was a blissful beat of silence before the inevitable howl.

"*Duuuuuuuu!*" Youuuuuuu!

She rolled over onto her knees and flailed for the reins. Oh! A swing and a miss. I sat back on my haunches, didn't wait for a second swipe. I was off! Racing out of the arena, past the stallions in pasture, and up through the vineyard. By the grace of God, the reins stayed around my neck, not tangling in my legs, and after the initial sprint through the rows of pinot, I downshifted to a canter . . . a trot . . . and finally, a semi-winded walk. I stopped only when I saw the grass.

My sides still heaving, I stretched down to sniff out a good patch and tore into it, shredding thin blades like an angry gardener. The reins slid down my neck and off to one side, collapsing next to me like a dead snake.

It wasn't long before I heard footsteps and labored breathing coming from behind, but I kept at the grass.

"*Tranquilo,*" Abel said. "*Está bien.*" Easy. It's okay.

He put his hand on my neck, slowly reached for the puddle of reins, and added, "*Buen chico. Comes hierba.*" Good boy. You eat some grass.

Needless to say, it wasn't the best of starts with the Wraith. It also wasn't the best of conclusions.

Most days, she'd cry, "*Nein!*" No! Then dig her heels into my side.

She was under the delusion I was testing her by not doing what she asked. The reality was, half the time, I didn't understand what she was asking. If I did not respond immediately to her abrupt aids, she yanked the reins or walloped my sides.

She may have been a sickly rail of a thing, but her contact was strong.

She set her hands like cement and never yielded. By not giving me my head or the space to move forward, she stole my balance along with my confidence. One day, after causing me to stumble so badly the two of us nearly landed face-first in the dirt, I cried my own, "*Nein!*"

I'd had enough. After regaining my footing, I promptly took off at full speed down the length of the arena, bending around the end corner at a precarious angle. I'd hoped she'd go flying into a potted cypress, but somehow she regained her own balance, yanked the reins, and spun me to a halt. I clenched my sides, readying myself for a kick or a howl. That's when I saw Frank.

His car was in the middle of the lane, its driver's door left wide open as he rushed toward us.

"Holy hell. Are you okay?"

"*Ja, ja.* No problem."

The Wraith now had me spinning and jigging in a small circle. My eyes and nostrils wide.

"Easy there, boy. Easy," Frank said. "That didn't look like no problem. What happened?"

"He just spooked."

"Jesus. At what?"

"Maybe a peacock."

"Damn birds. We have too damn many birds!"

I bristled at his words, worried Napoleon was in earshot.

"But you're okay?" he added.

"*Ja, ja.* No problem."

"Maybe that's good for today. He looks . . . well," Frank looked me straight in the eye. "He looks upset."

"*Ja.* We finish." She pulled back hard on the reins accompanied by a firm "Whoa!"

Frank held the reins as she dismounted. "That's enough excitement for me today. Nearly gave me a heart attack."

The Wraith flashed an insincere smile and took back the reins. "I take him back to the barn."

"Okay. Well, easy does it. Don't want anyone getting hurt."

As she led me away, Frank stood watching for a few seconds before returning to the silent Electric Pea.

The next afternoon, she arrived at my stall in a huff. I thought, *No thanks*, and hurried to the end of my run. Whatever time I could waste, I would.

"*Ich habe keine Zeit für deine Spiele.*" I don't have time for your games.

A breeze caught her sour scent and carried it to the end of my run. Suddenly, just like that time years ago with Sehnor Matos, I saw my grandsire before me. He was dancing with a bull, rushing sideways, goading the beast to try to keep up, catch him, touch him. In a flash, my grandsire swung round in a high and tight pirouette. The bull's horns narrowly missed his side. Confused, the animal locked his legs, creating a plume of dust as he skidded to a halt.

My grandsire swung back around to stare at the bull. For a moment, he stood stock-still. Then rushed head-on at the poor animal. His teeth sank into the bull's neck, and whether the attack was an act of courage, stupidity, or temporary insanity, it spoke to me. It said, if you can't outrun what threatens you—or even if you can—there comes a point when enough's enough.

The Wraith had reached me and was pulling the halter up and over my ears. I looked down at her, through her, as my grandsire had that bull.

She tacked me up in a hurry, neglecting to pick my hooves, and yanked me by the bridle toward the arena. The V of the snaffle dug into the roof of my mouth. At the same moment, the single cloud in the sky shifted and a sharp beam of sun caught her eye. Momentarily blinded, she lost her balance and stumbled back into me. I did not stumble. I did not step back. And when her thin, salty hair brushed my nose, I embraced the close proximity. Unlike what instinct had told me time and again, it now screamed, *Fight!*

She had started it, but I would end it.

She'd cinched a flash tight around my muzzle but had not spent enough time conditioning it. The dry, brittle leather was no match for my ire and when I curled back my lips and thrust open my jaw, the flash snapped in two like a fresh carrot. My grin wide, I sank my teeth into her bony shoulder. She squeaked like a sad little dog toy, but when she twisted around and raised her hand to slap my face . . .

"No!" Legs cried, running to my side and taking the reins.

The Wraith, forgetting about Abel's advice, mouthed off. "That horse. He is crazy. You saw him. He attacked me!"

The insults flew from her mouth like wasps from a rattled nest. She wanted Legs to believe I was the problem. Flawed, untrainable, unworthy. Never going to amount to anything because, above all, I was dangerous.

She said it again, "He is crazy."

"I've heard enough," Legs said. "He's out of the program."

Out of the program? Wait. Legs had believed her nonsense?

I'll never forget Legs's next words. She stared at the Wraith, her eyes narrowed, her voice cold.

"This is on *you*. Because, lady, he didn't try to take a chunk out of your arm for no reason."

The Wraith's jaw dropped.

"And believe you me, if he really wanted to hurt you, he would have. That was a warning. So get off your high horse and take some time to consider what he's trying to tell you. What all of these horses are trying to tell you. It's your *job*. And they all deserve to be heard. And respected."

Legs hadn't bought the Wraith's story. Legs was defending me. With a vengeance.

But why then . . . why was I out of the program? I needed to find Napoleon. I needed to understand what this meant. Thankfully, back at the barn, he was close at hand, pecking at fallen oats in my stall.

"Calm down, my friend," he said. "The First Lady has put too much time and effort into cultivating her program and this stable yard to let one bad apple spoil the bunch."

45

2010: Palo Alto, California

Relationships are like gardens. They need constant tending. Sadly, I'm a terrible gardener, quite bad at weeding and pruning and bringing things back to life after a frost. What had begun for Simon and me as warm and fuzzy companionship grew progressively colder after we married. A fact, along with many others, he had a hard time accepting.

Simon became less of a partner and more of a dependent, as if he didn't see the need anymore to pursue his ambitions or dreams. It was easier to be kept. Or at least that's how it felt to me. He used to like to say about other people, "Denial. It's not just a river in Egypt." The longer I knew him, the more I saw his inability to take a hard look in the mirror. I'm not sure he ever realized his "pot calling kettle black" hypocrisy.

He was eight years my junior and very much a "gonna-do" guy. Though I historically dated younger men, it had rarely been a good idea, and thus I'd been dubious of this May-December relationship. Obviously, not enough. After all the years, all the moves, all the boyfriends, all the dissatisfaction . . . I went and got engaged after less than a year of dating?!

The idea came up in early November 2007 (quick reminder: We met in December 2006). Simon's temporary work visa was soon to expire, and the thought of a premature goodbye loomed large. What if this thing we had could actually work out in the long term?

If only I'd had a crystal ball.

If only I'd paid attention to my gut telling me that, even at thirty-seven, I wasn't ready for marriage. Hell, I'd never wanted to be a bride.

If only I hadn't let the hint of Dickens's Micawber character in me surface to say, *You've had a good year with this Simon chap. Unlike your last boyfriend, who was eternally adventuring around the world and expecting you to be there for him with open arms when he returned home, Simon is here. He's present. He loves you. He loves the animals. Heck, even Bear has taken a shine to him.*

When I met Simon, I had two dogs: Beck, my soulmate of a Newfoundland, and Bear, my fearful, untrusting Chihuahua. I'd adopted her the year before after a friend plied me with wine and told me the story of some asshole kicking her, literally, out of his house because she peed on his precious floor. Sometimes, I really think I could murder a person.

Micawber wasn't wrong. The animals did adore Simon. He walked them, fed them, played with them. From what I understood, cleaning up after Bear if she had an accident in the house was nothing compared to the psychological human messes he'd dealt with in his past.

So, yeah, the misgivings scale tipped, and we got hitched. Our small wedding was held at the Woodside Town Hall, and we had a bagpiper pipe us and our nineteen guests—including six men and my wee one-year-old nephew, Declan, in kilts—across the street to the Village Pub, where we'd reserved the back room for dinner and drinks. I joke Steve Jobs was at my wedding. You see, when we walked into the restaurant and got a round of applause from the other diners in the main room, he was among them.

Simon and I had a lukewarm first year of marriage before things took that chilly turn.

Like many failed unions, we started to drift apart. I grew more and more weary and frustrated by his perpetual part-time work status and overall lack of motivation. I'm sure he grew more and more weary of my constant nagging to move, get going, pursue his dreams of organizing soccer camps abroad. Again, dreams that seemed to evaporate into thin air the moment we said "I do."

I spent more and more time at the barn. The one place I could breathe. He spent more and more time in front of the television or computer screen drinking wine and feeling sorry for himself.

When I was laid off from my job right before our second wedding anniversary, the chilly turn became a graveyard spiral.

The first time I kicked Simon out, it was after a girlfriend of mine told me he'd been hitting on her. The last straw on a growing pile of shit. He left to stay with a mutual friend and together they went on a bender. Already, he'd been drinking a couple bottles of wine a day, if not more.

A week later, he begged to come home, promised to quit drinking and clean up his act. He said he'd worked out a "schedule" to wean himself off the booze, and though I wanted him to seek counseling, I considered it something, if but a baby step. Too bad he knew nothing about detoxing. And frankly, neither did I.

On his second night back, we went out to see a movie, *The Ghost Writer*. On the drive home—three hours since his last drink—he had a grand mal seizure. When the convulsions stopped and he lay slumped over in silence, I thought for a moment he was dead. I hauled ass, not giving a shit about the speed limit, to the nearest emergency room. I kept repeating, "Simon! Wake up! Simon! Stay with me!" Like a line from a bad script.

That time, he stayed in the hospital for a week. That time, he was discharged with a prescription for valium and lorazepam and a tri-fold brochure on drug and alcohol rehabilitation. Nothing more. In short, *Adios, addict. Good luck with that.*

That time, it took him less than twenty-four hours before he started drinking again. Only, that time, he had a new cocktail: one part wine, two parts drugs. He was popping pills and acting stranger than ever. With each passing day, the gaslighting worsened and I began to wonder if the seizure had caused permanent damage.

"I'm not drinking," he slurred. "You're crazy."

"Do you think I can't smell?" I asked.

"Do you think I can't smell?" he repeated in a mocking, crapulous tone.

"What are you, two? I also found the empty wine bottles in your car."

"I had one fucking drink!" he exploded. "I think I've been good."

"Good? Like the 'Gatorade' in the fridge. That's good?"

Another new cocktail: Gutterade. He'd taken to buying Gatorade, dumping out half, and filling it back up again with Sutter Home wine or whatever other cheap plonk he could afford since I'd stopped bankrolling him.

"And what about the pills, Simon?"

"I've only had one today," he said like a zombie, his eyes half closed.

"Give me the bottle."

"No."

"Please, give me the bottle."

He thrust it into my face, insisting he'd had only one pill.

Opening it, I saw only a single pill remained. Four days earlier, when he'd picked up the new prescription, this time for Ativan, there'd been thirty. He was supposed to take a max of two pills in a twenty-four-hour period; there should have been twenty pills left. Everything coming out of his mouth was a lie.

It wasn't long before I asked him to leave again. He moved back in with his father and stepmother, who lived in the next town over. It also wasn't long before he was back in the hospital. Nearing the end of my tether and desperate to get him the professional help he needed, I gave him an ultimatum: rehab or else we were done.

Finally, he relented, but only, he said, if I were the one to take him.

I'll never forget picking him up and driving the twenty minutes to the rehab facility. Before I could parallel park in front of the nondescript building, he rushed to open the car door. Not to escape, but to puke up so much red wine someone could have mistaken it for the scene of a crime.

46

2013: Gilroy, California

There wasn't much blood . . . but once it was over, there was resentment.

Following the Wraith incident, I spent a week going from my stall to the hot walker to my pasture and back. If monotonous, I considered the change a small victory. At first.

The Wraith never touched me again. That was a great thing.

But no sooner had I begun to consider settling into this new routine than Legs and Frank arrived early one morning, out of turn.

"Hey, beautiful boy," she said as she slid open my stall door and stepped inside. "Today's a big day. But I promise, it's really for the best." She paused before adding, "And for what it's worth, I'm sorry."

Frank chimed in, "Stop being so melodramatic. He's going to be so much happier."

"I hope so."

"I know so. It's the right time. The right decision. The Dragon has to go."

"I know, I know," she said.

"No more second-guessing."

"I hear you. The Dragon has to go."

Sorry? Much happier? Has to go? None of it added up. I really needed to talk to Napoleon, but it was too late. Legs had already haltered me and was leading me out of the barn, handing me off to Abel, who stood beside a truck and trailer.

Once again, into the metal box I went. Once again, destination unknown.

As small consolation, at least the trip was a short one. The truck pulled into a wide, empty asphalt parking lot less than half an hour later. Before us stood a dull gray building. Not a barn. Not an arena. But somehow familiar.

Abel was quick to swing open the back gate of the trailer. He backed me out, turned me around, and started to lead me toward the building. A set of wide doors swung open, and the sharp smell of disinfectant smacked me in the face.

I put on the brakes. Abel stumbled. He looked toward the doors, then back at me. Adjusting his grip on the lead rope, he began to swing its end at my flank while clucking to urge me forward. But the more he clucked and swung that rope, the more I stepped back. I knew this place. Or at least this type of place. And I wasn't having it. Especially when a man dressed head to toe in light blue came out to *help*.

What happened that day is not something I care to detail. Not something I like to talk about. But let it go down in the history books, it was not my choice. And while in one way I did, I also didn't take it lying down.

In the end, my stay was brief. Only overnight. So, not the repeat quarantine I initially imagined, but a stay that forever changed me. Again, there was not much blood, but when I returned to Shangri-La, I was sore and a bit less myself.

But only a bit.

If they'd wanted the Dragon to vanish, they were out of luck. That fire burned deep within me, and even castration would not extinguish it.

47

2012: Duvall, Washington

At a certain point, you've gotta cut your losses. The weather had been a big reason to stay in California for as long as I did; somehow, almost fifteen years passed in a heartbeat. But at a certain point, no amount of sunshine could make up for the area's ballooning costs and self-satisfied attitude.

I'd walk down a street, and no one would say hello or smile. I'd hold open a door for someone at a restaurant or shop and they'd walk past without a word, without a nod of thanks, as if they were the bloody Queen of England. Not that the Queen would have been so rude. What's more, despite making a decent living, I couldn't afford to buy a house and have horses and eat.

For more than a few years, I'd been dying to find an escape hatch. So when a boss (and friend) relocated to Seattle and got another boss to okay me working remotely, it was go time. No more two-hours-a-day commuting. No more renting. And finally, the chance to have a house, horses, and eat my cake, too.

The supreme bonus: I would be moving back *home*, in a sense. My older brother, Eddie, had moved to Seattle in the mid-nineties (with his girlfriend, now wife, Heather) and he was the only one of us four siblings to have children—my amazing nephew, Declan, and niece, Siobhan. When my folks retired, it was all about being close to those kiddos. And partly about their lack of trust in babysitters and day care centers.

Two weeks after I'd been made the offer to move, I packed up life as I knew it into a rented U-Haul truck and loaded the horses into a northbound trailer. I knew I'd miss my friends and, sure, the sunshine, but my greatest misgiving stemmed from ripping those boys from their trainer, their routine, their home. It was a huge deal to decide to uproot them. And for better or worse, every decision comes with a cost.

For all its pros, Washington state came with a few surprises. To begin, I was shocked to discover so few boarding facilities offered pasture turnout. California had spoiled me in that regard. But even more shocking was how few had covered arenas. How did people expect to ride year-round? Oh. I see. They didn't. Huh?!

It's kind of how I ended up at a facility across the street from my parents' house (the way station during many months of house hunting). It had both. Kinda. The Pacific Northwest takes its toll on a place. The facility had a small covered arena and presumably year-round pasture turnout. One of its two barns, the upper barn, also had stalls with runs, which would allow the horses more space to stretch their legs when the pastures became muddy enough to be more dangerous than advantageous. I put myself on a waitlist for those and prayed space would open up soon. My boys were much too accustomed to pasture turnout and much too large for the twelve-by-twelve-foot stalls of the lower barn.

We'd arrived the week before Halloween in a relentless David Fincher rain. Had Bach's *Air on the G String* been softly playing in the background, I wouldn't have been surprised. The holiday came and went fast enough, but the rain remained. I remember standing at the bay window of my parents' guest room, looking down their driveway to where I could just make out Q and Ole. The pastures had not yet closed for winter—though maybe they should have?—and while I stood, warm and toasty, mug of Earl Grey tea in hand, there they stood, blanketed but huddled together at the edge of their sodden pasture. I wondered if all three of us were thinking the same thing: *WTF?*

For some reason, the Earl Grey also made me (and always makes me) think of violin lessons in Germany. They were almost always at Irene's house (Irene had been one of my best friends in middle school) and always in her father's downstairs study, where books lined the shelves that lined the walls. And the scent of Earl Grey filled the air that filled my memories. For some reason, it always stood out to me that her Italian father, who was a scientist, was shorter than her Dutch mother, who spoke five languages. But then, shorter still was Mitsue.

Petite but mighty, Mitsue was our Japanese violin teacher. She taught us the Suzuki method, and we met her because she was the wife of our middle school history teacher, Mr. Schmitt. I idolized her because when she'd pull out her vintage violin and play us a piece, all resonant vibrato and extended bow strokes, she sounded like an angel. I wish I'd known then to ask her to play *Air on the G String* for us.

She probably would have said no and then asked me why my *Minuet in G* still sucked so bad. And no, of course, she wouldn't have said that. That's just what I heard when she'd ask, "Erin, how much you practice this week?"

Uh . . .

And yet, she and Irene's folks and my folks couldn't understand why I didn't want to (and had repeatedly said I would not) play in a concert with all of Mitsue's other students, including the known prodigy, Mike. He made the rest of us sound like fingernails on chalkboards. Okay, maybe we sounded like that without Mike. But still.

If there's anything I don't like, it's being told what to do.

They still put my name in the concert brochure and when I didn't show (how was this a surprise?), Irene's mother came to me afterward with a reprimanding, "You should have been there. Your name was in the brochure and all!"

I didn't take kindly to the guilt-tripping, no matter how many Earl Grey teas she'd brought me in the past, and so I did what any self-respecting adolescent would do. I quit violin. A.k.a., cut off my nose to spite my face. And no, I can't help myself with the *Se7en* references.

Point being, at some stage I learned you have to do things you don't want to do sometimes. Like moving my horses from their home in California and, a year later, riding in a dressage clinic (more on that posthaste) that was anything but my cup of tea. Because in the end, both were for a greater good, despite what the relentless rain was telling me.

. . . Just shy of a year later

When the universe calls, I recommend answering. Same goes for when Aphrodite calls.

She phoned one day out of the blue in late September 2013.

"I know he's always been your favorite," she said. "If I offered him to you at the right price, would you be interested?"

"What's the right price?" I asked.

There were a dozen other questions I could have asked first, but this one cut to the chase. Was this even in the realm of possibility?

The fact her answer did not put an immediate end to the discussion was both amazing and overwhelming. I already had two horses. In no way, shape, or form did I *need* a third. Plus, as horse people know, the purchase price is one thing, but once you bring a horse home, they all cost the same. And that same is always: *everything*. All the money. All the time. All the energy.

I knew full well a third horse was completely out of the question. It was a terrible idea. Impractical on every level. There was just no way. So of course, my next question was, "Can I have a few days to think about it?"

That night, I lay awake, consumed with fear and anxiety. I was terrified I'd get another call from her saying she'd changed her mind and decided to keep him. Or much worse, she'd decided to sell him to someone else.

That night, I accepted a universal truth: When opportunity knocks in the form of a fairy-tale unicorn, the answer is always yes.

The next morning, I told Aphrodite yes, I'd be interested. As soon as we got off the phone, she booked me a flight to California for early the following morning. As she put it, I was to stay and be her guest for the weekend. When Aphrodite is on a mission, she doesn't mess around. She gets shit done. Pronto.

Since we'd first met on that fateful day four years prior, we'd become much more than acquaintances. We were friends, and I considered her a mentor. But for this trip, I was also a client. Not only did she come to pick me up at the airport, but back at the ranch, she laid out the red carpet.

Like a princess, I didn't have to lift a finger but had my mount delivered to me, spit shined and fully tacked in a traditional Portuguese bridle and saddle replete, respectively, with gold baroque buckles and studded ornamentation. A tight running braid along the crest of his neck had been woven with thick satin ribbon the color of paprika; the color paired beautifully with the mint-green saddle pad, gold stirrups, and fox *xairel.* Arty was a sight to behold, and I was a bundle of nerves.

All the fuss made me feel extra special but also extra anxious. Imposter syndrome is strong with this one—in more ways than one. At each turn, I was certain Aphrodite would rescind her offer, realizing I was a lousy rider, lousy person, lousy something or other.

When I said I was interested, I hadn't quite expected the invite for a final "test drive"—I'd ridden Arty on every past visit—but I also understood that, duh, this was different. She wanted me to be sure, and she wanted to be sure herself.

Sadly, she'd experienced seller's remorse more than once in the past. You'd be amazed at how many people make empty promises. "Oh, I'll see him every day." "I'll maintain the diet you recommend." "I'll work with the trainers, farriers, you name it, you suggest." "I'll be sure to keep in touch and send you photos and videos and report on his progress."

Mind you, once a contract is signed, unless stipulated, no buyer is obligated to do any of the above. However, if you can't do the bare minimum of consistently "showing up"—something I've witnessed too many times to count—I'll label you a shithead with zero hesitation. And that's not because of Aphrodite's or any other seller's wishes and hopes but because a horse deserves all our time, all our energy, all our love and devotion. They aren't toys. They aren't something to be pulled out and played with at our convenience or whim.

In short, Aphrodite wanted to find him his *person*. Someone who would be one hundred percent dedicated and could handle his newly acquired quirks.

"The program has been too stressful for him," she said. "He needs to learn to trust again with *one* rider."

That weekend, no quirks surfaced. He was a perfect gentleman, amazing to ride, and I fell that much more in love.

That weekend, Aphrodite made Sunny an offer she couldn't refuse. And it was agreed Arty would be coming home to live with Q, Ole, and me, little Miss Sunshine.

And yes, it seems ironic to *rescue* a horse from paradise and thrust him into a cold and wet Washington winter—once again, destabilizing his life—but I believed I could help him.

Looking back, how naive and arrogant I was not to have considered who the real savior would turn out to be.

48

2013, on the road again

I could tell Napoleon was gearing up for one of his pep talks. Not only did he flap his wings out to the side like a man unbunching starched shirt-sleeves from beneath a tailored suit jacket but he also cleared his throat with a strangled cocka-doodle-doo before launching in.

"Your mother," he started, and though I knew what he was about to say, I didn't interrupt, "she was telling you to find your rider, your person. And not necessarily your bullfighter. You know, just because you were born or bred or whatever you think for one thing doesn't mean you were meant to only do that one thing."

"Yes, yes," I said.

"No, really," he stopped me. "You may think you don't have a choice in this life, that horses don't get to carve their own path, but like your mother told you, you are your own horse. And if ever I've met a horse who could decide his destiny, it's you."

I lowered my head so we were eye to eye. "Thank you, Napoleon."

"I mean it," he said.

"I know you do, my friend."

"Okay, good"—he flapped his wings again before continuing—"because I need you to remember that. Now, it's about time I get back to the henhouse before they go and lock up for the night and leave me to hang out on some flimsy tree branch again."

"You'd better indeed."

He started to shuffle away and as he was about to turn out of the barn, he looked back and said, "You be good now."

"I'm always good."

"That's right. Good as gold," he said as he strutted out and into the early evening light, the sun only just starting to set. I dropped my head and got back to eating my hay.

Later that evening, long after dinner and as I was circling and pawing at my shavings, preparing to lie down, the overhead fluorescents buzzed back on. Legs and Abel walked into the barn and over to my stall.

Abel slid the door open, haltered me, and, though the air was warm, dressed me in a light stable sheet. It was blue and at least two sizes too big so it tugged at my withers. Legs joined us in the stall, stroking my neck and telling me what a good boy I was.

What's up with all the good-boy stuff?

She said something about how happy I was going to be as she and Abel led me out of the barn and down past the round pen, the covered arena, Oh Cherry, the old Ford truck, the foaling barn, the guest house and ponds, and on through the estate's wrought iron entrance gate.

They each turned on a flashlight at the edge of the property, and we headed into the caliginous night along the narrow road that led away from the ranch through a willowwacks of weeping eucalyptus. The smell was a surprise comfort, and I walked as Opa may have, a perfect gentleman.

Since arriving at Shangri-La on that wet, gray day four years earlier, I'd rarely traveled off the property, save for a few trailer rides to horse shows and the emasculating snip-snip trip. I'd certainly never walked down this road.

We'd not gone far before we reached a crossroads, where we stopped and waited. I stuck my nose high in the air and whinnied. No one answered. The only sound was the distant hum of the freeway.

"I think that's them," Legs said as a pair of headlights broke through the mist.

Abel nodded and gave me a pat on the neck.

The brighter the lights grew and the louder the rumble from the approaching truck, the more uneasy I became, stamping my feet and spinning around Abel.

"Easy," he said, holding tight to the lead rope. "Easy."

The truck pulled off onto the shoulder of the road and dust blew up around us, obscuring the driver as he climbed from his rig.

"Sorry for the delay, ma'am," he called out. "We hit some unexpected traffic around LA."

"Is traffic ever unexpected around L.A.?" Legs said.

The driver didn't have a response.

"I'm joking," she added. "Not a problem. Just glad you're here now. This boy's ready to go."

Go where? And am I ready?

"His name is Arty, and he's a very good boy," she said. "But he may be a little nervous."

"We're used to handling all kinds. Not to worry," said another man who'd opened the door to a long trailer and was lowering a ramp.

Another couple of minutes and I was on board. Abel stood with me while Legs signed some papers and handed them to the driver.

"Well, looks like we're good to go," he said.

Abel put his hand on my head and was quick with his farewell. "*Se bueno, amigo.*" Be good, friend. He turned and left to give Legs a moment alone with me.

She tousled my forelock, and I shook my head away. "Sorry, I know you don't like that. But you're going to like where you're going."

Where am I going?

"You're going to get special attention and lots of love. And the weather will be much, much cooler."

I don't need cooler weather. I'm fine.

"Okay, boy. Be good. I'll see you soon."

See me soon? I was so confused.

She walked down the ramp and into the night. She did not look back or make the sign of the cross like Nuno had. The driver's assistant shut the door, and a few minutes later, the truck and trailer rumbled on. From my window, I watched us drive farther and farther away from my home, my routine, my life, my friend. In that moment, I knew I'd never see that bawcock of a rooster again.

Napoleon had known the same, saying goodbye in the best way he could. As I looked down the long dark stretch of highway, I summoned up his final words and tried to imagine what choices I had. But try as I might, I saw only darkness ahead.

49

2013: Enumclaw, Washington

The next day, the rig pulled into the parking lot of an equestrian facility. The wrong way.

It was late afternoon, and I was growing restless as the trailer shook back and forth with abrupt stops and starts. Loud voices debated over how best to turn it around without knocking down trees and fences or crashing into a line of nearby cars.

With nothing more to do, I stared out my window, looking beyond the gravel lot toward acres of fenced green pastures. In the distance, a white-capped mountain touched the clouds.

When the rocking finally stopped and the trailer door swung open, I was shocked to see a familiar face. There, standing next to the truck driver, all smiles and nervous energy, was none other than Sunny.

The driver handed her a clipboard and pen. "Erin, I presume?"

"That's me," I said.

"Just need you to sign here." He pointed to the bottom of the sheet.

My hands shaking, I signed. "There you go. Now—"

"Now, just give me a second to find his lead rope, and I'll have him right out for you."

"Okey dokey," I said like a dork.

"Beautiful horse, by the way."

It was good to see someone had good taste, and once he clipped the rope to my halter and unhooked the bar to my travel stall, I stepped down the ramp like a gentleman. Also like a gentleman, I raised my head high and whinnied greetings to a group of horses who were grazing in a nearby pasture. Perhaps a little louder than intended. Not only did some of the horses whinny back, but a couple of concerned humans took double takes.

I could feel the eyes on us. No one came to say hello or welcome. Letting insecurity get the best of me, I guessed they were simply and silently judging from afar, likely questioning whether or not I had things under control. But distant whispers be damned! I thanked the driver, swapped him a tip for the lead rope, and walked off with my boy. My. Boy.

She led me to the edge of a pasture, where my heart fluttered and my legs buckled as I dove into a banquet of lush green grass. While I ate, she peeled off my travel sheet and began to stroke my neck and scratch my back. It felt good after all those hours crammed into that metal box.

"Wow," she said. "You are here. You spectacular, amazing, good, good boy."

I let him graze for a good while, trying to take deep breaths, relax, and enjoy the moment, but when the sun began to dip and I began to worry about too much grass upsetting his stomach—because I must always find as many things to worry about as possible—I decided it was time to get him settled in his stall, wherever that was. I'd tried earlier to find out, but unfortunately, the couple of folks I'd run into in the parking lot had no idea, and when we walked back to and into the barn, I got an earful in more ways than one.

As soon as we set foot in the barn, a horse came at us from the left, lunging against the metal bars of his stall, teeth bared. Arty squealed and struck out in a one-two-style punch with his front legs. I may have also squealed. But there's no doubt not one but two women—where had they been before?—ran over to lecture me about walking past stallions.

Had my nerves not already been shot to hell and my throat killing me from a budding cold, I may have argued. As far as I could see, there was nothing—no person, no sign saying do not enter or beware the "angry" stallion—to indicate the entrance was off-limits. I wish I'd also had the presence of mind to give them shit about the fact my horse or I could have been injured.

I was half proud of and half hated myself for simply saying, "Sorry."

The important thing is I found Arty's stall. It didn't have a run but was double the size of a normal stall, and with a storm brewing, that was probably for the best.

My stall gave me a tantalizing view of the mountains—and all that grass. Sunny—or rather, Erin—threw a fresh new stable sheet over me as the sun sank and the air turned brisk. While she hooked the front clasps, I stuck my nose on her head and breathed in. Her hair smelled of musk and flowers and somehow reminded me of Brazil. She kissed my nose, promised to return first thing in the morning, and whispered in my ear, "I love you. Be good. Stay safe."

After she left, I spun around a few times and pawed at the thick shavings before lying down to have a good roll. A sudden commotion made me quickly pop up and rush to investigate. The metal bars made it hard to see down the row, but when I heard a familiar *swoosh,* I knew it was dinnertime. Grain was on its way.

Not a minute later, a stranger arrived, looked at me, looked at a Ziploc bag full of grain, and said, "I guess you're Arty?"

He reached through the bars, and before he could finish dumping all the bag's contents into a feeder in the corner, I began to gobble them down. The rest of the night, I nibbled on timothy and wondered what was happening and why I was there. I missed Napoleon and wished for him to appear in a flutter to tell me all the latest news and gossip. But of course, that didn't happen.

By morning, the white-capped mountain was gone, concealed behind a wall of gray fog. It wasn't raining, but it wasn't not raining, either. If anything, it was mizzling. Like a giant cloud had descended upon the barn to deliver an unwanted wet kiss. *Welcome to Washington State,* I thought, *where the weather—rain or shine—holds a certain gravitas.* And neither Brazil nor Florida nor California had prepared me for this more honest October day.

As promised, Erin returned early. Only, she was not alone.

Wicked early that morning, I'd driven to the airport to collect Aphrodite, who'd flown up to watch me and Arty ride in a clinic. One of the terms of his purchase was that I "clinic" with a Brazilian trainer, who—lucky me—was scheduled to be in the area the day after Arty arrived. So, not only was I to ride my new horse—who'd just traveled nine hundred miles—but I was to do so with a clinician I'd never met and in front of a bunch of strangers. It was not a dream scenario; I could feel the storm clouds forming outside and inside the barn.

As other riders gathered in the barn aisle with their steaming mugs of coffee, it became clear Erin and I were to be the first ride of the day. She did not look well when she came to my stall. Her voice was hoarse, hands fidgety, nose a wet red bulb. While she brushed and tacked me, she prattled on about how nervous she was.

"I'm not sure this is the best idea," I told Aphrodite, secretly hoping to weasel my way out of riding. "Maybe he can just ride instead."

"You'll be fine. It'll be good for you," she responded, neither taking the bait nor letting me off the hook.

"I'm sure you're right," I said while thinking how riding in front of a crowd, even under the best of circumstances, is not something I enjoy. Hence, why I don't compete. But just as I'd taken that "let's get this over with" leap of faith, there was a problem. From down the barn aisle, a lady yelled, "He's been held up at another barn. Shouldn't be long."

"Hurry up to wait," I said. "Maybe it's a sign."

"It's not a sign," Aphrodite said. "It's the horse world."

And so, we waited. Then waited some more. Until finally, Erin decided to untack me and let me go back to my breakfast. Outside, the weather worsened. The mizzle turned into a steady downpour that the wind heaved in sideways through the barn's open doors.

First, I'm in warm, sunny California. Next, I'm in cold, wet Washington. I'm loaded, unloaded, tacked, untacked. Breakfast didn't hold my interest, and I began to pace back and forth in my stall, once again contemplating my choices. I didn't see many, but in a way, thought maybe Erin felt the same. She seemed about as ready to bolt as I.

Two hours later, the clinician arrived without apology. Definitely not his fault. The other barn was to blame. When he came to meet us—or, really, Aphrodite—he wore a tinny grin along with a floppy fur cap that made me wonder if he'd made a pit stop somewhere in the Yukon.

He ignored me but embraced Aphrodite. "Please, please tell me about your horse from Brazil."

"Well, he's not mine anymore," she said, "but I think you will enjoy him. He comes from fine lines."

Since he didn't seem to have any interest in me, I decided to spend the time tacking Arty up. Again.

I listened in as Fur Cap and Legs discussed my lineage, level of training, and some of the issues I'd been having. He said he knew my bloodlines and liked my look; he was even kind to compliment my profile. He did not, however, much care for my saddle. Or my bit. Both, he said, were too narrow. I agreed, and yet, it's what we had to work with, and it was well past time for the lesson to begin.

To get to the small arena, Erin led me through a narrow aisleway, directly past the stall of yet another pinned-ear stallion. The two of us exchanged "words." I wasn't happy. Erin wasn't happy. And to heighten the tension, the rain had begun to come down hard. It sounded like a small battalion marching across the barn's tin roof.

Erin presented a decent case for having Fur Cap hop on first for a test drive, and when he said yes, she exhaled for the first time all day. She stood in the middle of the arena as he climbed aboard and began to wax lyrical about investing in connection.

"A horse will round himself when you have a good, reliable, quality connection."

I tested his theory by shaking my head, rooting, and waiting for him to jerk back on the reins. He never did. I appreciated that, as well as his edict on anger management: "You can never, ever get angry with a horse."

The lesson was going okay, not great. I had trouble taking the correct canter lead at times, and as I downshifted into a huge trot at one corner, Fur Cap and I nearly took out the clinic videographer. Poor thing gasped and fumbled backward. Other spectators began to chatter. But what did they expect? I'd just traveled nine hundred miles to this strange, cold, wet land. I was tired. I was anxious. I didn't know Fur Cap from Black Hat. All I wanted was to be back home. And that's when Fur Cap halted me, dismounted, and handed the reins to Erin. "Your turn."

I could feel her nerves, her trepidation as she climbed into the saddle, but she gave me a pat, asked me to walk on, and proceeded to do her best to follow Fur Cap's instructions. He was not unkind, but he was also not kind as he continued to repeat, "Connection! Where is the connection? I don't see the connection!"

To be fair, he was right. Erin was far too delicate with the reins, which made it hard for me to understand what she wanted. Still, she was trying, and luckily for her, for me, for all, when the next rider entered the arena and mounted her horse, Fur Cap finally looked at his watch.

"Ah yes, we can be done," he said to Erin.

For only the second time that day, I heard her take a breath. She hopped off, loosened my girth, and whispered in my ear, "You were amazing. Thank you."

One of the auditors approached me and Arty as we were leaving the arena.

"You're quite brave," she said. "That boy's a big mover and you wouldn't have seen me get up on him under the same circumstances. That rain alone. Did he really just arrive last night?"

"He did indeed. And thank you. That's really nice of you to say. But I don't deserve any kudos. I was a nervous wreck. He's the brave one. A true superstar."

The rain kept Erin from taking me out to graze, and I spent the rest of the day and night in my oversize stall. I ate the timothy and grain they gave me, but I didn't lie down, didn't rest, despite how tired I was. Occasionally, a horse would pass, and I would either whinny or pin my ears. What can I say? I like some horses, not all.

The next day, Erin and Legs returned early, and Fur Cap was not late. During the lesson, he made Erin stick to walk and trot, concentrating on how to make that first step toward connection. The skies had not cleared, and the rain continued to pummel the tin roof, but by the end of the lesson, there was a hint of a different kind of connection. It was as if, in some way, we'd weathered our first storm together.

50

2013: Duvall, Washington

The next morning, the rain persisted. The mountain stayed hidden. And the barn's gutters turned into overflowing, spurting fountains.

Erin arrived early, sans Legs, but with two women I'd never seen. As Erin gathered my few belongings—my oversize travel sheet, a brush, and a hoof pick—they led me from the barn, through puddles the size of ponds, toward another, much smaller trailer. Water splashed my belly, and I let out an ear-piercing whinny and began to passage.

One of the women shook her head. "Amateur's horse, you say?"

"I had nothing to do with it," said the other.

They were hasty, likely wanting out of the wet as much as I. No sooner was my halter clipped to the trailer and the door slammed behind me than off we went with a rattle and jolt. This tiny trailer, I quickly discerned, was no air-ride. I focused on keeping my balance, hoping wherever we ended up would be warmer and drier.

After just two days in Washington, I'd already had my fill of rain. The smell of it reminded me of the big stone barn and that day the wind had breathed life into a stiff gray tarp—but not what lay beneath it. When the foals had gathered close to their mothers, seeking shelter from the prickling hail. When I pawed at rough straw in a dark corner, only to collapse upon a cold, damp floor.

Bam! A bump in the road knocked me off balance, not only interrupting the memory but also causing me to let loose a spray of watery poo. I'd also had my fill of these shaking, swerving metal death traps.

Fortunately, it wasn't too long before I felt the curves in the road tighten, the incline steepen. We slowed nearly to a halt before taking a final sharp turn into a property where, through the bars of the trailer window, I saw moss-covered fences and trees pointing like arrows toward the brumal sky, reminding me of the persistent gray, as if daytime here were but one long gloaming. We came to a stop after a small round-about, and the trailer door swung open.

The same woman who'd loaded me clamored inside, but when I turned my head to look behind, she gave a hard yank on the lead rope, screeching, "Whoa! Whoa now! I don't know what you've been taught, but around here, we back out of trailers, buddy!"

Buddy? I didn't like her tone but did as asked and backed out in a hurry. She slipped on the slick, wet ramp and let out another loud "I said whoa!"

My haunches swung left, then right, left, then right with each fresh snap and tug of the rope. I wasn't sure what she wanted but finally stood square, quivering in a small gravel parking lot.

The rain had not masked the scent of mares. But intermingled with poo and pee and pine, I sensed a strong female presence and looked around to find its source. A nearby barn had stalls with gnawed Dutch doors facing the parking lot. Curious horse heads began to poke out. I let out another whinny, shrill enough to doff the flaking paint from the barn's battered exterior. This place, I also quickly discerned, was no Shangri-La.

The rain came down harder still. And though Erin's truck had pulled into the parking lot, the woman did not wait for her and hustled me toward another barn. She walked me down a long concrete aisle with an arena to one side and a row of a dozen stalls to the other. Metal bars across the stalls prevented these horses from peeking their heads out, but many kept a watchful eye. In particular, a big black horse with an oddly huge, fuzzy white star gave me a convivial neigh.

Mine was to be the last stall in the row, next to a disinterested chestnut who didn't even raise his head from his hay when I walked past. The space was small—less than four by four meters—and while there was an attached run, the Dutch door to it was closed. A pile of hay sat in a corner, perhaps to bait me, but when the woman reached to remove my halter, I pulled back, reared, and sent her scurrying out of the stall.

"He needs to learn some manners!" she said.

"His manners are fine," I corrected her. "He's just scared."

And so was I. Scared to death he'd hurt himself but doing my best to remain calm.

I reared again, this time completing a half pirouette before landing and kicking out at the neighboring-but-not-neighborly horse's stall.

"Whatever you say."

Who is that woman? And who are these other women? Between my stall bars, I watched a small crowd of strange faces begin to gather and gawk.

"Well, he's quite full of himself," said a lady in a bright yellow raincoat. "I've never seen a horse rear like that in a stall. I hope he doesn't hurt himself."

"What is he?" said another. "He's quite agitated."

"Looks like a handful," said yet another. "Where'd he come from?"

The questions were coming rapid fire, as if I were holding a press conference when all I really wanted was to be left alone with my horse.

"Well, just now, we came from a clinic in Enumclaw, but he arrived a couple of days ago from California. It's been a long haul for him, and this is all new and scary, and I'm pretty sure this weather isn't helping."

"He doesn't like rain?" asked the barn's resident quidnunc.

"Let me guess, you do?" I said, pointing to her yellow rain slicker. In my head, I was saying, *Be nice, Erin.* But my tone came out a bit more *Suck a bag of dicks, lady.* Interestingly, she didn't seem to notice. Too bad.

"Are you going to ride him today?" she continued.

"Yeah, no. Not today."

Erin turned toward me and rolled her eyes. I understood immediately. This woman was one of those. I may have always lived at private farms, but I'd seen enough visitors to understand. She was a prodder. And if I were to guess, not a great rider. But that was just a guess. Call it horse sense.

"He may be better if you exercise him."

"You don't say." Erin stuck her face between the bars of my stall. "Don't worry, Arty. You don't have to do a goddamn thing today." She reached in and held out a treat, which I snatched from her hand before returning to whinnying and spinning in circles.

"He's going to work himself into a lather with that sheet on," Yellow continued.

"Would you like to go in and take it off?" Erin asked.

"I was just saying—"

"I'm going to give him a few minutes to settle down."

"So, what breed did you say he is again?" one of the other women asked.

"Lusitano."

"Ah, Spanish."

"No, not quite. I mean, Lusitanos are related to the Spanish Andalusians; both are Iberian . . . but back in the late sixties, the Spanish and Portuguese stud books were split. Lusitanos are the Portuguese national horse."

"So, he came from Portugal?"

"He was actually bred in Brazil."

"He came here on a ship?"

"No. He came on a plane."

"He flew?"

"Yes," Erin said. "But that was a few years ago."

"I guess he's used to traveling."

"I suppose. But he's been in the same place for a few years and so this is all still new and confusing to him."

"He looks like a lot of horse. What if he doesn't work out for you?" Yellow was back at it.

"Doesn't work out? That's a weird thing to say."

"I mean, he seems very different from your other two."

Other two?

"Variety . . . the spice of life, right?" Erin started to open my stall door.

"So, you're keeping the others?"

"Oh my god." Erin stopped and turned to face Yellow. "What's with the twenty questions? Of course, I'm keeping my boys."

Her boys?

"I was just saying—"

"I've got a question for you," Erin interrupted her.

I started to circle less, listen more.

"You've got two kids, right?"

"Yes," said Yellow. "A son and a daughter."

"Okay. So, when you had your son or your daughter . . . which one is older?"

"My son's the oldest."

"Okay, riddle me this. When you had your daughter, did anyone ask if you were getting rid of him?"

"I think that's a bit different."

"Well, I don't. These are my babies. And they've got me for life, like it or not. Though I pray they like it."

Yellow was quick to continue her offense. "Well, I think most people are more flexible."

This woman is getting on my last nerve.

"Oh, I see," I said, taking a second before adding, "actually, you know. No, I don't see. I think too many people see horses as a commodity. They're an object, a possession, and as soon as they no longer serve a human's purpose or pleasure or whim, they're discarded."

No one in the small crowd said a word.

I took the helmet I'd been holding and put it on before sliding open the stall door and walking in—and away from them. Arty stretched out his neck, sniffing me for more treats.

"Well, of course I have treats," I said, handing him a few while taking the opportunity to reach under his blanket to check for sweat. Good, all dry.

The others began to disperse.

"Good luck with him," said one.

"Can't wait to see you two together," said another.

Just when I thought they'd all take their leave, Yellow turned to add a final thought. "For most people, if it's not a match, it's better to let the horse go."

Not turning around, Erin simply said "okay" before taking a deep breath, looking me square in the eye, and adding, "And cool people don't make snap judgments, and they also give others the time and space to enjoy a new horse."

A cat slipped through the slight crack in the stall door and began rubbing against Erin's leg.

"Hey, buddy, maybe not the best place for you to be right now." She picked him up and set him outside, but he came back in.

"Don't say I didn't warn you, cat," she said before turning back to me. "Maybe he wants to be your friend. I sure know I do. And my only wish is you'll be happy here. Because I promise. I'm not sending you anywhere."

I glanced around, unsure if that was a good or bad thing. No one had asked me if this was what I wanted. All I knew was this place was cold and dark and musty. Cobwebs hung in uniform rows in every corner of my stall like little sawdust hammocks. Above, large sections of torn insulation flapped like plastic flags, each gust of wind threatening to set them free and freak me out. A mouse the size of . . . wait, was that a rat? Whatever it was, it scurried across the stall as the cat, instead of chasing it, pawed again at Erin's leg.

"Buddy, I swear, I don't have anything for you."

The cat meowed and Erin added, "I'm sorry."

She shouldn't have because what that fat lazy cat had just said was, "Useless human. I shall find your truck and pee on its tires."

I bent down to the cat's eye level, my ears flat against my head to let him know what I thought of his intention. Erin was quick to react.

"Okay, fat cat, out you go. Once and for all." She scooped him up and placed him back out in the aisleway.

Lucky cat. Now, where was I? That's right, searching for treats.

"You are hilarious. Nothing against cats—well, maybe, they do make me sneeze—but he's pretty ineffectual as a barn cat."

We agreed on one thing.

She stayed with me for hours, re-braiding my mane and simply hanging out, but nothing about this place felt like home. There was no "En Aranjuez con Tu Amor" drifting from overhead speakers. There was no Napoleon to give me the lay of the land. I would have to wait and see what the next day brought.

To begin, it brought Erin, early as usual. And finding me in a calmer state, she opened the doors to my small run. What lay before me was nothing I could have expected.

Rather than a majestic mountain, I spotted a lone, rangy calf—definitely not a bull—on the opposite side of a drooping fence about thirty meters away. He gave a nervous, forsaken moo just seconds before a sudden cacophony of *rat-tat-tat, rat-a-tat-tat* gave me, the other horses, and Erin a start.

"Goddamn hillbillies!" Erin yelled. "You're gonna get someone killed."

I had no idea what Arty thought, but I could have imagined. He'd come from beautiful Shangri-La and was now in the boonies of Duvall, where people randomly fired off guns and the sun was loath to make an appearance between October and April. I was anxious to get him moved as soon as possible to a better stall, where he'd have a longer run and, hopefully, be next door to either Q or Ole. Fingers crossed.

51

2013: Duvall, Washington

For weeks, the rain did not let up. The ground caved, unwilling and unable to soak up more moisture. The end of my run swelled into a murky green pond, where surface tension held fallen pine needles afloat and adrift. They swirled like tiny castaways, round and round, round and round, until a strong gust embedded them into a mound of gravel or poo.

And still, I preferred to stand outside, where I could see the other horses. And that scrag of a calf. Oddly, he gave me mild comfort. At least I wasn't him. And at least I had a blanket, even if it, too, was on the verge of surrendering. While it had done its best to keep my core dry, it was no match for the constant deluge and had permanently shifted to one side, hanging askew like an ill-fitting saddle. Needless to say, I was never truly dry and rarely very clean, despite Erin's efforts. Or, as she called them, Sisyphean efforts.

"A gray horse in Washington. What was I thinking?"

Thing is, with the certainty of the daily drizzle came another certainty: Erin's arrival at the barn. She lived off-property, as Nuno had, but came every day to spend time with her "boys," of which I was supposedly now one. Well, at least to her. Don't get me wrong. Erin had never been anything but kind, but I'd been misled by kindness and good intentions in the past and didn't have it in me to make haste in warming up to anyone. Neither Erin nor her equine fraternity.

Three weeks into my stay, a stall became available next to Q, the big black fellow who'd nickered greetings to me on my first day. As it happened, he was Erin's "first son." It didn't take long to see this firstborn had a sixth sense about his mama's daily arrivals. Q could be out in his run taking a nap when all of a sudden, his head would pop up, his ears would swivel around like someone had just called his name, and off he'd hustle back into his stall. Ready and waiting. Minutes later, I'd hear the rumble of her truck, followed by the boo-beep of a car lock, followed by the deep whinny of son number one.

It reminded me of Brazil. How I'd always hear Nuno before I saw him. How the routine of his singing had comforted me like a lullaby. How now, despite my urge to not want anything from anyone, I'd begun to count on that rumble and whinny.

Erin's other son, Ole, was less vocal, but when Q headed in, he wasn't far behind. Ole's stall was closest to the door. So when Erin rolled in, she'd greet him first, with Q next and me last. At first, I didn't take offense to the order, but with each passing week, I grew more and more impatient, occasionally kicking at my stall door to encourage her to hurry along. After all, she always came bearing treats. Treats to say hello. Treats for letting her clean my hooves. Treats for a good ride. Treats right before she left each evening with the parting words, "Be safe, have fun, I love you, and I'll see you tomorrow."

My growing attachment didn't escape Q's notice. Late one night, when we were standing in our runs beneath a wet, starless sky, about as close as we could get while remaining safely separated by the electric fence, he said to me, "You know. She means it."

"Means what?"

"That she loves you and will be back."

"I don't really care."

"You sure about that?"

"All I know is maybe she means it. Maybe she doesn't. I've had a lot of tomorrows not end up as I'd hoped."

"Well, tomorrow, she'll be here," said another, more distant voice. "And the day after that, too."

I looked past Q. The night was so dark I could barely make out Ole's outline, but his voice was clear when he continued, "Forgive me if I assume incorrectly, but while this place may not be the type of fancy you're used to, it's a good home, she's a good mama, and she isn't going anywhere. Or sending you anywhere."

"How do you know?" I said. "You don't even know me."

"No, but we know her," they said in unison.

"And who are you for me to trust?" I asked.

And thus, the history of their fraternity began to unfold.

Despite appearances, they weren't real brothers, at least not by blood, and still, they shared an uncommon kinship. Rain or, well, rain, they stood side by side in their runs every day, often touching noses and sharing hay beneath the hot wire. They'd been together half a dozen years now and had grown closer than they'd been to any other horses in their lives.

"This one's the best friend I've ever had," Q said.

"I'm the only friend you've ever had," Ole joked.

"Well, that, too," Q quipped back.

"How Q ended up as Erin's first horse is a question for the ages. My guess, the answer lies somewhere between craziness and naivete."

"Funny," Q said.

"Do you even know what Q stands for?" Ole asked me.

"I've heard her call you Quantrill."

"Yes, Quantrill," Ole said. "As in William Clarke Quantrill and his infamous Raiders. As in ride with the devil. She calls him that on rare occasions."

"I'm not following," I said.

"My apologies. I digress. Let me start at the beginning." And Ole went on to recount the day Q and Erin first met.

Q had been parked out on the front lawn—yes, front lawn, not pasture—of his previous owner's mini farm, eating fresh green grass and in no mood for disturbances. When the poor woman (not Erin, but the previous owner) went to collect him to show him off, he let out a kick so swift and high he narrowly missed scalping her.

"That is Q," Ole accentuated before continuing. "Believe it or not, or so the story goes, that bit of misbehavior was not why he was for sale. The previous owner, an endurance rider who preferred small Arabians, had bought Q for her paunchy husband."

"Who, thankfully," Q interjected, "took no interest in me."

"Despite the near beheading she'd witnessed, Erin fell for Q. Hook, line, and stinker."

"Apparently, she's a sucker for bad boys with pretty faces," I said.

"Now you're catching on," Q said.

"How old were you?" I asked.

"Oh, I don't know. Six, maybe seven."

"What about before that? Where were you born?"

The questions hung in the air, which had suddenly turned cooler. Q wasn't much interested in talking about that, but Ole asked, "Can I at least tell him about the auction?"

"Suit yourself."

"I was sold at an auction, too," I said.

"I somehow doubt this was the same type of auction," Ole said before relating Q's "discovery" story.

His had indeed been a very different experience to mine. It was the type of auction where if the general public failed to bid on any horses, a seedier side of mankind would slither in to pay the bare minimum and, consequently, haul off whatever living carcasses they could to resell to slaughterhouses. It was not a profitable endeavor. Often, they might make only enough profit to buy a case of beer and a carton of cigarettes, but to them, a horse's life wasn't worth more.

"And that's as much as I care to talk about that," Q interjected. "And frankly, more than I care to remember. Life is good now, and I'll take that."

I understood and didn't push but instead asked, "And Ole?"

"Ole fan Sil," Q said. "The good son. Now there's a better story."

Ole was the Friesian of Erin's dreams. Regal, imposing, and feathery-footed, he was as mild-mannered and sound-minded as they came. Q painted a vivid picture of Ole's fairy-tale debut. The quaint, faraway farm. The love of three Dutch women: his first owner, his breeder, and of course, his mother. And then, there had been the sudden disappearance of his owner and the lonely months before another woman came to see him. This time, an American woman. And when she did . . .

"Stars aligned. Double rainbows appeared. That is Ole," Q said.

"And you've always been friends?" I asked.

As Ole explained, getting introduced into a two hundred–acre pasture with a herd of thirty-some other geldings was stressful. But that was the default setup where Erin boarded.

"No way around it," Ole said. "Despite the space to run and romp, it's not easy to assimilate at the beginning and yet, for some reason—maybe because Erin had told him to be good to me—Q always had my back. And early on, liked to try to take a bite out of it."

"It's what you do," Q said. "You establish a pecking order. Pasture scuffles are part of the process."

"I think it was also that Q wasn't used to sharing. If Erin came to get me and not him, he'd follow us all the way to the pasture gate, and without fail, as she'd be trying to close the gate while keeping him in, he'd bite my ass."

"Here we go," Q said.

"Here we go?" I asked.

"One day, I decided I'd had enough—" Ole started to say.

"And would you believe it," Q interrupted, "this behemoth double barrel kicks me. Square in the chest."

"Got you good," Ole added. "Left hoofprints and all."

"Ouch," I said.

"Got my attention for sure," Q said.

Both agreed, from that kick onward, a friendship grew, and as Erin would say, they became "thick as thieves." If another horse chose to mess with one of them, he chose to contend with the two of them.

I was intrigued by their loyalty and had so many more questions, but that was all the storytelling I was going to get for the night. The rain had started to pick up, and Q and Ole decided it was time to head to their stalls and hunker down in a pile of shavings. I followed their lead and did the same. It was the best rest I'd had since arriving.

52

2014: Duvall, Washington

Some days were dull enough to notice drifting pine needles in puddles. Others tested my tolerance for excitement. Or more so, commotion.

The woman who'd trailered me to the barn turned out to be its resident trainer. She gave basic equitation lessons in a voice that could strip paint from a wall. It boomed across the arena, always finding its way to the end of my run, where I went to escape it and the comings and goings of her students, most of whom were children. Children who giggled, blubbered, or raced through the barn screeching things like, "It smells like poo!" "But I want to ride that horse!" "It tried to bite me!"

To her credit, Trainer Lady showed more than a modicum of patience in those moments. She'd busy the little hellions by handing them a brush or directing them to grab a bridle from a musty locker. It was her business, after all. And yet, her tolerance had its limits. If a student repeatedly ignored her instructions—this happened often—the boom would turn to a bark, and that bark had teeth.

"Pull hard and turn right. No! Your other right. No. No. Noooo! Stop. Just stop! Pull and stop! I said pull! With both hands! Now!"

I had little . . . wait, scratch that. I had zero sympathy for the students. In the short time I'd been at this new barn, I'd watched more than half of them take their first and last lesson, at once. It seemed the biggest lesson they learned was that riding wasn't for them. It wasn't easy. It wasn't about just sitting atop an already-groomed tacked horse, expecting the horse to do the rest. Riding was work, and it took focus, fortitude, and finesse. Plus, in this case, some resolve to handle the swing in moods of Trainer Lady. One minute, pleasant as warm sunshine. The next, irritable as Senhor Matos without his afternoon snack.

I reserved my sympathy, along with a degree of respect, for the lesson horses. They numbered at least half a dozen and did their job with patience and grace. And, I could only guess, a tinge of resignation. I didn't know their individual stories, but I saw each of them accept the many different riders, doing their damndest to interpret the mixed signals they were given. Kicks and yanks and plops atop.

Respect indeed for their fortitude. Envy? No. I'd experienced that similar revolving door of riders, and it wasn't for me. Not that it's really for any horse, but if a stranger were to enter my stall, saddle me up, and lead me to the arena, I dare say, they'd be in for an altogether different kind of ride. As a prey animal, I also disliked and was prone to flinching when strange little faces suddenly popped up outside my stall. Once, a young girl went so far as to grab my halter, slide open my door, and begin to chase me down before Trainer Lady caught sight and belted out, "No! Not that one! I said the chestnut with the white blaze."

That kid was lucky not to have gotten sideswiped into a stall wall, and thankfully, there'd been no further near disasters . . . to date. Most often, when newbies came to the barn, they paused at Ole's stall. I could hear them oohing and aahing. No doubt for the fact he was such a tall, dark, and handsome horse, but also because there was a sense of recognition.

"Oh, it's a Friesian!" *Good guess!* "They're from Denmark, you know." *Try again!*

As the breed experts would continue down the aisle, they'd either pass right by me without a second glance or point and proclaim, "Arabian!"

Me, with the convex profile of a Roman god, an Arabian? Not even Veiga-ly.

Nothing against Arabians, I wanted to tell them, but Arabians don't fight bulls. Could someone please set the record straight?! And suddenly, someone did.

"Nope, not an Arabian."

I was standing in the crossties, the bitter smell of burnt hoof filling my nose as a cloud of white smoke engulfed me. Beneath me, the farrier moved quickly but with practiced ease.

"Then what is he?" asked the skeptical pro.

Pivoting toward his anvil, the farrier proceeded to deliver a few sharp clanks before plunging a still-red-hot shoe into a water bucket. It hissed and bubbled like a mini hot spring before he looked back and over to the pro.

"That there is a Lusitano."

He pointed his tongs toward me and then toward Erin. "Isn't that right?"

I'd been standing at Arty's side, silent, wishing for the little know-it-all to go away when another child whipped around the corner, one arm outstretched and pointing at Arty, "Araaaaabian!"

"Slow down!" I scolded. "Spook a horse, and you could end up hurt!"

The know-it-all smiled and, ditching the conversation, turned to catch up with the other little brat.

My farrier shook his head. "Kids. What do they know?"

"More like, what do they hear? I've told both of them he's not an Arabian. Why do I even care?"

"You care because he's not an Arabian. He's a bullfighter."

I pawed at the ground. *Yes! I am a bullfighter.*

"See, he knows what I'm talking about." Closing the door on the roaring orange fire of his forge, he continued, "It's in his blood, his DNA. His type was born for the fight. Incredible athletes. Super brave."

"I didn't know you were such a fan of Lusitanos," Erin said.

"How could I not be? You know, I've seen them in the ring."

"The ring?"

"Yeah, the ring. The bull ring."

"Stop it! Where? When?"

"Mexico."

I pawed again, as if to say, *Go on. Tell me more.* Besides Mother telling me the story of my grandsire's fame, I'd heard very little about the bullfight. And I'd never met anyone willing to share a firsthand account. My ears pitched forward. I wanted to catch every word, every detail he might reveal. I prayed Trainer Lady was not about to start a lesson.

"I want to know everything," I said.

Besides my dad, who'd seen a bullfight in Mexico when he was stationed at Fort Huachuca, Arizona, in the sixties, I'd not known many people who'd been to one. My dad said he was told it was Portuguese-style fighting, and the main event was a big white horse like Arty, who moved at just the right angles so the bull would narrowly miss him. At the end, the horse and bull faced eye to eye for the final thrust of the sword.

"Like, are they just gruesome?" I probed. "Horrifying? Or . . ."

"They're a mixed bag. That's for sure," my farrier said.

"Like awful, but oddly riveting? Or even beautiful in some strange way?" Immediately, I felt I'd misspoken and so tried to explain. "I mean, *beautiful* is the wrong word because it's impossible to ignore the abuse of the bulls and even the horses at times."

"Yeah, I once saw a horse gored."

A horse gored? Say it ain't so.

"Okay, maybe I don't want to hear more," Erin said.

Maybe I agree.

"It's okay. He lived."

Phew.

"But maybe that's just it. He could have died," she said. "Everyone in that ring walks or dances or whatever you want to call it along that fine line. Stupid humans by choice. Brave horses and bulls, well . . ."

"Like I said, for the Lusitanos, it's in their blood."

"And then, there is blood."

"Yes, there is blood."

"And still, the skill of the riders and horses fascinates me."

"It's a spectacle," he said. "No doubt about that."

"That's a good word," I agreed. "People love spectacles. Like, was the bull goring a horse your most vivid memory?"

"Actually, when I hear *bullfight*, the first thing that comes to my mind is the smells."

"The smells?" Now he was talking my language.

"Yup, first thing," he said. "There was always this mixture of animal sweat and dirt and . . . adrenaline. Adrenaline not just from the horse and bull and rider, but from the crowd. Probably most of all the crowd."

"What the heck does adrenaline smell like?" I was desperate

to know what he meant, how he would describe it. He didn't let me down.

"Imagine fear and anxiety and excitement all mixed together. It flowed from one end of the arena to the other like a wave. No, like *the* wave. And then of course, the smells from the concessions. Like at a baseball game, the food vendors walked around, hawking their 'fares.' Pistachios. Corn nuts. Cerveza."

More memories spilled out. He said he'd spent his childhood, back in the seventies, in the border city of Tijuana, Mexico. His family bought season tickets to the bullfights like an American family might buy tickets to football games. It was a tradition, a time for them to all go out together, be entertained, get swept up in the thrill and excitement of the spectacle.

"I'll never forget the year we finally got seats on the shady side of the arena," he said. "It was the moment I knew we'd arrived."

"Seats in the shade," Erin echoed. "That's pretty cool. Pun not intended, but now, I wish it had been."

"My father would have loved to tell you all about the fights. He knew the history, the bullfighters, the horses. Bullfighting horses have to go through an extremely rigorous selection process, and my father used to say they needed to be more than athletic and brave. To be the best, they had to have a sixth sense about the bull, a sort of telepathy."

"Maybe they did."

"Maybe. Maybe not. I don't know. But it was a different time. Strange how long ago and yet, give me a second to think about it, and I'm right back in that stadium."

He spoke of the hum of the crowd and how it grew in intensity as the day progressed and perhaps as more cervezas were consumed. The loud marching bands played different music for each stage of the fight. In fact, each song represented a different facet of the fight.

"So, you enjoyed it?" Erin asked.

"I did. Very much." He paused. "Until the day I saw a very bad fight. I was probably fifteen, and the rider was terrible. There was no artistry. No skill. No care. The fight was unwatchable. Just butchery."

"Oh, God."

"Yeah. I mean, I'd been going for years. I'd admired other riders, those my father knew and respected. And their horses, they were magnificent. But that day, when I saw that bull tortured, I was done. I never went again."

Is this the other side of the fight Mother never had a chance to tell me about? The bulls are tortured?

"Makes me think of this French folk song, 'La Corrida,'" I said. "Such a beautiful but sad song."

Back in 1994, a friend from grad school introduced me to the songwriter Francis Cabrel and his album *Samedi soir sur la terre*. Of all its evocative songs, "La corrida" had been my favorite by far. But never could I have predicted I'd be standing telling a farrier about it while he hammered shoes onto my "bullfighting" horse.

"Don't know it," he said.

"It's told from the bull's perspective. And after the song opens . . . first, with these haunting melancholic strings and then a single, exaggerated guitar strum, we find him, the bull, waiting in a dark room. He can't see anything, but he can hear loud laughing and singing as someone leads him down a corridor and right before they thrust him into the bright light of day. That's when he sees this massive crowd and hears, as you said, marching bands. At first, he's confused and thinking he just has to defend himself, but after the door closes behind him and he sees there's no way out, he begins to understand and asks the question, 'Is this world serious?'"

"Good question."

"Yeah. Right?" I said. "And then there's this beautiful line where he remembers the prairies of Andalusia, surrounded by cactus, and the moment when he chooses to fight this bunch of puppets until finally, their blows level him. Then, when his head hits the sand, he says, 'Isn't it crazy how this could feel good?'"

"The world is crazy."

"I wish there could be a bullfight without a bull. Or maybe, not a fight. I have no idea what I'm saying."

Yes, what are you saying? A bullfight without a bull?

"The good thing about Lusitanos," the farrier said, "is they don't need to fight bulls."

Wait! What happened to 'It's in my blood, my DNA'? I stepped forward, stretching the crossties to their limit.

"I think he took offense to that," Erin said.

"What I meant was, they don't have to fight bulls because they can do anything. They've got the mind, the conformation, the sensitivity to excel at any discipline."

Hard to argue with that.

"I guess the question is, what do you want to do with him?" he asked.

"Well, we're obviously not going to fight bulls. So, maybe classical dressage. If I could find the right trainer. Or working equitation. If I could find any trainer. I'm not quite sure."

"Too bad you can't just ask him." The farrier pointed to me with his rasp.

"Right?" she agreed.

I'm standing right here, constantly telling you things. All you have to do is listen.

53

2014: Duvall, Washington

Finding a trainer who understood Lusitanos had become more than a difficult task; it had become a near impossible one. With so few Lusos in the world, not many people had met—let alone trained—one. They were an unknown quantity, and people, it seems, prefer the familiar. It brings them a sense of comfort and perhaps control. That was issue number one.

Issue two was most people I'd been meeting had a singular drive: to compete. And more so, to win. They were fueled by the pomp and circumstance of shows, points, blue ribbons, and engraved championship trophies, none of which held any appeal for me.

Three: Few seemed to know piaffe from passage.

Four: I needed to find the right match for Arty. Almost without variance, people would mistake his intelligence, sensitivity, and even generosity for what they dubbed naughtiness. "Oh, isn't he a naughty one?"

Them's were fighting words! The phrase stung me like a hot poker, sending me into prickly word battles every time I heard it. And I heard it often. Too often.

"Naughty?" I'd ask. "What exactly makes my boy naughty? Please expound."

"You said yourself you're having trouble finding a trainer."

"That wasn't my question."

"I just meant . . ."

"Just meant what?" I would threaten.

"He's very hot."

"And?"

"Well, a hot horse has a lot of energy, sometimes too much."

"So, a lot of energy is a bad thing?"

"Well, yes, if the horse doesn't listen and takes off."

"When have you seen Arty take off?"

"Okay, not take off, but I've seen you have trouble getting him to pick up his right lead?"

"His right lead?"

"Well, it's not good he doesn't pick it up when you ask."

"It's also not naughty."

"But it gives you grief, no? That he won't pick up that lead?"

"Grief? No, it doesn't give me grief. It gives me something to work on."

"So, you're never frustrated?"

"Not with him. It's not his fault. He's trying his damndest. If anything, he's giving me an opportunity to learn something."

"If you say so."

"If I say so?"

"If you say so."

"What's the alternative? Call horses naughty and perpetuate some misbegotten notion they throw tantrums and live to disobey us?"

"Some horses do misbehave."

"They let us ride on their backs, for Christ's sake! That's a goddamn miracle. But yeah, if my horse doesn't pick up the correct canter lead every time I ask, he's misbehaving. Sure."

"You're not listening to what I'm saying."

"Because you're not making sense. What you don't seem to see is how horses try so hard to give us what we want. I mean, have you ever considered what they've given to us? And by us, I don't even mean you or me. I mean mankind."

And there it was. The mankind card. The tack that discomfited even the most stalwart of "naughty" supporters. Plus some. I quite enjoyed listening to these conversations. If I were a human, I may have grabbed a bowl of popcorn and sat back to watch the fireworks.

"These impossibly majestic, selfless creatures have carried us on their backs in so many ways," Erin would say. "Plowing our fields so we could eat; transporting us across plains, over mountains, through forests and rushing rivers so we could explore; onto battlefields, all so we could prevail while they, what? Died, badly."

At this point, some reacted with a quiet "Okay, point taken." Others gave a sardonic "Alrighty then." Once, someone loudly and disingenuously applauded before asking, "Did it take you long to write that speech?" (As Erin later said, "What a B.") Most, though, stood in silence before slowly walking away.

Since my arrival in Washington and as evidenced by her willingness to give a speech on the debt mankind owes to horses, she'd been so ready and apt to defend me, impervious, at least it seemed, to the many "known" whispers behind her back. The ones that went beyond people calling me naughty and ventured to question her competence. "She's in over her head." "Why would anyone get a wild horse like that?" "Her riding is not correct."

They reveled in finding fault and dispensing unsolicited advice. Yes, for whatever reason, the schadenfreude was strong in this barn. And baffling. As if any of the other boarders or resident trainer, for that matter, held haute école credentials and a true ability to discern, let alone judge, correct riding. Their skills were not even a vague match for those of a master. I never saw their horses sprout wings like Pegasus or a spiral horn like a carousel unicorn. Quite the contrary. Most days, all I saw was athletic potential snuffed out like a lit wick in a cold wind. A rider's ignorance of equine biomechanics or fear of self-injury prevented honest progression. So, instead of casting aspersions, I'd say the catty barn whisperers would have done better to look in the mirror and reconsider their own motives, actions, and, most of all, shortcomings.

But at that point, if I'd learned anything about people, it's that they're like water: They take the path of least resistance. It was easier to parrot another's misguided opinion and label me naughty—a horse who varied from their norm—than to spend time getting to know me. And perhaps the same held true for whips and spurs and twisted bits; they were other default mechanisms. If a horse refuses to advance, apply more pressure, increase the pain.

Erin's methodology was different. She had always shunned shortcuts and undue pressure . . . which is why it made it almost inconceivable that first she had invited this new trainer to the barn at all. A woman who was now on my back. And second, hadn't moved, hadn't spoken to intervene and advocate on my behalf. *What is happening?!*

I had stopped, unable to put another foot forward. My body trembling. My chest slick with a white lather of foam. Every crack of the whip sent me collapsing further inward. *Why can't this woman see this wasn't defiance? This isn't disobedience. This is me not understanding her language.* And the louder she wailed with whip and spur, the faster I slipped away until . . . like the bull . . . I was elsewhere. Mother's sweet scent filling my nose. Maysa's tender lyrics caressing my ears. And me asking myself, *Is this world serious?*

With every kick to his side, smack of the whip, I wanted to scream, *NO! STOP! THIS IS WRONG!* But I just stood there. Mute. Unable to move. Just like Arty.

"He literally won't move," the new trainer yelled.

Steam from his neck and haunches enveloped her.

"That's . . . no . . . I should have . . . I don't . . ." Words finally started coming from my mouth. None of them right.

"It's like a circuit blew," she said.

More than a circuit had blown. He'd completely shut down. Gone somewhere else.

"I'm not sure how he's been trained," she continued. "I just don't get him."

I went into autopilot. I took the reins. I watched her dismount. I thanked her for her time. She had no ill intentions, but she was right about one thing. She didn't get Arty.

I lead Arty to the crossties. I untacked him. I draped a cooler over his back.

It took nearly an hour for him to be dry enough for me to curry his salt-crusted coat. When I finished, I was the only person left in the barn and I was freezing.

"I'm so sorry, Arty," she said through chattering teeth. "That was awful. I thought I could do this, but I don't know. I keep getting it wrong."

It was the first time I'd seen her defeated, and it took me aback.

"I just wish you could tell me what to do, what you want."

Since bullfighting seems out . . .

"I mean, maybe you are telling me."

. . . dinner would be nice.

"And I'm just not getting it."

I can't argue that point.

"And what if I never get it?"

The corners of her mouth turned down. Her brow furrowed. *Uh-oh.*

Before any tears could fall, I nudged her in the chest. A little harder than intended.

She stumbled sideways, knocking into a water bucket. Water splashed over its side and onto her shoes. But instead of pushing back or reprimanding me, she started to laugh.

"I fucking deserved that. And I fucking love you."

She threw her arms around my neck.

"I know what I'm going to do. And it's gonna be good," she whispered. "I promise."

54

2014: Alentejo, Portugal

I don't win contests. Like, ever. But this one. I knew I had to win. Somehow.

It had been almost a year since I'd brought Arty home, and while surfing the web one day, I came across a new Lusitano website that was having a "launching competition." The site's creators, two young Swedish women named Hanna and Andréa, had found sponsors for prizes, and if you wanted to enter, you had to answer four trivia questions and explain your "motivation" for entering.

The grand prize was a week's stay in Portugal at a beautiful hacienda, Herdade Pero Viegas, in the Alentejo region with daily riding lessons (for two) with a working equitation and dressage pro, Nuno Avelar. (No, not Brazilian Nuno.)

I did the only thing I could think to do. I had Arty write them a letter.

Dear Hanna and Andréa,

My name is Artilheiro do Vouga. I'm a nine-year-old Lusitano and I live in Washington state with my new owner, Erin. Though we've only officially been together since last October, Erin fell for me five years ago, on the first day we met.

At the time, I was living on a beautiful ranch in California. My previous owner wanted to introduce Erin to the Lusitano breed and invited her to ride several of her stallions, including me. While I mightn't have been the biggest or zippiest or most advanced, I had presence, personality, and a canter to die for. See, today, everyone calls me Arty. Back then, my nickname was Dragon. I huffed and I puffed and I strutted like I belonged in a royal court.

Erin was hooked.

Over the next several years, she came to visit as often as she could, always thrilled to try different horses, but always leaving, pointing to me, saying, "Still my favorite boy." Even when she learned I'd begun to develop some trust and anxiety issues, losing a bit of confidence under saddle, not always wanting to go forward, it didn't matter to her. She still dreamed of taking me home—only never fathomed it a real possibility. But then there come those times . . . when you put something out to the universe, the universe answers you.

Through luck, fate, generosity, timing . . . Erin and I found our way to one another—and it's for the long haul. I finally have my own devoted person. We work together every day and, to try to help me overcome some of my anxiety, we've gone back to basics. Thing is, I'm very capable of "d, e, and f," but I'd kind of forgotten how to do "a, b, and c." The goal is a partnership, which Erin hopes to achieve through classical dressage, long chats in my paddock and pasture, and lots and lots of carrots and kisses.

I know not everyone who enters this contest may have the good fortune, as she does, to work every day with a handsome (ex) stud like myself, but I do hope you'll still please consider her for the win.

Erin just wants to do right by me. She realizes we Lusitanos are highly intelligent, talented, emotional, and complex, and she has so much to learn to be a better owner and rider. The opportunity this contest presents to work with professionals who have a deep knowledge of the breed, its strengths, its idiosyncrasies, could provide the answers we need for our future progress.

Muito obrigado por sua consideração.

When Hanna and Andréa emailed to let me know I'd won, they told me I had one year to book my trip. So, once again, I did the only thing I could think to do. I called my best friend, Heather (a.k.a. Bubbles). Yeah, I may have killed her Sour Cherry buzz, but she's since thanked me for that *favor*, time and again.

"I need a partner in crime for a trip to Portugal," I said. "You in?"

I won the contest in August. We landed in Portugal a month later. We figured it would be a cool experience. We were wrong. It was a once-in-a-lifetime experience. And one that never would have happened had it not been for a horse. A horse who insisted on writing that letter. Because only he could. It wasn't the first time I found myself trying to see the world through Arty's eyes, or imagining I could speak his language, but the fact is, that letter planted a seed, which slowly (but often, not surely) grew into this book.

Our flight landed at Lisbon airport in the early morning, and Nuno picked us up, all matter of fact and hustle, hustle. He'd left his car in the pickup lane—along with his girlfriend, Carolin—and was keen on making a speedy exit.

"It is one and one half hours to the Alentejo. Are you hungry?" he said as he heaved our overstuffed suitcases into the car's trunk. Before waiting for a reply, he added, "We stop for donuts."

I don't have much of a sweet tooth, but when in Portugal . . . We stopped at a strange little rest-stop bakery, where I ordered *pastéis de nata*, vanilla custard tarts, and a much-needed coffee. Back on the road, it wasn't long before the landscape changed. Urban became rural. Dense forests lined our path. And tree after tree began appearing in various states of deshabille. Midsections stripped to their red cores and spray-painted with a single white number from one to nine. Branches as gnarled and gangly as arthritic fingers offered subtle shade but not a modicum of modesty.

"They are cork trees," Nuno said, before explaining that a tree can be harvested every nine years, and the number represented the last year it had been harvested. Because cork is a renewable resource, and healthy trees can produce cork for hundreds of years, he added that inheriting a cork farm was a bit like winning the lottery. And I supposed, opting for annuity payments.

"I wish I had a cork farm," he said.

"Me, too," I said. "Me, too."

In addition to donuts and easy money, we talked about why Heather and I had wanted to come to Portugal. I offered a condensed version of how easy it had been to fall in love with Arty but how difficult it had been to find a trainer who knew enough about Lusitanos to help me better understand and work with him.

"I'm afraid of failing him," I admitted. "And though Arty may have been born in Brazil, his roots run deep here. I'd guess even deeper than those of the cork trees."

Not one for sentimentality or excuses, Nuno said we would work on many things that week, and he would pair us with the horses he believed could teach us the most. "Don't worry. You will learn much."

The regular schedule would be breakfast, a morning training session, lunch, an afternoon training session, and finally, dinner. Both lunch and dinner would be taken in the main *Ponderosa*–meets–*Downton Abbey*–style dining room with the ranch's matriarch and her son. The place had been in their family since the nineteenth century, and I really wished I'd learned to say more in Portuguese than *bom dia* (good morning) and *obrigado* (thank you).

After arriving at the ranch that first day, Nuno led us into the grand white manor house and down a long dark tiled hallway to our room. The opening verse of "Hotel California" entered my head and didn't leave for the duration of our stay. It wasn't that I felt trapped but, rather, transported.

"Please, unpack," Nuno told us. "I am going to the barn. Change and meet me there in one hour."

"To ride?" I was surprised.

"Yes, to ride," he said. "You are here to learn, no?"

He was right and I should have been elated but my nerves and jet lag were getting the best of me. I'd been hoping for a nap before an early dinner, not to be immediately put on a horse. But duh. This was not a vacation.

For better or worse, we closed our eyes for fifteen minutes before splashing water on our faces, donning our trousers and boots, and heading out into what had become a windy afternoon. On the short walk from the main house to the barn, we passed peacocks out for a stroll, stallions sticking their heads out from barn windows, and mares grazing in nearby fields with young foals. We made a conscious effort to take deep breaths and encouraged one another by saying, "This is going to be fun." Followed quickly by, "Right?"

Heather had not been on a horse since selling hers a few years earlier, and though I rode on a daily basis, I worried Nuno would see my every fault and realize I didn't deserve Arty. Oh, the awful things we tell ourselves.

The covered arena was gorgeous. As were the two gray Lusitanos in the crossties when we arrived. Nuno introduced us to the horses, Ulysses and Xilene, showed us the tack room, and told us to grab boots for the horses' legs.

"Heather, you will ride Ulysses." He pointed to the girthier of the two horses. "Erin, you will ride Xilene. He is very sensitive, but you like sensitive, no?"

Uh, again, had I said that?

Nuno, we quickly learned, liked to crack jokes, but he also had a knack for pairing riders and horses. That afternoon, he worked with us to figure out the horses' buttons, and which ones to push when and how much. And not to say all of the horses I went on to ride during our stay weren't incredible "teachers" in their own right, but Xilene became my favorite. Beautiful and sensitive, he challenged me to focus, feel, trust, all while stealing a little piece of my heart.

The first time I cantered him, Nuno yelled, "Slower!"

I sat a little taller, gave a gentle squeeze on the reins, and Xilene slowed right up. I thought, *Wow, cool, I found the button* . . . until Nuno yelled again, "No. Slower!"

I was thinking, *If I slow down anymore, I'm going to come to a grinding halt.* But Xilene rose (or slowed) to the occasion. And voilà! Just like that, I was riding a carousel pony. I could have cried. And, in fact, did many times throughout the week, including the first night at dinner (always three courses) when Nuno told me Xilene had been a test.

"He has had some traumas. He needs a rider with a light touch who does not overreact. You did well today."

Admittedly, I'm a super sap, but that horse brought me to tears for all the right reasons. I still get a little choked up thinking about him and what Nuno taught me.

By the end of the week, I was feeling my way in and out of

pirouettes on Xilene and doing two-time tempi changes on Nuno's prized stallion, Bogota, learning where to put the pieces of my body and when to ask and when to just follow the horse. Slow is golden, and less is more.

While long rides, lingering meals, and opportunities to watch Nuno train the horses were more than enough to fill our days, there were also plenty of amazing places to explore nearby.

One morning, Nuno took us on a field trip to Coudelaria de Alter Real. It is Portugal's royal stud farm, founded by Portuguese King João V in 1748 and home to the line of stunning bay Alter Real Lusitanos used by the Portuguese School of Equestrian Art. We walked its palatial grounds, marveling at the impressive riding rings, row upon row of picturesque, vaulted stalls, and, above all, the magnificent horses.

Another afternoon, Carolin drove us to a nearby lake, Barragem de Maranhão, where a charming waterside taverna offered the perfect spot to enjoy cold beers, a friendly feline, and a beautiful sunset after a long day in the saddle.

Five days into our trip, two Finnish women arrived at the ranch. There are three things I remember most about them.

One.

They were *very* serious, and after watching one of our lessons, one of them asked us why we smile and laugh so much while riding.

"Because it's fun," I said. "You don't smile when you ride?"

"No, it is not part of our culture."

"Well, you're a beautiful woman and a fabulous rider, maybe you should try it. The culture police won't arrest you here. Plus, the horse will feel it."

Two.

Because the other woman had partial paralysis in one leg, Nuno decided to pair her with Xilene. I understood, but when she started to complain about him after only one ride, I couldn't hold my tongue. Her nitpicking and desire to fault-find reminded me too much of those who consistently labeled Arty "naughty."

I set my dinner glass down hard enough on the table for water to splash over its edge. "Xilene is my favorite horse here. So talented, so kind. That's too bad you didn't have a better ride, but have you considered your role in that?"

Nuno backed me up, and whether it was this woman's competitive nature or not, the following evening, she raved about Xilene. I hate to admit it, but it also irritated me, and the next morning, I asked Nuno for a favor.

"I know she'd prefer to ride him today. *Now* that she sees how great he is. But it's my last ride and I love him more."

Without hesitation, Nuno said, "He's all yours."

Three.

While watching *Jaws* in the guest living room after dinner one night, one of the women got up, walked past me, and at point-blank range let loose a savage fart. It took me a minute (or a day) to regain my composure, but when I did, I thought, *How interesting.* Smiling while riding is frowned about, but practically shitting in a stranger's face, all good. No *anteeksi* required.

I mention the Finns not to bash them but because they taught me something, too. No matter how much we think we know, there's always more to learn, and maybe, just maybe, I had something to offer as well. The next day, the farting Finn smiled and laughed (and who knows? maybe even passed a little gas) during her lesson. She was stunning.

55

2014, Duvall, Washington

Following the unforgettable but regrettable "whip happy" trainer experience and the trip to Portugal, Erin had "very few shits left to give" about what other people thought. She took her act solo, inviting no new trainers to the barn and putting unsolicited advice where it belonged—in the "thanks, but no thanks" suggestion box. A.k.a. where the sun don't shine.

She tried hard; I'll give her that. She showed up. She sat in the saddle. She never pushed me too hard or too long. She rewarded generously and often. But still, it wasn't all sugar cubes and alfalfa.

An exemplar of misinformed *légèreté*, she sometimes rode with too loose a rein, a practice that belied a couple of simple truths. Looseness does not equal lightness, and lightness does not begin and end in the mouth. When ridden, a horse wants connection. And direction. Much like a kite, we need a tether and skilled pilot to stay afloat. If properly guided, we will do more than follow. We will dance.

I was not opposed to having Erin as a dance partner. Ever so slowly, I was growing more fond of her. The sound of her car had become a harbinger of treats, scratches, and kind words, all of which prompted me to kick at my stall door, demanding attention and imploring her to hurry along past Q and Ole.

Nothing against those two. They were decent cats, and not half bad for stepbrothers.

Over the summer and into fall, the three of us had spent the majority of our days turned out in adjacent pastures. They in theirs; I in mine, solo style. We mostly grazed in silence but for the swish of tails fending off niggling flies and mosquitoes. Occasionally, we teased one another with bared teeth and warning kicks on either side of the fence, which, like the barn, was showing its age, so worn that even a sideways glance could have split and leveled its boards. Repairs were a near-daily necessity, and truly, the only thing keeping us apart was inertia.

Unlike Napoleon, Q and Ole weren't much into or up on gossip. Maybe a gripe here and there about a new and funky batch of hay or an obnoxiously loud lesson, but otherwise, they simply enjoyed trying to get my goat by saying how Friesians were cooler than Lusitanos or telling me the woes of being black horses in California.

"We're part draft. That automatically makes us cooler!"

"We'll take the rain and snow over that brutal southern sun!"

I told them if they hadn't been to Brazil, they didn't know heat, but I also had to agree with them on one thing: the snow.

The first time I saw it, falling light and soft as goose down, it was a revelation. It covered the mud and crud in a sparkling white quilt and brought an unexpected tranquility. Besides the barn hand, who complained of it making stalls harder to muck, and Trainer Lady, who complained it hurt her business—few students dared drive in the stuff—not a single horse protested. No lessons, no problem.

On one of those quiet post-snowstorm mornings, during my second Washington winter, Erin arrived extra early. The sun had risen, bright and strong, and so, too, had the mercury. Just enough. Thick icicles dripped like hungry fangs from the gutters above the exit to my run.

"Jesus," Erin said. "These things could poke an eye out."

She took a broom and knocked them down. She checked my water buckets to be sure they hadn't frozen over. She removed my blanket only to put it right back on again after a quick brush. Yet, no matter the sun, brooming, grooming, and general fussing about, she shivered as if unable to shake a bad feeling. Something was afoot.

Or someone.

Erin had moved me to the crossties and was picking my hooves when I heard the muffled crunch of tires followed by the *ca-thunk* of a closing car door. Uneasy, I jerked my leg from her hand and began to prance and sway.

"Easy, buddy, easy."

At the barn's entrance, I saw what I thought was a small Christmas tree floating our way. I only realized my mistake when the figure crossed into a ray of sunlight. This was no holiday conifer but an elflike woman, enveloped and disguised by a floor-length green puffer coat and equally oversize pom-pommed wool hat. I could not see legs but assumed she had them, as what I did see were a pair of paddock boots. Notably, without spurs attached. *Good.*

Unlike so many other visitors, her first words were not "What is he?" or "What level is he?" Her first words were a compliment.

"Well, would you look at that profile! A perfect 10 of a Roman nose if I've ever seen one."

I liked her immediately. I hoped Arty did, too.

"Isn't it just?" I extended a gloved hand to shake her mittened one. "Pleasure to meet you, Carol. I hope you didn't have any trouble driving down."

"Snow tires and all-wheel drive. All good. Pleasure to meet you and"—she said, turning to Arty—"this magnificent boy, whom I take to be the famous Arty."

Magnificent? Famous? Oh, Christmas Carol, what have you got up those long sleeves of yours?

She peered at me through round wire-rimmed glasses, tilting her head right, then left, as if a director contemplating a scene.

"With that square frame and regal appearance, he would have fit right in at La Grande Écurie of Versailles, dancing with the best of King Louis XIV's mounts."

"That's too weird," Erin said. "First time I saw him, I thought of the Sun King, too. Could you imagine?"

I think she just did.

"And those classic almond eyes. So expressive, so curious."

Yes, curious to know what is happening here. Is this woman for real? Is this flattery to be trusted? Or is she just here to ruin my peaceful snow day?

"Tell me about him. How did you end up with a Lusitano? And more importantly, this Lusitano?" she asked.

Finding Carol was a byproduct of my trip to Portugal. One connection led to another, and I'd been amazed to learn of a classical dressage trainer who lived nearby *and* knew Lusitanos. I had crossed my fingers, hoping for the best, but was also super anxious. And then, from word one, she brought such a lovely, kind energy I thought of how the resident quidnunc could learn a thing or two from her. Carol showed a genuine curiosity. Not judginess.

"Good questions," I said. "Man, where to start . . ."

I offered a condensed version of the story of me and Arty. The love at first sight. Arty not thriving with a rotating roster of riders. The surprise and generous offer to buy him. My YOLO decision to go for it.

I also told her about the clinic with the Brazilian. The attempts to find a local trainer. And maybe a bit too much about my doubts, fears, and sleepless nights wondering, *Am I up to the task?*

"He's so different from any horse I've experienced," I said. "More excitable, more animated."

"More generous?" Carol asked.

"Yes! Exactly. I mean, not to say my other horses aren't. I'll introduce you to Ole and Q later. They're amazing and try very hard, but with Arty, it's like he doesn't know he doesn't have to do so much. He takes it to eleven. Every time. Especially with the canter. At that first clinic, I was told, 'Don't canter him for three months. Work on trot.' So, I did. But then after three months, I was like, well, now what? I can't say anything really changed in that time."

"What happens when you ask him to canter?"

"Total box of chocolates."

"Chocolates?"

"You know, Forrest Gump, never know what you're gonna get."

"Aha."

"Some days, he'll launch into this crazy big forward canter," I tried to explain, "but it always starts with him doing this weird thing with his back legs. Like he's the Road Runner, gearing up to take off. Then he's off like a shot, off to deliver a message to the king!"

"I see."

"Other times, he'll kind of canter in place, doing this up, up, and *not* away thing. Or the worst is when he'll just shut down and not move. I don't know if I'm supposed to push, not push. He's not being bad . . ."

"No, of course not."

"It's more like he's lost, and I don't know how to help. Like I'm missing some essential cue and making everything worse. I'm so afraid I'm confusing him and letting him down and making him sad."

She took a quick look at Arty and stopped me from going down that rabbit hole of self-doubt by saying, "He doesn't look sad to me. And you're not letting him down."

"How can you be so sure?"

"Because you're asking for help and admitting you don't know it all, which, by the way, none of us do. But if I had to guess, I'd say maybe he's just a bit skeptical, but also, look at how attentive he is. He's tuned into every word we're saying."

She wasn't wrong there.

"Here's the thing about horses. Life with them is a journey, not a destination. There will be ups. There will be downs. When you start to teach them a new exercise, a new trick, a new anything, as they begin to master that, something else may start to fall apart a bit. That's okay. Progress doesn't happen in a straight line. It's not all meant to come together at once."

"So, you're saying this is normal?"

"Well, I'd never call anything about a Lusitano normal," she smirked. "What I'm saying is if you get too caught up with progress, progress, progress, you'll snub the process. And if you snub the process, you're not only missing the point, but you might be missing out on some incredible moments. Even if they don't include a perfect canter every time. But if you trust the process and follow it daily, the results will come."

"I don't think I have a clue what this process is," Erin said. "Because I'd take a normal canter any day."

"Well, it can be different for every horse, but I think it should always include consistency, patience, and gratitude for every effort."

"Like the Baucher way? Deliberate, calm, and kind training."

"Yes, I believe elements of Baucher's Second Method are essential. But to be clear, I also don't believe in strictly following a singular philosophy or methodology. Our knowledge of horses is constantly evolving. So we try different things, see what works, what doesn't, and always look to the horse to tell us what's needed."

"I'm in. Where do we start?"

"How about with your normal routine. Show me what you usually do."

Erin hurried to finish grooming and tacking me. Her eager energy put me a bit on edge, and as she led me to the arena, I reached over to nip her arm.

Having watched from behind, Christmas Carol asked, "Does he do that a lot?"

"The nipping? Maybe, sometimes. Is it terrible?"

I really only caught a little piece of jacket.

"No, not terrible."

See. Minor infraction.

"I mean, is it bad I don't really do anything about it?" Erin asked.

"Well, it's a far cry better than smacking him in the face. Now that wouldn't be good."

Not good at all!

"But," Christmas Carol continued, "I wouldn't ignore it altogether. He's trying to tell you something."

"Like he hates me?"

I don't hate you.

"I think it's more like a child tugging at his mother's sleeve, seeking attention or reassurance. He's nervous and wants to be sure you're there for him."

Maybe.

"You've only had him a little over a year now, right?"

I nodded.

"It takes a year, sometimes two, for a horse to adjust to a new home, especially if he's been moved around a lot. Think about it. They don't know what's happening. They've had no choice in the matter. It's extremely stressful for them, and I wouldn't doubt he's waiting for the other shoe to fall."

"Other shoe?"

"He may not yet trust this is home. That you're his person. For him, a trailer could arrive at any moment and—"

When Carol said this, it hit me. I knew exactly what she meant. As an army brat, I'd felt this on many different levels. There were times, especially in high school but also beyond, when I simply lost faith, gave up, stopped caring or wanting to care for anything or anybody. On top of that, there had been a sense of not belonging, not fitting in, all combined with an impulse to defy, resist, rebel.

Before she could say another word, I interrupted her. "I would never sell him! God forbid, not unless I truly thought it was in his best interest."

My best interest?

"The two of you will be fine. I only point that out because it's an opportunity to communicate with him. When he nips, you don't have to 'take it.' Give him a little pinch on the neck to say, 'Hey, quit that.' It won't scare him or make him head shy, but it will grab his attention."

I was tempted to nip Christmas Carol, too, but she was slightly out of reach. Erin walked on and into the arena to demonstrate our usual routine.

"Since horses take in different information with each eye, as, duh, I'm sure you don't need to be told," Erin said, "I always start by hand walking him around the arena, once in each direction. That way, he can see if there's anything new or different or scary."

"Good idea," Christmas Carol said.

"But honestly, he's so not spooky."

"He's brave. A true Lusitano."

"Yes. And, well, after we've done that, I usually get up. I mean, sometimes I'll longe him, but . . ."

"That's fine. Let's see how he goes."

And here we go.

Once mounted, Erin walked me around the arena a couple more times before asking for a trot. The squeeze of her legs sent my neck and knees high in the air, and before we made it once around a twenty-meter circle, Christmas Carol interjected.

"I see he's rushing the trot, not keeping an even tempo. But I also see you are rising very high and sitting very deep into the saddle as you post. Let's try this. As you post, imagine a raw egg in the saddle you don't want to crack. No need to post very high, and when you sit, it's light and delicate as opposed to deep and heavy onto his back."

When Erin abided her instruction, I felt the difference immediately. My back had room to rise, and, less constrained, I slowed my pace and lowered my neck. Not quite stretching out and seeking contact with the bit, but also not avoiding it altogether.

"Does that feel better?"

"Yes, definitely."

A few strides later, I popped my neck up again.

"No problem. That's totally normal," Christmas Carol said. "He's going to go up and down as he gets used to this. Just keep sitting lightly, and remember, riding is not a static exercise. It's about constant adjustment. And less is more when it comes to helping him with his balance."

"Understood. Less is more. Less is more," Erin repeated.

"And now, deep breath, and see if you can gently bring him back to the walk."

Downshifting wasn't the easiest for me. Once I got going, I didn't want to walk, and I most certainly didn't want someone pulling or clinging to my mouth. I rooted the reins from Erin's hands, and she immediately pulled them back.

"Let go there," Christmas Carol said. "When he roots, give him the reins, give him his head."

"I thought I wasn't supposed to let him root."

"Who told you that?"

"The world."

"Just like the nip, if he's rooting, he's telling you something. His neck and head are his balance. If you're to gain his trust, because it's trust over obedience, you need to show him he'll have his head when he needs it. It's part of the process."

"Ah, the process."

"I promise, if you do this now, he will stop rooting much faster than if you continue to pull back on the reins."

"Got it," Erin said.

She let the reins loose to the buckle. I lowered my head to the ground and let out a deep breath.

"That's nice," Christmas Carol said. She came over to pat my neck, and I realized the urge to nip her had faded. "I have some other ideas for you, too, Mr. Arty."

She explained how the *world* often misinterprets a horse's actions, labeling things like nipping, rooting, you name it, as bad behavior when, really, they are anything but. Most often, if a horse is seen as not doing what someone wants, it's not because the horse doesn't want to. It's because he's scared. And if he's "misbehaving" under saddle, it's likely he's just trying to save himself from falling down.

"Signs a horse is out of balance," Carol said, "can be tension in the reins, bracing in the poll, speeding up, motorcycling around a turn, drifting out, breaking from one gait to another. Our position in the saddle isn't important because it's pretty. It's important because it's what will help a horse keep its balance. Think about it this way. What's the difference between training a dog and training a horse?"

"Well, we don't ride dogs," I suggested.

"Exactly. With dogs, we train their brains. With horses, we have to train their brains *and* their bodies. And they have the grace to let us try."

Something about her felt so familiar.

"I'm guessing you don't want to see his canter?" Erin joked.

"No, no. No need to canter today. I can imagine," she said. "I'm thinking we work on some relaxation exercises. Horses should be moving with relaxed muscles, and I can see he's very animated and carries a lot of tension in his back and neck. But really, all tension starts in the jaw. So, until he learns to release his jaw, he won't ever release the poll. And without a supple poll, there can't be a soft and supple neck and back."

With Erin still in the saddle, Christmas Carol stood in front of us and delicately lifted both sides of the bit with her hands. When I opened my mouth, she immediately released the bit.

"These are called jaw flexions, and the objective is to get him to open his mouth and chew on the bit when I ask. And only when I ask."

I already tended to champ on the bit when not asked, so at first, it was hard to calm down and open my mouth only when she moved the bit. But I figured it out.

"See? Look how fast he's gotten it. A very quick study."

After finishing flexions that encouraged me to stretch forward and down and left and right, Christmas Carol suggested some horse yoga.

"You want me to do yoga on him?"

"No, not that. It's for him. Yoga for the horse. To get him to stretch and relax even more," she said. "Do you know how to ride shoulder-in, counter shoulder-in, renvers, and travers?"

"Yes, I believe so."

"Okay, I'm going to have you start with shoulder-in to renvers on the circle. These two exercises will help with straightness. After that, we'll move to counter shoulder-in and travers, which help with collection."

Still mounted, Erin led me onto a twenty-meter circle to the left, abruptly putting me into a shoulder-in position.

"Remember, this is yoga," Christmas Carol said. "And no one does yoga fast. So, take your time."

Using her outside rein, Erin asked me to move my shoulders closer to the center of the circle such that I was moving on three tracks and crossing my back left leg over my back right leg. I wavered here and there, swinging my haunches too far out or collapsing my shoulders too far in, but for the most part, I maintained a correct position.

"Nicely done. When he's going well like that, try to coast. Let him carry himself, even if it's only for a step or two."

We'd made it around a couple of counterclockwise circles when Christmas Carol said, "Now gently ease him into renvers."

Erin pulled my head too quickly to the outside of the circle and without supporting my hind end with her leg. I veered sharply left, falling into the circle.

"No problem," Christmas Carol reassured Erin. "He's a sensitive boy. So think of doing everything in millimeters. Gently. Slowly. The more you rush, the less you'll accomplish. Slow and steady. And remember, in shoulder-in and renvers, your weight is where?"

"I've been trying to sit square in the saddle. Is that not right?"

Christmas Carol explained that horses will follow the rider's weight and asked Erin to think of the saddle as having four quadrants.

"In shoulder-in and renvers, you will adjust your weight slightly toward the outside front quadrant to help the horse continue moving around the circle without falling into it. It may seem counterintuitive, but try it. When we get to travers, which is the basis for pirouette, you will want to shift your weight more to the inside back, as if it's the pivot point."

Say what?

"Sorry, my brain isn't computing. Do you think . . . I mean, could you show me from the saddle? I'm a much more visual learner."

"Sure. No problem," Christmas Carol said.

Nothing seemed to be a problem for her. And I liked that she never raised her voice. She took off her long sleeping bag of a coat and handed it to Erin before taking the reins.

"You look cold," she said to Erin, "and it's very warm."

Erin didn't hesitate to put it on over her jacket.

In the saddle, Christmas Carol guided me through the four movements with simple shifts in weight and leg position. Her voice was calm and encouraging. "So smart," she said, again and again. "He's like riding a unicycle on a tightrope. You have to be so precise in how you sit and what you ask. Again, adjustments are by the millimeter. And it's about relaxation. Until he's relaxed, there's no point in asking for more. Relaxation must always come first."

She also broke down every exercise for Erin. For example, she explained that renvers on a left circle would be useful in correcting my left half pass, as the movement would help shift weight to my right side and mobilize my haunches. She saw that travers left was trickier for me; I would rush and try to escape by swinging my haunches right.

"You could do these exercises for hours. They aren't physically strenuous. Just remember to always take lots of breaks to let him walk and stretch out his neck and back. If you haven't noticed, he's starting to walk much straighter than when you first started today."

"Little by little," Erin said.

"Exactly! You don't need to cram in every gait, every exercise every day. Be thoughtful. Listen to what the horse is telling you each day. Classical dressage is a lot like making beautiful music. If you were to sit down at a piano and play all the notes at the same time, all you'd get is noise. It's the space between the notes that allows the melody to emerge. It's the space between your aids that allows the horse to respond, and dance.

"And of course, as I say that," Christmas Carol added, "I have one more thing I think would be good to try today. It's called the counted walk, and the reason I want to show you today is because I think he'll be very good at it, which is another important thing to remember. If you're ever doing anything and your horse seems to get worried or frantic, always go back to something you know he does well. Arty is a proud horse and it will help build his confidence. And yours. So why don't you get back up in the saddle."

With Erin once again on my back, Christmas Carol told her, "With the counted walk, the idea is to slow down so it feels you could stop him with one of his feet still hanging in the air. Think about your core more than your seat. Sit up tall, breathe in. Hands higher to keep his neck high, but not so high it hollows his back."

Erin gave a slight squeeze with both legs, and I began to walk, at first with trepidation, hesitation, but then more so with deliberation, as if in slow motion.

"Yes, there you go," Christmas Carol said. "And always keep your arms and hands moving, even if minimally, with his neck until . . . ever . . . so . . . slowly . . . you begin to feel the diagonal beat of the trot. And, yes! There it is! You just went from the counted walk to the piaffe."

Erin was mesmerized. "This is so cool."

Heck, I was mesmerized. And feeling more relaxed than ever. Perhaps I'd judged Christmas Carol too quickly. Once again, she told me how smart I was and called me a lamb as I stretched my head around to take a treat from Erin's hand. For a moment, I felt very safe and very proud . . . and that's when it hit me.

That elusive sense of familiarity. The words she had chosen. Generous. Brave. Proud. It was Mother. She reminded me of Mother.

56

2015: Duvall, Washington

Stories of the centaur go back millennia. In Greek mythology, these half-man, half-horse creatures were said to live in the lawless land of Thessaly. They hunted bulls in the forest for sustenance and, sadly, also let their weakness for wine aggravate an innate propensity for violence. Even the smell of it riled them. At their core, these creatures were but unruly savages with a serious drinking problem. Not exactly the lot you'd want to be associated with. For that reason alone, I preferred the story Christmas Carol told on a subsequent visit. And to be fair, it also didn't hurt Mother had shared a similar chronicle with me all those many years ago.

I swear to God, Arty was as mesmerized by Carol as I was. Her visits were never solely riding lessons. She was equal parts dressage instructor, horse trainer, historian, storyteller, and, whether she knew it or not, therapist. She exuded calm and gave me (and Arty) much-needed reassurance. At the same time, she proved to be so knowledgeable and entertaining I invited my dad, a history buff, to swing by for a listen.

After his first *lesson*, he became a regular auditor. It reminded me of when I was a kid in Germany. He was always the one who took me to my weekly riding lessons. I think he enjoyed seeing his little girl casually hop up on big-ass warmbloods, all smiles, no fear. Ah, yes, the halcyon days of youth when, thanks to horses, I was able to be less in my head, more in the moment. With Carol, I think my dad started to understand more about the intricacies of riding. As he likes to say now, "Riding is more complicated than golf."

Indeed, Dad. There certainly is much more to it than meets the eye, and lest anyone forget, while golfers may want to be one with their clubs, those clubs don't have a mind of their own. Still, a rider can aspire for a centaur-like connection. That's how I've felt since hearing Carol give a brief history on the subject, which went a little something like this . . .

Back when the Romans were out and about invading the world, they landed on the Iberian Peninsula, where, much to their surprise, they were met on the battlefield by a cavalry so unique, it forever changed the face of Roman combat. The defender's horses were incredibly swift, their riders possessing such skill that as they advanced, spun, and retreated, they seemed to move as a singular, seamless creature, effortlessly outmaneuvering the Roman soldiers. A man-horse bond so perfect it inspired the myth of the centaur. A myth, in this case, not marred by tales of debauchery and misconduct but spurred by a deep and unrivaled cross-species partnership.

Like I said, this version was better. What's more, Christmas Carol also said, as Mother had, the centaur had sprung from the valley of the Tagus River, where mares were sired by the wind. In "reality," the horses of this region lived in close proximity to wild bulls. To survive, they walked a fine line, learning to keep just close enough to the bulls to dissuade attacks from larger predators but not so close as to instigate an actual bull attack. It was this ebb and flow, this undulating dance, that helped them develop and hone, generation after generation, a "cow" sense that has made them . . . us . . . me . . . adept and fluid in the bullfighting arena. Yes, those were my Iberian ancestors. Attentive, agile bull aficionados.

But what did cow sense and centaurs have to do with a dressage lesson? Christmas Carol's mind worked in mysterious ways.

She was teaching Erin how to ride the passage and wanted her to understand the importance of not going against my movement.

"A similar thing happened in the New World," Christmas Carol said. "When the Aztecs saw the Spanish conquistadors for the first time on horseback, they thought they were seeing a new life-form. A singular entity. And this is key.

"Like the centaur," she continued, "you must go with, not against, your horse. Once you ask for something, it's okay to be passive for a moment. Give him the chance to answer. And when he does, don't interfere. Yes, like that!"

Erin let go, releasing the tension in her body. My body responded in kind. My jaw suppled, my back lifted, and my legs came under me such that I had the balance and power to push up and forward. For a few strides, we were floating.

"Brava!" Carol said.

"Now *this* is fun," I admitted. "Such a good boy."

"He certainly is, and you should definitely enjoy it! But also, always keep in mind, the passage is not something to be overly influenced. When you see riders moving too much. Pushing. Fussing. Kicking. They create resistance that goes against the natural movement. Contact is about connection, not obedience. So, once again, sit up, let go, and ride that beautiful wave."

It was interesting. Carol's visits weren't frequent—maybe once a month, twice in a good month—but they were grounding. She was helping me regain confidence. Not only in my riding but also in my decision-making.

When I got stuck in my wishy-washiness, she'd point to her heart and say, "Trust this. It will guide you."

Funny how even though Carol was the visitor, she exuded this xenial quality that made time with her feel like a homecoming. Maybe even an awakening. Her stories inspired me to think beyond work in the arena and even to dream up stories of my own like I had when I was a child. For example, when my brother and I were *old* soldiers, sporting feathered tricorn hats and brandishing swashbuckling swords (a.k.a. long blocks).

"Take him out on the trails. Go have some adventures," she said. "Horses like adventures."

Do we? I wasn't sure. But I was soon to find out.

When spring arrived and the days grew longer, Erin started to take me out into the neighborhood trail system, which weaved for miles through a dense forest of moss-covered trees. Most often, it was just the two of us. Erin sometimes pretended we were scouts for the Union army, gathering intelligence on Johnny Reb's movements and, apparently, terrorizing as a side job.

"We must move like sharks and be but ghosts," she said to me, "who prey and creep and put fear into their hearts."

It was probably good we were alone.

Other times, we were English gentry, crossing the moors, apparently in capes, headed for a spot of tea at some duke and duchess's manor house.

"I hear the stable hand is quite kind. He will cool you out and if you are very good, which I know you will be, he will slip you sugar cubes and a handful of oats," she promised.

But I never saw a single sugar cube or a manor house, for that matter. And the stories didn't end with menacing scouts or cloaked upper crust.

We were also pioneers, bound for a better life, in search of the perfect plot of land to call our own.

"What do you reckon, Arty? Do you like the look of that river? We could build a log cabin right here and you could have that glorious pasture under the shade of those maples."

Again, like there were no sugar cubes, there was also no grand river. Only a skinny creek leading to what looked like a murky pond. And pasture? There was barely a patch of grass in sight. This woman had a vivid imagination, I came to realize. Because . . .

We were also, on more than one occasion, a king's knight and his valiant steed, riding under cover of darkness, risking life and limb to deliver a wax-sealed ciphered correspondence. To be clear, we never rode in the dark. Erin hadn't fallen that far off of the "safety first" wagon. She just thought it made for a better story. And I can't lie, it did.

These trail rides and off-property adventures became part of our new routine. Or as Christmas Carol preferred to call it, our ritual.

"There is greater intention and purpose behind a ritual. It's not about getting something done or out of the way. You never want to rush rituals. They are meant to be cherished. Something to look forward to. Something that brings a sense of calm through consistency."

Following our preliminary arena walk, once around in each direction, our daily ritual became jaw flexions and horse yoga. In a way, it all made the seemingly mundane meaningful. It was something to depend on. Something I knew how to do. Something that made me feel good and eased me into my workouts. No doubt, it also helped calm Erin. She had a plan, she stuck to it, and, lo and behold, my half passes improved.

My box-of-chocolate canter began to contain fewer and fewer nuts. And my passage . . .

They say good things come to those who wait. I think Erin had waited a long time to meet someone like Christmas Carol. Before, I'm not sure if Erin had been patiently waiting and not wanting to ask for too much too soon or if she simply didn't know how to ask for a passage. But now, when she asked, I obliged.

Erin raised her hands and let the reins slide forward ever so slightly.

"Legs also forward," Christmas Carol counseled. "Now leave him alone. Let yourself hang there."

Again, we were floating.

These moments were not flukes. Not happenstance. They were earned. Erin and I were going places. Maybe not for high tea and sugar cubes, but more and more, season after season, it felt like we were heading down the right path.

57

2015: Duvall, Washington

Spring's pluvial debut blossomed into a warm bluebird of a summer. The pastures reopened, and Q, Ole, and I delighted in the return to our designated side-by-side acreage. These were our fields, where once again, we spent long, languid days, mostly munching on green grass and wild dandelions, occasionally giving one another a "what for" flattened ear and wide-eyed glare for no better reason than perhaps not wanting to fully relinquish old habits. And yes, despite the fact we had our own small realms, more often than not, we huddled en masse at the common fence line.

Little by little, my apathy faded and what had once been a somewhat superficial kinship deepened into something more, something earnest. I still vied for Erin's attention but felt less threatened when she spent time with them. It was not a mark against me, and really, something about the contrast made her appreciate each one of us all the more.

"*Vive la différence,*" she said to those who asked why she had three horses. And to those who dared ask her to name a favorite, she said she didn't play that game. If they insisted, "Oh c'mon, if you had to choose. . ."

"How about I put it this way," she'd say. "*Sophie's Choice* was not my favorite movie."

For whatever reason, that tended to shut them up. But I still wondered. Did she have a favorite?

I had favorites. My favorite treat: Mrs. Pastures cookies. My favorite place to be scratched: just above the withers. My favorite season: summer. Without contest. In Washington, June through September was the best time of the year. There was no better weather, no better light.

And then there was fall.

It crept in like a fox in a henhouse. Inching closer, closer, and then, *pounce!* In for the kill. The pastures closed. The rain fell. And on the penultimate day of October, Ole stopped eating and lay down.

Later that night, he was gone.

58

2015: Snohomish, Washington

Small intestine strangulation is one of the worst types of colics a horse can have. That's what Ole had.

When we got him to the animal hospital, the on-call surgeon performed a quick ultrasound before announcing that, if Ole were to have a chance, he would need to go into surgery immediately. I did my best not to throw up as I signed all the necessary paperwork. Next, I sat in a cold, dark waiting room while Ole was hoisted onto an operating table and gutted. His intestines squeezed clean like a tube of toothpaste and reassembled into his belly like a bowl of bloated *pasta scotta*.

Five hours later, the vet emerged to say Ole hadn't died, but now, it was a matter of waiting and seeing.

"Go home. Get some rest," he added. "No news is good news. So hope for no calls. We'll be in touch after morning rounds."

One of the worst complications a horse can develop after colic surgery is gastric reflux. That's what Ole developed.

In layman's terms, reflux means whatever you put down comes back up, whether due to intestinal stasis or another obstruction. But to truly appreciate reflux, I say remove the letter *l*. Because all this evil bastard does is fuck you, again and again. That's what it did to my Ole.

For four days, he had remained relatively stable, and then, on his fifth night in hospital, things took a turn—for the better. He'd barely had any reflux, and they were even hoping they would soon be able to remove his nasogastric tube, which had been inserted post-surgery to drain fluids.

"Go home," the medical staff told me. "Get some rest. This is a good sign."

I was so tired, I agreed to leave earlier than usual, letting myself feel an ounce of relief on the forty-five-minute drive home. When I got there, I had more good news. They'd sent me a photo of a poop pile. It had been Ole's first since surgery.

Rejoicing, I went to bed and actually slept for the first time since he'd colicked. Overnight, there was no more news. I took to heart the "no news is good news" mantra.

That morning, I drove to my mom's to pick up a cheesecake on my way to the hospital. She's a phenomenal baker (I am not), and I'd asked her to make it for the staff. The sun was shining, the air was crisp, and hope had finally stopped feeling like a four-letter word.

But when I walked into the clinic, the world went dark.

The vet, who was not one to mince words, told me, "The reflux is back. Something's wrong. We need to open him up again."

Someone took the cheesecake from my trembling hands before pointing me toward Ole. They'd already been prepping for surgery and another attendant was leading my big, beautiful boy from his metal cage into the operating room. I ran to hug him before I watched him walk away.

59

2015: Duvall, Washington

On that same penultimate day of October, Trainer Lady had hosted a Halloween barn party for her students and their families. All afternoon, little ghouls and goblins raced around the barn, snatching mini carrots from plastic jack-o'-lanterns and haphazardly lobbing them at our faces. Each time a horse spooked, spun, and shot out into its run, the ghouls squealed like foreboding banshees as their oblivious parents gulped Monster Mash punch from red plastic cups.

Unimpressed, Q and I positioned ourselves at the far end of our runs. No carrot was worth that bedevilment. It hadn't struck us as odd that Ole hadn't joined. He was always far less bothered by such commotion. But then, we heard two trucks arrive and saw Erin leading two unfamiliar, serious faces into the barn.

I remember the exam. The vet did not delay pulling on a long plastic glove that went up to her armpit. What she did next did not look pleasant for either her or Ole. "There's a hard mass, a definite impaction," she said. This was not good news.

I remember the fear. It spread across Erin's face like a solar eclipse when the vet asked if she had a trailer to get him to the hospital sooner rather than later. The vet's assistant put a hand on Erin's shoulder and said, "A trailer ride may be just what he needs. Shake things up a bit."

I remember the shavings. They still clung to Ole's mane and tail as

Erin led him out of the barn toward a trailer Trainer Lady had quickly hitched up.

I remember the whinny. It was sharp, distinctive. Q was calling to his friend. I saw Ole's ears swivel back. He'd heard but lacked the energy to do more.

60

2015: Snohomish, Washington

An hour after Ole's second surgery began, the surgeon came out to find me in the waiting room.

"There's dead tissue at the intersection of the small and large intestine," he explained. "To resect would require a heroic effort for a one-in-a-million chance of survival . . ."

For a split second, I was Lloyd Christmas, believing there was a chance. I waited for the vet to continue, but he only looked down and slowly shook his head.

I can't. I can't do this. This can't be real. Not my Ole. Save him. Please. Please, God. You have to save him. Those were the words that raced through my head, but all that came out was "Fuck!" And "No!" And "Fuck!" again. And "No, no, no." As if I were an actress trying different ways to work a scene.

Somewhere between *fuck* and *no* and trying to remain upright, the surgeon said I could go into the operating room to say goodbye.

Goodbye?! But I don't want to. I distinctly remember hesitating, thinking if I didn't move, somehow this beast of a nightmare would go away.

What I don't remember is if Ole's eyes were open or closed when I kissed his face and told him I loved him and not to be afraid. Even though I'd never been more afraid in my life.

The surgeon was standing in the doorway as I went to leave. I grabbed his face with both hands and said, "Thank you for trying. Thank you for everything you did." And then I couldn't breathe. The air had left the room and all I could do was run.

61

2015, Duvall, Washington

Five days after Ole left in that trailer, there was a sudden, clamoring kerfuffle behind the barn. Every horse darted from its stall into its run, and we all saw something big and black fly past. And when I say fly, I mean fly. It was swift and winged.

Snorts sprang up and down the row. Half the horses scampered back into their stalls, trying to figure out what they'd seen, if all was safe. But Q, like a parent searching for a lost child, let loose a primal scream. That's when I knew for sure. The beautiful black flash had been Ole. He'd come to show us all, but especially Q, that he had shuffled off his mortal coil and was now more glorious than ever.

Now, he could fly.

For hours, Q stood at the end of his run, head in the air, alert, sniffing at the wind. It was a futile search I had known all too well. Even when our evening flakes were served and the dark and cold crept in, he stayed outside until, eventually, he lowered his head, in defeat or acceptance. Maybe both.

Since Ole left, Erin had made it to the barn every day. She didn't stay for long but always reassured us Ole would be home soon. That day, we never saw her.

62

Hot Shot was my first truly personal horse death. That was back in 2000. One day, he was there, with his horrendous mouth-cancer breath, protruding ribs, and dull chestnut coat. The next, gone.

He used to always stand alone at the barbed wire pasture fence line, seemingly ostracized from the herd. The same herd Q and Buddy belonged to. He was old and small, but so sweet. After learning his owner had abandoned him years before, I made a point every day to give him pats, feed him a small carrot chunk if he would take it, and tell him he was beautiful. Because he was.

When I turned up one evening after work and couldn't find him, I was shockingly devastated.

"Old Hot Shot? Yeah, they put him down," I was told.

How had I been so naive? I had to have known horses didn't live forever, right? I was thirty years old, and I cried all the way home. In a way, Hot Shot marked the end of my innocence.

After his, the deaths came with frightening regularity.

One busy weekend, there was an argument in the mares' catch pen. Too many moody horses had been corralled into too small a space. I was walking to my tack shed when a scream and a scuffle caught my attention. I turned to see one mare kick another in the leg. The force snapped the leg near in two. Like a wind chime, it dangled in the air as the mare fought to stay upright on her remaining three legs.

Someone screamed for a gun. *A gun?!* I thought. *What century are we in? Is this the Wild West? Is there no other option?*

As if reading my mind, someone else yelled, "A vet will never get here fast enough."

I was still inexperienced enough to think there was hope. That she could have been saved.

Next, there was the gelding who stepped in a mole hole out in the pasture. No one was quite sure how long he'd been standing there, but he was wet with sweat and shaking uncontrollably by the time someone found him. So it had to have been a while. There wasn't much blood, but what there was had started to scab around the obvious compound fracture at his front fetlock. Beside him was his best buddy, standing guard, refusing to leave him.

Again, I held on to hope: "If we could get the trailer. . ." Again, I was wrong.

That was the first time I watched a vet inject the drug that stops a heart. Despite his heroic effort to stay upright and alive, the brave boy finally collapsed to the ground, and I cried all the way home.

There were many deaths after. Colics, mostly, but also quality-of-life euthanasia, other bizarre incidents. In all these years, only once have I known of a horse who truly went out on his own terms. His name was Snort, and he was well into his thirties. Quite the ripe old age for a horse. His owner was an older doctor but also an old-school cowboy. He'd done everything with that horse. Roped, wrangled, heck, maybe even rodeoed. It was a partnership to commend and aspire to.

One morning, Snort was found curled up next to the creek that ran through the middle of the pasture.

"He looked like he'd simply gone to sleep," the kind doctor told me. "I couldn't think of a better, more beautiful way to go."

I agreed, and it was the first time I didn't cry all the way home.

But with Ole . . . nothing had prepared me for losing him.

November 4, 2015: Snohomish, Washington

That day, death followed me home. Unlike a vampire, he didn't need an invitation to invade my home, my life. He stormed right in, ready to maraud and ravage.

He crept into every nook and cranny of my being. Every daily routine.

In the morning, he stood beside me in the shower, as I brushed my teeth, as I pulled on my pants, tied my laces. Throughout the day, he followed me to the kitchen, the store, the barn, whatever *necessary* activity I could manage. At any moment, he threatened to send me into a panic.

Even at night, when I thought sleep could be my refuge, he'd slip under the sheets and suddenly take hold of me, shake me awake. But no matter how much I kicked and thrashed and begged him to let go, he refused to release his grip. Because that's the thing about Death. Once he arrives, he becomes a permanent resident.

Everywhere I looked or turned, he was there as a constant reminder Ole wasn't.

"Dying is not unique. It's universal," my dear friend Camille told me after she'd lost her mother. "Yet it feels so personal and singular. All of it is such hell."

She couldn't have been more right. What fresh, all-consuming hell it is.

I'll never understand, dear Ole, how you existed one moment—heart beating, lungs breathing—only to fall silent and still the next.

I see you everywhere. In every bird, every falling leaf, every brilliant orange and red and blue Pacific Northwest sunset. But as Death is only too quick to remind me, you're also now but ash and bone in an oak box sitting on my bureau, collecting dust.

July 22, 2015: Fife, Scotland

Not long before Ole died, I was reminded of a final line in an E. E. Cummings poem, "Since feeling is first": "And death I think is no parenthesis."

Turns out, he was right. Death is no parenthesis. It's a double period.. Like not one but two nails in a coffin..

On an otherwise unremarkable day in July, a friend texted me: "Simon died.."

Simon died. Dot. Dot. For some reason, those two dots stood out. As if maybe there were more to come. But how could there be? No matter what my friend said next, it wasn't going to change the fact he was dead. Dead as a doornail. Period. Full stop.

I was standing in Macy's, looking at a purse, when I got the text. I felt shocked but not surprised. Dizzy, but also dull. My mom was with me, and she asked if I needed to get home. I'm not sure why but I said, "No, I'm okay."

I wasn't okay but just hadn't realized it.

Is that shock?

My divorce from Simon had been finalized four years earlier. It had been acrimonious at best. He'd threatened to take my horses, my dogs. He'd threatened to kill himself. He'd told me he'd hired a private investigator to follow me. For what reason? Who knows?

Shortly after we'd separated in the summer of 2010, I moved

apartments and naively gave him a key. But after I filed for divorce later that year and the threats began, I changed locks on doors and told everyone at the barn to be on alert should he show up and try to do anything with the horses.

Meanwhile, he continued to cycle through booze, hospital, rehab, booze, couch surfing, DUI, jail, hospital, rehab, booze . . . until finally he moved back to his native Scotland in 2012. With the distance, both physical and emotional, I felt safe enough to exchange a few amical emails with him, but the "ceasefire" was short-lived. His mother convinced him to sue me for fraud because she didn't think he got a fair shake in the divorce. Simon had been right about one thing: Denial. It's not just a river in Egypt.

They did not win the case, and though he emailed me numerous times after, I never responded. Through the grapevine, I heard he'd returned to the boozing-and-hospital cycle . . . until finally, the cycle ended. With organ failure.

He was thirty-seven years old.

Ole had been eleven.

Despite the so-called natural (unnatural, if you asked me) causes, I was at a loss to comprehend either of these deaths, even though one of them was a beloved I got to say goodbye to. And with no answers to be found, it got pretty damned dark, pretty damned fast. Had it not been for a certain white horse, who knows.

63

2015: Duvall, Washington

Long after the last lesson of the day, I heard pebbles popping from beneath tires. Like Q, I knew the sound of her truck, and I hurried into my stall, ready to greet her. The engine's roar cut off quickly, but it took longer than usual for the car door to open and close, for the alarm to beep, and, despite a steady rain, for her to walk around the barn to its side entrance.

She heaved the heavy metal door open but, once inside, struggled to slide it shut. Her hand slipped on the wet handle and the bag she was carrying fell to the floor. Carrots and apples rolled off in every direction.

"Mother f'er!" she said, groping for the light switch.

The overhead fluorescent tubes buzzed to life with all the willingness of a warmblood on a hot summer day as she bent down to salvage the fallen produce. It had been two days since she'd last visited, and I banged my hoof against my stall door, anxious for treats and attention.

"Hold on, sweetie," she called out. "There in a sec." But when she got up, she stopped before reaching my stall.

Ole's stall stood empty but clean. Ready for his return.

Were you ever really here? Or was it all a dream? I thought, not at all ready to confront this altered reality. Not at all ready to confront a lot of things.

I'd come to the barn late for a reason. I knew I'd have to see people eventually, but I wasn't ready for the handfuls of dirt they'd throw on his coffin. A.k.a. the pitiful eyes and sympathy hugs. The "I'm so sorrys" and "if there's anything I can dos." But worst of all, the past tense. "He *was* such a great horse."

Ashes to ashes, dust to dust. He was gone, but I was still here. Why?

And oh my.

I stared at the block letters of his nameplate: OLE FAN SIL. I had to catch my breath at the sight of all the flowers and condolence notes hanging from or taped to his stall door. They may not have matched the sea of those left for Diana at Pont de l'Alma, but they were beautiful, heartening, and reaffirming. Ole had existed, and he had touched hearts beyond my own.

I slid open his door and stepped inside. I wanted, if only for a moment, to live in his skin, see what he had seen. I spun around once, twice, imagining what he felt when he came in from his run and before settling in for a meal or down for a nap. Sometimes, it's the little things we cease to notice on a normal day . . . The scratched wooden walls. The hooks holding fast a pair of full water buckets. The tattered insulation precariously dangling from the ceiling. And most profoundly, the strands of his mane caught in the jagged splinters of the weather-worn door frame. Like a forensic investigator in search of answers, I carefully pulled them out and tucked them deep inside my pants pocket.

I wanted to puke.

Despite my clamoring, she didn't rush over. When I heard her stop at Q's stall, I turned and went outside, where I saw her meet him under what had become an increasingly cold rain. Her hands reached up to cup his jaw, and Q jerked his head away as if not wanting to hear or accept the truth. She said, "I miss him, too. I miss him so much."

Then he stood, still as a statue, letting her kiss his wet nose. A whisper on the wind said I needed to steady myself.

When she finally came to my stall, she extended a carrot and an apology. "I'm sorry it took me so long, sweetie. How you doing? You warm enough?" She reached to touch my ear. It was her way of checking my temp, so to speak. "Oh, good. Nice and warm."

Generally, I pull back when she does that, but this time, I lowered my head, so my left eye was level with hers. In the only way I knew how, I let her know, "I see you, and I've got you." Like Q, I stood stock-still.

Unlike Ole, who never seemed to mind, Q and Arty were not fans of having their faces touched. So I tried to avoid doing it. That night, however, I felt this incredible need to touch their faces, drape my arms around their necks, and hold tight. Both obliged without protest, which may seem a small thing, but it meant the world to me.

There may be no "scientific" proof, but I'm convinced horses not only possess varying levels of extrasensory perception but excel at feeling our emotions, reading our minds, and responding to us in ways that may seem *unbelievable*. Sure, we know they are masters at reading body language, easily able to suss out confidence, arrogance, timidity, you name it, in us humans, but there's more to it than that.

In the wild, horses can synchronize their heartbeats with their herd to help sense stress and, ultimately, guard against danger. It's been said they can do the same with their human guardians. This heart coupling, mirroring, whatever you want to call it, is something

I've only experienced with a horse. It's more than extraordinary. It's how Julian Barnes describes love in his book *Levels of Life*.

"Love," he says, "is the meeting point of truth and magic."

Truth and magic. If ever there were two better words to describe what it's like to be in the presence of a horse, especially one who trusts you, I don't know what they are.

People have told me, too many times to count, I'd never truly know love until I had children. The presumption used to infuriate me. That's a lie. It still infuriates me. But what I've realized is every single one of them never had a relationship with a horse. I suppose I could try to argue they'll never know love until they have horses, but why bother? Love is not a competition.

Besides, it's easier to just shank a bitch for saying dumb shit.

It's also easier, sometimes, to try to joke or make light or digress to the point of not remembering where you are or what you were saying or how you were feeling, which at that time was me wanting to jump off a bridge. Or in front of a truck. Or into the deep end of a lake, wrapped in a Chicago overcoat.

It had been almost two years since I'd brought Arty home, and I knew it was a precarious time. Like Carol had said, it can take a horse a year or two to adjust to a new home. Arty had been slow to trust, slow to acclimate. Even his body had refused to grow a winter coat those first winters, something that can happen when a horse is moved from a southern to northern climate. Generally, their coats adjust within a year. But Arty, special as he is, stayed sleek as Greek marble for much longer. While his habit of banging on his stall door irked some, it had become part of *our* routine, and it made me feel wanted.

That night in his stall, Arty's energy shift, from stall-door-banging impatience to a rare and quiet stillness, spoke volumes. He was offering me a lifeline, something to hold on to. And just when I thought tears were unavoidable, that beautiful boy . . . headbutted me so hard in the solar plexus I nearly toppled over.

I couldn't help myself. The tension was killing me.

I couldn't help myself. All I could do was laugh. Bury my face in his neck. And cry.

Ole's death pulverized me. Because he'd been so young, I felt I hadn't only lost what he'd been but also everything he was yet to become. I found myself missing all the memories we'd never make, all the adventures we'd never take. It was as if I'd been stripped of my very identity. But what can you do but accept what you know to be true?

There's a part in *A River Runs Through It*—what can I say? I love the book, and maybe even more so, the movie—when Reverend Maclean asks his oldest son, Norman, if he's told him everything about the death of his youngest son, Paul. Norman says, "Maybe all I really know about Paul is that he was a fine fisherman." To which the reverend replies, "You know more than that. . . . He was beautiful."

To me, those few words encompass a universe of love and loss. And because I could never write anything better, especially about the incomprehensibility of a life snuffed out too soon, I'll borrow again to say, Ole was beautiful.

64

"Should I kill myself, or have a cup of coffee?"

—Albert Camus (or so I always thought)

Years ago, my friend Julia volunteered at an animals-as-therapy program, where she was paired with a fourteen-year-old girl who'd recently tried to kill herself.

"Her mom lived in a motel and had serious drug problems. Her dad was in jail. Her brother was on the run from the cops," Julia told me. "So, yeah, she'd had more than her fair share of trauma. And she was pretty angry. And sad. And scared.

"The first time I met her, I was all like, 'Hi, my name is Julia, let's walk around together and pet this here horse.' Basically, there was nothing about her life I could relate to besides her love of horses. And yet what I eventually saw, and it was powerful, was for one hour every week, she got to have some semblance of control. The barn was her time to shine and grow. That horse gave her a reason to live. And live better than she'd ever thought possible."

Like Julia, besides horses, there's little I could have related to in terms of that girl's home life. I may have had some instability growing up, but I also had an amazingly loving and supportive family. My mom didn't have a drug problem. My dad wasn't in jail. My brothers weren't on the run from the law. At least not so far as I knew.

Call me lucky, call me fortunate, just don't call me #blessed, my family has always been there for me. They've taken me on adventures, endured my mercurial temperament, encouraged my kaleidoscopic interests—save for that time I asked for a piano shortly after quitting violin—and even if they don't get the horse thing, they get it's *my* thing, and they know better than to ever tell me I don't know what true love is.

In addition to horses, I've always loved the painting *Napoleon Crossing the Alps*. For some reason, I long assumed I'd seen it for the first time in Paris. In my mind, it had to have been at the Louvre, in the same hall as Delacroix's *Liberty Leading the People* and another of David's renowned works, *The Coronation of Napoleon*. But the problem with that "memory" is not a single version of the painting, of which there are five, resides at the Louvre. I also know I couldn't have seen it nearby at the Musée Nationale des Châteaux de Malmaison because I've never been to the Musée Nationale des Châteaux de Malmaison.

So, where oh where?

I got my answer when I called my dad to ask him about another memory: our "field trip" into New York City to see the National Horse Show at Madison Square Garden. Founded in 1883, it was America's oldest indoor horse show and, as described in two different *New York Times* articles from the 1970s, was "first held in the gaslight era when the beasts hauled taxicabs on the New York cobblestones" and "the New York skyline was bathed in the soft yellow glow of gas light." How awful to describe them as beasts and yet how romantic to imagine horse hooves hitting cobblestone beneath a lambent flame.

"Dad, did we go to the Garden in '80 or '81? And do you remember the gray pony they were raffling off?"

"It was 1980," he reassured me, "but it wasn't a pony. It was the Courvoisier horse."

"The Courvoisier horse?" I questioned, not having a clue.

"Don't you remember all the posters?"

"Posters of what?"

"Of *Napoleon Crossing the Alps*. The painting was in all the Courvoisier ads. They were posted all around the arena."

"Holy shit!" I said in disbelief. "*That's* where I saw that painting for the first time."

"I have no idea about that, but Courvoisier was the sponsor for the raffle," he said. "They were giving away an Arabian, like the horse in the painting."

Of course, I had to immediately look up the ads. The copy for at least one said, "Character is destiny—as true of Courvoisier Cognac as of history's conquering hero. For Courvoisier is *The Brandy of Napoleon*. Its character has destined it to be the choice of kings and statesmen. And its matchless flavour and bouquet reward you with *une sensation splendide*, cherished by all who can command the finest."

Ah yes, the finest . . . like a white horse.

That day in 1980, my dad bought me a handful of raffle tickets. I clung to them all night, barely able to pay attention to the rest of the show, convinced I was going to win.

But as written in the book of Ecclesiastes, "There is a time for everything." For me, the time to bring home a white horse was not as a ten-year-old in 1980. I'm sure much to the relief of my dad, whom I also recently asked, "What would you have done had I won?"

"I have no idea."

My dad knows me well. Even now (four decades later), he dared not say, "Well, I guess we'd have sold him."

What's also interesting about that painting is how it's drawn wide criticism over the years, many calling it propaganda rather than art. (But can propaganda not be art?) To the critics, I say, be damned. Or maybe just, I beg to differ. Because I love it. I absolutely love it. For the actual image and the story behind it.

Whether it's historically accurate or just rumor, it's said Napoleon was not keen to sit for the portrait but instead advised the artist to paint an equestrian portrait. He offered but one further detail. He wanted to appear "*calme sur un cheval fougueux*." Calm on a fiery horse. I've also heard Napoleon was inspired by Alexander the Great, and I can't help but wonder, did he also admire Helios and his fiery steeds?

When I left the barn that second night of the rest of my life without Ole, I gathered the flowers and the cards. In one, someone had written, "It's good you have a white horse. They bring light and life. Let Arty be the light in your darkness."

Some love stories were never meant to be. Some love stories don't last. But this love story, which began with a fiery arrow, will conclude (but only here) with a thank-you.

With all my heart, I thank you, Arty, for being my cup of coffee.

ACKNOWLEDGMENTS

I have so many to thank for their support, their ears, their ideas, their memories, their insights—and maybe most of all, their patience.

To Dad, for being reader numero uno for anything I write, like it or not. You've tolerated my endless iterations and aren't afraid to say, "Nope, I don't like that." But more often, you tell me you do—especially when something makes you laugh. That's always my favorite.

To Mom, for saying, "I'll read it when it's published" and "I'm sure it's great"—because you always believed I would finish, even when I most certainly didn't.

To Bjørn, for (almost) always saying, "It's up to you." For being the calm in my storm and the buoy in all other storms. Without you, I would most certainly drown. I love you.

To Elizabeth Rosner, without whom this book would not be what it is. You helped shape the story into something I never saw. And you gave me the courage to talk about myself, which never seemed a worthy subject. *So, enough about me—let's talk about me.*

To Renee Lee, Abby Croteau, and Robyn Atkins—my forever pony pals and greatest cheerleaders. You make me feel necessary. You make me howl. You make me know it's FINE. I adore you.

To Heather Schulze, for being my partner in crime for longer than either of us can quite wrap our heads around—and for being there at the start of this whole wild adventure, and always when it matters.

To Camille Bossenberry, Heather O'Malley, and Wedge Martin, for taking the time I know you don't have to read my words, for offering such thoughtful feedback, and for making me want to keep writing.

To Diego Baccino, for your technical acumen and eye for detail. Because let's be honest: Mama D. knows best.

To Sarah Abbot, for always making me laugh. Ess Snow. Beautiful.

To Heather Gillette, for bringing horses back into my life. We'll always have B&B.

To Carol Lynn McArdle, for truly seeing Arty. Time with you was never just a riding lesson—it was a history lesson, a life lesson, a treat.

To Nuno Jose Avelar, Hannah Larsson, Andréa Julie Kjellberg, Carolin Kircher, and Nuno Sa, for a once-in-a-lifetime experience that planted the seed for this book.

To Ruben Davalos. No foot, no horse. Thank you for sharing your master skills and childhood stories.

To Dany Bert, for putting the dressage and Iberian bugs in my ear. You were right: I did need to meet the Lusitanos—and yes, they rule.

To Barbara Liebeck—where do I even begin? For your insane generosity and faith in me. You set me down a life-changing path, and I'll be forever grateful.

To Julia Glass, for the wild, unwavering love you've shown all my babies.

To Tammy Stafford and Jo Jones—for standing in my place when I was brought to my knees. I'll never forget.

To Iris van Werkhoven and Anneke Bradley-Kloosterman, for trusting me with your angel.

To Patricia Wood, for helping me get to the point. Bam.

To Kip Mistral, for being the first to say, "I think you have a book here."

To Brooke Warner, for being the first to say, "I'd like to help you publish this." Thank you for your wisdom, your guidance, and your belief that this story was worth sharing.

To Lindsey Salatka, Carol Odell, Lisa Cheek, Laura Munson, Mikayla Butchart, and everyone at She Writes Press—for your talent, kindness, and support.

To Emi Battaglia, for saying yes and letting me buzz with the excitement of possibility.

To Caroline Gilman, for "getting" me, laughing *with* me, and always going above and beyond.

And to the great loves of my life: Winnie, Q, Beck, Bear, Izzy, Ole, Atticus, Tully, Arty, Xairel, Louis, Bella, and Donatella. You've made my life rich beyond measure.

Thank you, all.

And if I forgot to name you—*mi scusi.* My brain isn't what it used to be, which either is, or isn't, saying much.

About the Author

photo credit: Diego Baccino and Abby Croteau

Erin O'Malley is a lifelong horse lover and reluctant extrovert. She began her career in Paris, working for Hearst Publications on titles like *Harper's Bazaar*, *Marie Claire*, *Cosmopolitan*, and *Town & Country*, before transitioning into tech, where she focused on marketing and content strategy. She credits her love of telling stories to her upbringing as an Army brat—always moving, ever shy. *The Brat and the Bullfighter* is her debut, told from two perspectives: a girl and the horse who saves her. She lives near Seattle with her husband, two horses, and three dogs.